To learn to classify is in itself an education — ALEX. BAIN

ABRIDGED

Decimal Classification

and

Relativ Index

by

Melvil Dewey A M LL D

for libraries and personal use
in arranging for immediate reference
books, pamflets, clippings, pictures, manuscript notes
and other material

Edition 5

revised to correspond
to the few changes in meaning of numbers
in ful tables, edition 13

by

Dorkas Fellows, Editor
Myron Warren Getchell, Associate editor

Forest Press, Inc.

Lake Placid Club N. Y.

1936

Publisher's Note

Simpler spellings used ar strongly recommended for general adoption by both American and English filologic associations, including nearly all prominent scholars in English now living. We regret prejudis which certain readers wil feel against these changes, but after careful study of all objections urged, we find the weight of scholarship and reason wholly in their favor, and feel compeld to bear a share of the prejudis which some must endure before the great benefits of a rational orthografy can be secured.

Fuller information free from Education Foundation, Lake Placid Club, Essex Co. N Y

The *Decimal classification* is copyrighted, and the right strictly maintaind, not as a source of income to either author or publishers, but wholly to protect users

CONTENTS

	PAGE
INTRODUCTION	3
Explanation	3
Suggestions to users	5
Variations	11
Other uses	12
SUMMARIES	15
TABLES	17
INDEX	71

Abridged Decimal Classification[1]

EXPLANATION

Before beginning to use the classification read carefully at least the paragrafs in large type. The smaller type givs stil farther information.

THIS abridgment is to meet a strong demand for a very simple form for small libraries. Even they ar likely to hav a few books or pamflets on limited topics found only in the fullest tables, which aim to provide for all subjects treated in books, pamflets, or articles. As minor subjects differ in each library, obviously no condenst or selectiv classification can meet every want of even small collections. A library needing subdivisions for its specialty should ask the publishers for a fuller table of that subject.

Change from short to ful form These short forms can be changed to ful class numbers at any time without other alteration than adding extra figures to those here given.

Plan This classification divides the field of knowledge into 9 main classes, numberd 1 to 9. Cyclopedias, periodicals, etc. so general as to belong to no one of these classes, ar markt 0 (naught) and form a 10th class. Each class is similarly separated into 9 divisions, general works belonging to no division having 0 in place of the division number. Divisions ar similarly divided into 9 sections. Thus 512 means class 5 Pure science, division 1 Mathematics, section 2 Algebra, and every algebra

---

[1] The confusion and annoyance to the many users of this system caused by printing unauthorized variations hav forced the publishers to insist strictly on the protection afforded by copyright. Every library and individual user has, however, entire freedom to make such variations as he thinks he needs, under the simple restrictions found necessary to protect the rights of others as on page 11, Letter notations for changes.

is numberd 512. Its class number, giving class, division and section, is applied to every book and pamflet in the library.

Where o occurs in a class number, it has its usual numeric value. Thus a book numberd 510 is class 5, division 1, but no section; i. e. the book treats of division 51 (Mathematics) in general, and is limited to no one section, while geometry, which is so limited, is markt 513; 500 indicates a treatis on science in general, limited to *no* division or section. A number beginning with o means 'not limited to any class'; e. g. a general cyclopedia treating of all 9 classes.

Books ar arranged on the shelvs in simple numeric order. Since each number means a definit subject, all books on any subject must stand together. These tables show the order of subjects. Thus 512 Algebra precedes 513 Geometry, and follows 511 Arithmetic.

Summaries The first page of tables shows the 10 classes into which all topics ar divided. The next page shows the 9 divisions of each of the 10 classes, and is useful as a birdseye view of the whole scheme.

Tables Following these 2 summaries ar the annotated tables which repeat in proper order all the classes, divisions, sections, and subsections, if any. Synonymous terms, examples, brief notes, and various catchwords ar often added to the simple heds to giv users a fuller and clearer idea of the field which each number covers.

Relativ subject index Following the tables is the most important feature of the system, an alfabetic index of all the heds, which refers by class number to the exact place of each in the tables.

What the relativ index includes This index includes also, as far as found, all synonyms or alternativ names for the heds, and many other entries likely to help a reader find his subject redily. Even a user who knows just where to turn to his subject in the tables, if he consults the index, may be put on track of valuable allied matter which he would otherwise overlook.

Most names of countries, towns, animals, plants, etc. hav been omitted, the Index containing only those in

the tables; e. g. it can not enumerate all species of articulates, but when the classifier has found from the proper reference books that Remopleurides is a fossil articulate, the index wil send him to 565 and he can classify his monograf on that subject.

Relativ location By relativ location and decimal class numbers, the simple arabic numbers tel of each book and pamflet, both *what* it is, and *where* it is.

Books ar arranged on the shelvs by class numbers in decimal numeric order. Books on the same subject and therefore having the same class number always stand together, but ar farther arranged alfabeticly by authors' surnames; e. g. United States histories ar all 973, but Bancroft, Eggleston, McMasters and Wilson would stand in this order. (*See also* p. 9, Book numbers) Shelvs need not be markt, but the beginning of each subject is shown by a bold class number on a movable carrier just under or before the first book bearing that number.

Sizes on shelvs Shelv octavos and all smaller books together in one series, and arrange in parallel libraries only quartos and folios, which ar too tall for the regular shelvs. A size letter prefixt to the book number shows the series in which any oversize book is put; e. g. 749 qB shows that book B on Artistic furniture is too large for the regular shelvs, so is placed in the 'q' or quarto series. Another way is to use a wood or pasteboard dummy to show location of a book not in its regular place.

Suggestions to users

In referring to tables, hold the book in the right hand and turn with the left. The class numbers then show very plainly on the left margin and reference is greatly expedited. But however the book is held, the eye should follow the left margins wholly.

How many figures to use In very small collections 2 figures might do til growth required farther division; but it is economy, and saves handling the books a 2d time, to use at least 3 figures at first, even in the smallest collection.

Familiarity with tables   Get a general knowledge of the scheme by learning the 10 main classes (you wil soon know the 100 divisions also without special study), so that you can tel to what subject a given number belongs from its first figure without referring to the tables. Familiarity with subdivisions wil come gradually, but rapidly, from use.   Using the tables alone, and then always verifying your result by the index, you wil more rapidly learn the classification and gain facility in using it.   To do this, decide first to which of the 10 classes the subject belongs; next, take that class as if there were no other, and decide to which of its 10 divisions the subject belongs; then in the same way select its section, thus running down your topic in its groovs, which become tenfold narrower at each step.

Use of index   *As a check against error, use the index freely*, even tho familiar with the scheme.

> By consulting the index of the ful classification, subjects omitted in this abridgment wil be found assignd with allied subjects to the proper hed.   The ful subject index wil decide at once most doutful points, and no topics omitted from the abridged tables and index should be numberd without such reference, as otherwise great annoyance may result from finding that the number used conflicts with that in the great mass of printed and ms catalogs, cards, indexes and other bibliografic aids arranged by this system.

Subject of a book   To determin the subject of a book consult:

1   **The title**, since it is generally chosen to show what the book is about.   But, as many titles ar misleading, never class from title alone, but always examin also

2   **Table of contents**, which is the best guide to the true subject.   If there is no table of contents read

3   **Chapter heds** or marginal topics.

4   **Preface**   Unless alredy certain, glance thru preface to catch the author's point of view, and verify impressions gaind from title and contents.

5   **Reference books**   If preceding means fail, consult reliable bibliografies, clast and annotated catalogs, biografic dictionaries, histories of literature, cyclopedias,

reviews, etc. for information about the caracter of the book.

6 Subject matter If the 5 shorter methods above fail, examin the subject matter of the book itself, and if stil in dout, to avoid mistakes, put aside on an 'Under consideration' shelf til you can examin more thoroly or consult

7 Specialists Experts, competent to define true subject and relation, ar usually glad to examin any new books in their departments enuf to class them. Old ones they know where to put alredy.

> After deciding what the book is about, find this subject in the tables, either thru the index or by using the tables directly; e. g. Pollock's *Land laws* might naturally be clast from the tables alone as '333, Land; ownership; rights; rent,' which seems exactly to fit this book. But the index shows 2 numbers for land laws; viz, 347, from the legal, and 333, from the economic point of view. The object of this book, as seen in the preface, is to giv a popular presentation of English statutes pertaining to landholding, not to discuss the history and theory of land laws from the economist's point of view; so it should be clast '347 Realty,' which might hav been mist but for the index.

Assigning class numbers 1 Practical usefulness is the chief object. Put each book under the subject to the student of which it is most useful, unless local reasons 'attract' it to a place stil more useful in your library. See p. 8, § 7.

2 The content or real subject of a book, not the form or the accidental wording of its title, determins its place.

> Therefore put a filosofy of art with Art, not with Filosofy; a history of mathematics with Mathematics, not with History; for filosofy or history is simply the *form* which these books hav taken. Their true content or subject is Art or Mathematics, and to the student of these subjects they ar the most useful.

3 Always remember that the question is not where one would probably look to find a particular book, but under what subject is the book of greatest value; e. g. it is of little consequence whether one would be apt to look under 595 for Darwin's *Formation of vegetable mould*, but of much consequence that one studying earthworms should find that book in **595** Worms, since it is chiefly

valuable as a study of the habits of earthworms. Any one wanting that special book should look for it in the catalog under Darwin.

4 Assign every book to the most specific hed that wil contain it; i. e. do not mark all ancient histoiy 930, but put history of ancient Rome in 937, of anciant Greece in 938, etc.

> If there ar only 10 books on a given subject it is useful to hav them stil farther groupt by topics or form of treatment, for other-wise, they hav only accidental order, which servs no one. If a reader wishes a specific subject, he is sent instantly to the exact place by the subject index; if, however, he wishes a specific book, he should go, not to the shelvs, but to the name catalog, where he can find its place quickest. If he wishes to study the library's resources at the shelvs, he wil be *greatly helpt by close classing.*
>
> Whether there ar 1 or 1000 books on any topic, they take no more shelf space if clast minutely, and the work is done once for all. When large accessions come, even if a century later, this number wil not hav to be alterd. In a relativ location, the number of books you hav on any subject has no special weight; any num-ber of consecutiv topics without a book yet in them, wastes no space on shelvs, as the numbers ar merely skipt. This plan not only does no harm, but has the considerable value of showing that you hav nothing on the subject; a piece of information second in value only to finding something, for one need no longer search. It takes just as many figures to mark all mathematical works 510, costs just as much labor in most cases and, if one wants the one calculus in the whole library, he has to search thru the 150 volumes in 510, when he would find it instantly if markt 517.

5 The predominant tendency or obvious purpose of a book usually decides its class number at once. If, how-ever, a book treats of 2 or more different subjects, assign it to the place where it wil be most useful.

6 If 2 subjects hav distinct page limitations, class under the first, unless the 2d is decidedly more important or much greater in bulk; i. e. always put a book under the first subject, unless there is good reason for entering it under another.

7 Consider not only scope and tendency of each book, but also the nature and specialities of each library.

> Any subject on which a library specializes naturally attracts allied subjects; e. g. a book on fishing which an agricultural library

puts under 639, has also a place in 799, where the sportsman wants it.

8 If a book treats of 4 or more sections of any division, giv it the division number, insted of the most important section number; e. g. class a volume on light, heat and sound, under the hed most fully discust. But if it treats also of mechanics, class as 530, or general physics.

9 To secure uniformity, make notes for future reference of all difficulties and decisions; for it is even more important to *put books on the same subject together* than to put them in the absolutely correct place.

> Such notes should be written either on the margins of the classification tables, or on an interleavd copy, or on standard-size slips arranged by class numbers. (See also p. **13**, Index rerums)

10 Separate collected works, libraries, etc. and class the parts as independent works; or keep them together, and assign them like individual books to the most specific hed that wil contain them; or assign them to the most prominent of the various subjects of which they treat. Of these 3 plans the first is the best, unless the books ar titled and volumed as a set.

11 Class translations, 'tales from,' reviews, keys, analyses, answers, and other books about a specific book with the original book, as being there most useful.

Book numbers With this abridgment the arrangement below of books in each class by author's surnames is recommended; tho some experienst library organizers strongly advise, as simpler and easier, omitting book numbers entirely and using author's surname in binder's title or written on label for arranging books on shelvs and charging loans.

Under class number on back of each book put initial and first figure of its author's surname taken from Cutter or Cutter-Sanborn author tables; e. g. English history by Gardiner 942 G1. Use the *same initial and figure* for all books by the *same author in any one class;* e. g. if in class 942, History of England, Gardiner's *Outline of English history* were G1, Green's *History of the English people*

would be G8, and Green's *Short history* would be G8s. On the shelf these books would then stand

GARDINER	GREEN	GREEN
Outline	History	Short history
942	942	942
G1	G8	G8s

Class and book number together make a short 'call number' identifying every book in the library. 942 G1 'calls' for Gardiner's *Outline*, as no other book in that library has exactly that number. A glance at the shelf list translates any call number into author and title. If any class outgrows this abbreviated plan do not hesitate to apply the full book number as given in the author table. Practis need not be uniform in all classes but exceptions should be plainly noted.

Biografy book numbers   To keep lives of the same person together, assign book numbers in individual biografy from name of person written about insted of from name of writer.   *See* notes to 920 in Tables.

Fiction numbers   For fiction in English, omit the class number altogether and alfabet by authors' surnames. Number both fiction and biografy by the Cutter (or Cutter-Sanborn) author table.

Class fiction in foren languages with the literature of its language; e. g. Hugo's *Les miserables* in French with 843, but put an English translation in its alfabetic place in unclast fiction.

Form distinctions   Except for a few cases shown in ful *Decimal Classification* and to a less extent in *Abridged*, the following form divisions may be added to any subject number: 01 filosofy, theories etc.; 02 compends, outlines; 03 dictionaries, cyclopedias; 04 essays, lectures, letters etc.; 05 periodicals, magazines etc.; 06 societies, associations (transactions, reports etc.); 07 education, study, teaching, training etc.; 08 polygrafy, collections etc.; 09 history and general local treatment. This series of form division numbers is extensivly subdivided on p. 1629–31 of unabridged *Decimal Classification*, edition 13, as part of Appendix table 2, Common subdivisions. If the numbers to which these form divisions ar attacht end in 0 this figure (as part of the form division) is not

repeated: *e.g.* theory of economics is 330.1, *not* 330.01; a geologic periodical is 550.5, *not* 550.05.

Divided like   The numbers below may be subdivided as in the following tables and in many cases may be farther subdivided as in ful *Decimal Classification*. Also many numbers not subdivided at all in *Abridged* may be extensivly subdivided as in ful.

016 and 375 may be divided like ful classification; *e.g.* Bibliografy of engineering 016.62, Political science in the curriculum 375.32.

Numbers divided like 930–999 ar: 015, 309.1, 327, 342, 349, 354 (for governments outside the United States), 374.9, 376.8, 581.9, 591.9, 911, 912; *e.g.* Publishers weekly 015.73, Social conditions in London 309.1421, Roman law 349.37, Vassar college 376.8747, Map of Louisiana 912.763.

Numbers divided like 940–999 ar: 274–279, 314–319, 324, 325, 328, 336, 373.4–.9, 378.4–.9 (except 378.99), 379.4–.9, 508.4–.9, 554–559; *e.g.* General church history of Belgium 274.93, Foren population in Illinois 325.773, Scientific travels in Brazil 508.81.

353.9 may be subdivided by states like 974–979; *e.g.* Government of Virginia 353.9755.

924–928 may be divided like 400–800; *e.g.* Biografies of astronomers 925.2, Biografies of American poets 928.11.

Certain numbers may be divided like certain other numbers or groups of numbers representing allied subjects: *e.g.* 299 is divided ethnicly like 491–499, *e.g.* Egyptian religion 299.3; 561 like 580 Botany, *e.g.* Fossil ferns 561.7; 562–569 like 592–599 Zoology, *e.g.* Fossil reptils 568.1; 619 like 636 Domestic animals, *e.g.* Diseases of horses 619.1.

Each of the numbers above may be subdivided more minutely by use of ful tables, where many farther examples of ' divided like ' numbers may be found.

Variations from printed scheme

1   Letter notations for changes   Copyright does not allow printing our numbers with changed meanings. If you wish to alter them, ad a letter for your new meaning. But remember that this elementary form does not furnish data enuf for intelligent criticism. The subdivisions of the ful *Classification* make apparent many reasons which this abridgment can not show.

This plan of introducing letters or other symbols wherever each user pleases, wil giv all needed freedom to the personal equation

and desire for originality, and meets all real wants for peculiar classification in peculiar cases.

Fiction   As half the circulation in popular libraries is often fiction, omit the class number entirely and use merely the book number, as described on p. 9–10.   *No* class number then means fiction in the English language, whether original or translated.

Juvenils   Class juvenils exactly as if for adults, with J prefixt to class number.   In juvenil *fiction* prefix j (small) to prevent confusion with capital of book number; e. g. jJ6 Johnson's *Williams of West Point*.   Then arrange juvenils in a parallel library by themselvs, so that J942 comes between J941, juvenil history of Scotland, and J943, juvenil history of Germany.

> Or put J books by themselvs at the end of each class number; or put them in alfabetic order among other books on the same subject.   In this last case J is useful only to call attention plainly to their juvenil caracter.

2 Broken order   A common and often desirable variation for shelf arrangement is to break sequence of numbers, either to put books most used (fiction, juvenils, and biografy) nearest the delivery desk; or to bring together Sociology (300) and History (900), Filology (400) and Literature (800).   The strict theory is to keep the whole 1000 numbers in exact sequence; but a higher rule to be obeyd everywhere is to sacrifice any theory for a substantial gain.   There need be no hesitation in breaking regular order if enuf is gaind, but posters or dummies and charts should show clearly where to find any group removed from its natural place; e. g. after 520 a dummy saying 'In observatory.'

Other uses

Scrapbooks   Use scrap sheets of uniform size, with class number of subject written in upper front corner of the page.   Mount clippings on the sheet as in a common scrapbook.   When one sheet is full, insert another next it.   Thus perfect classification is kept up without blank sheets, and at the smallest outlay of money and trouble. These sheets ar then arranged numericly like a **clast**

card catalog, the sheets of each class being farther arranged, when required, under alfabetic subheds. Scraps thus mounted ar shelvd either in pamflet cases or in patent binders, or ar kept in vertical files.

Index rerums These ar best made on the standard P size (7.5 x 12.5 cm) card or slip. Light weight catalog card stock is best for private indexes, etc. It costs only half as much as hevy bristol and takes only half the room.

> Where durability and convenience of handling ar less important than cheapness, common hevy writing paper may be used; but most novises greatly diminish the usefulness of the card system by using ordinary machine-cut cards or slips varying in hight so much as to make quick and accurate manipulation impossible. The extreme variation that should be tolerated is 1 millimeter or $\frac{1}{25}$ inch. This wil be understood by placing a 7.4 cm card between two 7.5 cm cards. The fingers make a bridge across the taller cards and miss the lower one entirely in rapid turning. Cards must be accurately cut or they wil lose half their value, and in many cases make it necessary to recopy the material at a cost tenfold greater than to hav thrown away at the outset the imperfectly cut cards or slips.

Class number is written in upper left corner, any alfabetic subject hed follows at the right, and notes fil the card below. The cards ar then filed in order of class numbers, the cards of each class being farther arranged, like the scrap sheets, according to alfabetic subheds. Paper the size of scrap sheets, 20 x 25 cm, arranged and stored the same way, may be used insted of cards. Scores of devices for convenient handling and storing of these slips and sheets and pamflets ar manufactured. The full descriptiv and illustrated Library Bureau catalogs and the catalogs of other library supply houses giv details.

Topical indexes D C class numbers ar used to index books red. The number takes the place of a series of words, and the results can be handled, arranged and found much quicker because of the simple numerals. Such entries may be kept separate or combined with the index rerum.

Fuller explanation and discussion may be found in the Introduction to the unabridged *Decimal classification*.

CLASSES

0 General works

1 Filosofy

2 Religion

3 Social sciences

4 Filology

5 Pure science

6 Useful arts

7 Fine arts

8 Literature

9 History

DIVISIONS

000	**General works**	500	**Pure science**
010	Bibliografy	510	Mathematics
020	Library economy	520	Astronomy
030	General cyclopedias	530	Physics
040	General collected essays	540	Chemistry
050	General periodicals	550	Geology
060	General societies Museums	560	Paleontology
070	Journalism Newspapers	570	Biology Anthropology
080	Polygrafy Special libraries	580	Botany
090	Book rarities	590	Zoology
100	**Filosofy**	600	**Useful arts**
110	Metaphysics	610	Medicin
120	Special metaphysical topics	620	Engineering
130	Mind and body	630	Agriculture
140	Filosofic systems	640	Home economics
150	Psychology	650	Communication Business
160	Logic Dialectics	660	Chemic technology
170	Ethics	670	Manufactures
180	Ancient filosofers	680	Mechanic trades
190	Modern filosofers	690	Bilding
200	**Religion**	700	**Fine arts Recreation**
210	Natural theology	710	Landscape gardening
220	Bible	720	Architecture
230	Doctrinal Dogmatics Theology	730	Sculpture
240	Devotional Practical	740	Drawing Decoration Design
250	Homiletic Pastoral Parochial	750	Painting
260	Church Institutions Work	760	Engraving
270	General Hist. of Christian church	770	Fotografy
280	Christian churches and sects	780	Music
290	Nonchristian religions	790	Amusements
300	**Social sciences Sociology**	800	**Literature**
310	Statistics	810	American
320	Political science	820	English Anglo-Saxon
330	Economics	830	German and other Teutonic
340	Law	840	French Provençal
350	Administration	850	Italian Rumanian
360	Associations and institutions	860	Spanish Portuguese
370	Education	870	Latin and other Italic
380	Commerce Communication	880	Greek and other Hellenic
390	Customs Costumes Folklore	890	Other literatures
400	**Filology**	900	**History**
410	Comparativ	910	Geografy and travels
420	English Anglo-Saxon	920	Biografy
430	German and other Teutonic	930	Ancient history
440	French Provençal	940	Europe
450	Italian Rumanian	950	Asia
460	Spanish Portuguese	960	Africa
470	Latin and other Italic	970	North America
480	Greek and other Hellenic	980	South America
490	Other languages	990	Oceania and polar regions

(940–990 bracketed as **Modern**)

General works

010 Bibliografy

Including both bibliografies and catalogs. Bibliografies show what books hav been written by certain authors (011), or in certain countries (015), or on certain subjects (016);
but often not what books there ar in any one collection (Catalogs 017–019)

011 General bibliografies   Universal catalogs

Entries in author order; if in subject order class in 016
Properly a catalog is of a special collection and so tels where the works may be
found. A bibliografy disregards actual location and tels what there is, but its contents can seldom be found in any one library
012–016 include both bibliografies and catalogs. 017–019 is limited to catalogs of
general collections

012 Of individuals

Alfabeted by subjects of bibliografies (bibliografees), not by compilers; e. g. Chaucer,
Dante, Ruskin, etc. A bibliografy of an individual may include either works about
or by the individual, or both

013 Of special classes of authors

e. g. Jesuits, members of French academy, Yale alumni

014 Of special forms: anonyms, pseudonyms, etc.

e. g. Frey's *Sobriquets and nicknames*

015 Of special countries

Books publisht in the country. Publishers' lists, current publications. Bibliografy
of books publisht in England, as Lowndes or English catalog
The history of literature, i. e. belles lettres, poetry, drama, fiction, etc. goes, of course,
with those topics in 800; but the literary history of any given place or period covering the writings on all subjects, as wel as in literature, is bibliografy, and goes usually
in 015, tho the literary history of some special class of authors is 013

.7 American e. g. *Publishers weekly, American catalog*

016 Of special subjects

Put here also clast bibliografies (e. g. *ALA catalog*) and catalogs of libraries on special
subjects (026); but for other catalogs arranged by subjects, see 017 and 019

Bibliografy of

.1	Filosofy		.6	Useful arts
.2	Religion		.7	Fine arts
.3	Social sciences		.8	Literature
.4	Filology		.9	History
.5	Pure science			Including travel and biografy

017–019 Catalogs: library and sale

Class a catalog of any special subject, whether subject, author, or dictionary, under
its subject number in 016, which is the ruling hed wherever it conflicts with another.
017–019 therefore include only catalogs of general collections, limited to no one class
or subject

017 Clast catalogs: systematic or logical

Put any form of alfabetic subject catalog in 019. But put clast bibliografies and
catalogs of special subjects in 016

018 Author catalogs

See 011 for Bibliografies
Put author and clast bound together in 017. 018 includes accession, cronologic, and
any other forms (except subject and dictionary) of catalogs of collections

019 Dictionary catalogs: alfabetico-clast, etc.

020 Library economy

.5 Periodicals
.6 Societies, associations, clubs, conferences
.62 Local clubs
.7 Education Training Library schools

021 Scope, usefulness and founding of libraries

'People's university'; relations to clubs, etc. Also scope and founding of combined libraries and museums. Support, development

.3 Library in relation to schools and the young

This is mainly for relations of general public libraries to school work. Class a library ownd by and kept at the school in 027.8. Class general work for children with children's libraries in 027.6

.8 Libraries and the state Library laws

State aid: subsidies, free importation, cheap postage, etc.

.9 Support, raising funds, etc.

For state aid separate from local help see 021.8

022 Bildings

See also 727 Architecture of educational bildings; but class library bildings here. For care of bilding, see 025.9

.4 Storage and shelving
.9 Fixtures, furniture, fittings

023 Government and servis

Charter, bylaws, trustees, librarian, staf; duties, pay, etc.

024 Rules for readers

Qualifications, fees or free use, library hours, reference use, loans, special privileges; injuries and abuses by readers

025 Administration Departments

025 is for the librarian's part. The trustees bild and furnish (022); make rules for government and servis (023), and rules for readers (024); but the administration involvs questions of its own, which, however, ar closely allied to topics in 021–024 and elsewhere; e. g. the librarian must know his side of binding, and be able to giv proper directions and supervision, but need not know all the details of the binder's craft (686)

Administration includes .1 Supervision .2 Acquisition .3–.6 Utilization .7–.9 Preservation; i. e. the librarian's duty to books is to Get, Use, Keep

.1 Executiv General supervision

Finances, accounts, salaries (see 023); supplies, printing; publications, statistics, reports, bulletins; relations to readers, permits, privileges, visitors; correspondence

.2 Accession Acquisition

Selecting and buying books, serials, pamflets, efemera; prices, discounts, duty free importation (see 021.8); auctions, old book lists; sale duplicates, exchanges, gifts (see also 021.9); reception, checking bils, collation; plating, pocketing, embossing, private marking; accessioning; order slips, index and book, order and serial blanks

.3 Catalog

For printed catalogs themselvs, see 017–019. This is for *cataloging*
Printed, manuscript, or card; author, subject, title, clast; dictionary or combined; cooperativ rules; size notation; cooperativ cataloging; duplicated titles, print or fotografy; mechanical accessories, cards, cases and fittings, drawers, trays, blocks, checks, guides, labels

.4 Classification

For filosofic classification of knowledge, see 112 Methodology. This is for practical classing of books, pamflets, and notes, rather than theoretic speculation
On shelvs; in catalogs; in dictionary catalogs; systems of notation, figures, letters, symbols, combined; importance and advantages; difficulties; close *vs* broad classing; mnemonic features; basis of division; coordination of special subjects

025.5   Reference   Reference books   Aids to readers

> See 028 for general discussion of reading and aids. This is limited to library administration

.6   Loan

> See also 024 for Rules
> Indicators; charging systems, legers *vs* cards; book cards, marks, pockets; call slips, readers cards; notises, reservs; registers; interlibrary loans; mecanical accessories, slip cases, trays, tils, stamps, etc.

.7   Binding and repair

> See also 686 Bookbinding
> Materials, durability, tight *vs* spring backs, sewing, color, lettering; paper covers and temporary binders; restoring, mending, cleaning, and oiling

.8   Shelf

> See also 022.9 Shelving
> Arrangement; shelf numbers; shelf and book labels; fixt and relativ locations; sizes on shelvs; arrangement and preservation of public documents, pamflets, papers, manuscripts, maps, drawings, and plans, music, broadsides, clippings; injuries, heat, gas, insects; stocktaking; shelf lists

.9   Bilding   Care, cleaning, safety   Janitor   Police

> See 022 for bilding and fittings. This is janitor's department

026   Libraries on special subjects

> Histories, reports, statistics, bulletins, handbooks, circulars, and everything about the library not more required in one of the sections above; e. g. a Medical library, a Chess library; but the catalog of a Chess library is 016.7; blanks, etc. from any library go in 025, as more used in studying topics

027   General libraries

> This includes both circulating and reference; i. e. all not limited to special subjects. A private library is stil clast 027.1, after it has been sold or merged in a public library. But reports of a society library changed to a free public should class in 027.4 after the change; and if not too much earlier material aledy on the shelvs, change all to new number insted of making cross reference

.1   Private and family

.2   Proprietary: society, club, atheneum

> .2 is limited to libraries that ar semi-private, requiring an election for admission, while .3 includes all open to any one on payment of a fee. It is the difference between a club and a hotel. .3 is for libraries run as a business. A mercantil library, even tho it has endowments, if open without individual election, goes in .3 as a subsidized public subscription library. Many private subscription libraries go in **.2**

.3   Subscription   Circulating

> Mudie's, Booklovers, etc.

.4   Free public   Rate supported   Endowd

> Public library commissions. See also 331.8, and 027 last note

.5   State and government

.6   For special classes

> Children, institution, prison, reformatory, asylum, blind, monastic, workmen, factory, railroad, sailors, lighthouse. A workmen's library of books on engineering goes in 026, not here, as the subject is more useful than the class of readers

.62   Children's libraries   Storytelling

.7   College

.8   School   Sundayschool   Parish

> See also 371.6 Libraries as school equipment; 021.3 Library in relation to schools and the young; 028.5 Reading of the young

.9   Free newsrooms and reading-rooms

028   **Reading and aids**

       See also 374 Self education

    . 5   Reading of young   Juvenils

       Both discussion and lists of books

029   **Literary methods and labor savers**

       Much in 025 and 028 belongs equally under 029 in its ful meaning, but practical convenience is best servd by keeping such material under those heds insted of separating a part here

030   General cyclopedias

       Subdivisions of 030–050 ar by language, not by country

031	American	036	Spanish
	e. g. Americana, International		
032	English	037	Slavic
	e. g. Britannica, Chambers		
033	German	038	Scandinavian
	e. g. Brockhaus		
034	French	039	Other languages
	e. g. Larousse		
035	Italian		

040   General collected essays

       Bound pamflets (essays, addresses, etc.), scrapbooks, etc. too general for any one class 041 American, 042 English, etc. like 031, 032, etc.

050   General periodicals, magazines

       051 American, e. g. Atlantic, Century, Harper's, Scribner's; 052 English, e. g. Athenaeum, Blackwood's, Contemporary; like 031, 032, etc.

060   General learned societies, transactions

       061 American; 062 English, like 031, 032, etc., except use *068 for Other countries* insted of limiting it to Scandinavian

069   Museums   Museum economy

070   General newspapers   Journalism

       071 American, 072 English, etc. like 031, 032, etc.

080 Polygrafy   Special libraries

Including sets or 'libraries' so constituted as not to be redily scatterd by subjects, and miscellaneous information; but class in 803 *literary* questions and answers, even the not alfabetic. Collections conditiond by terms of gift on being kept together ar better clast as a parallel library distinguisht by a letter; e. g. the Doe collection D010–D999

081   Individual polygrafy

Complete or partial collections of an author's works, treating of various subjects. If they treat exclusivly or mainly of one subject they ar clast with that subject

082   Collectiv polygrafy

Distinct works of several authors, treating of different subjects and publisht in a collection

083   Official publications

Official publications of countries, states, provinces, cities and other public bodies and powers may be clast together here but ar much better clast with subject treated or, if too general for that, with body by which issued

087   Publications for various classes of readers

Children's collections may be clast here but ar much better kept as a separate collection markt J, the separate books being given their regular subject numbers (see paragraf relating to Juvenils, in Introduction, p. 12)

090 Book rarities

For books about these topics, and those chiefly valuable because of their rarity; but class a rare early edition of Shakspere in 822.3

091   Manuscripts   Autografs

Class in 096 mss important chiefly for illumination. Fotografs of mss, when more valuable for subject matter, go with subject rather than here. For diplomatics and paleografy, see 417, and special languages, 421, 431, etc.

092   Block books
093   Books printed before 1500   Incunabula
094   Rare printing

Aldines, Elzevirs, Caxtons, etc.; privately printed or unique books

095   Rare binding

By noted binders, with costly ornament, curious bindings

096   Rare illustrations or materials

Illuminated. Illustrated by inserted plates. Printed on vellum, silk, bark, etc., in gold or silver letters, etc.

097   Ownership   Book plates   Ex libris

Noted or rare. See also 025.2

098   Other classes of works, based on inner caracteristics

Prohibited, lost, imaginary, etc.

099   Other classes of works, based on outer caracteristics Curiosa

Minute size, etc.

Filosofy

100 Filosofy in general
Works limited to none of the 9 divisions

101   Utility

102   Compends   Outlines

103   Dictionaries   Cyclopedias

104   Essays   Lectures   Addresses

105   Periodicals   Magazines   Reviews

106   Societies   Transactions   Reports

107   Education   Study and teaching

108   Polygrafy   Collected works   Extracts, maxims, etc.

109   History of filosofy

110 Metaphysics

111   Ontology
        Nature of being.   Substance and form

112   Methodology
        Filosofic classification of knowledge.   Terminology.   For book classification, see 025.4

113   Cosmology

114	Space	117	Matter
115	Time	118	Force
116	Motion	119	Quantity Number

120 Other metaphysical topics

121   Theory of knowledge   Origin   Limits

122   Causation   Cause and effect

123   Liberty and necessity
        See also 159 Wil

124   Teleology   Final causes

125   Infinit and finite

126   Consciousness   Personality

127   Unconsciousness   Automatons

128   The soul
        See also 218 Natural theology; 237 Future state

129   Origin and destiny of individual soul

130 Mind and body

For alternativ scheme see 159.9

131 Mental physiology and hygiene

New thought, psychoanalysis

132 Mental derangements

133 Occultism   Witchcraft   Astrology   Magic
Palmistry   Clairvoyance

Psychic fenomena, telepathy, spiritism

134 Mesmerism

Hypnotism, animal magnetism

135 Sleep and wakefulness   Dreams   Somnambulism

136 Mental caracteristics

See also 131 Mental physiology

.7   Childstudy   Paidology

137 Personality   Grafology

Temperaments, idiosyncrasy

138 Physiognomy

Expression of mentality thru the body

139 Frenology   Mental fotografs, etc.

140 Filosofic systems

The heds 140–149 ar for discussion of the systems as such.   The filosofic works of authors
of these various schools ar clast 180–190, not here.   From these heds refer in the catalogs
to authors clearly falling under them, without attempting to label each writer as an
exponent of some one system

141 Idealism   Transcendentalism

e. g. Plato, see 184, 888; Berkeley, see 192; Fichte, see 193; Emerson, see 191, 814

142 Critical filosofy

e. g. Kant, see 193

143 Intuitionalism

e. g. Reid, see 192; McCosh, see 191.   See also 156 Intuitiv faculty; 171 Ethics

144 Empiricism

e. g. Descartes, see 194; Bacon, see 192

145 Sensationalism

e. g. Locke, see 192

146 Materialism   Positivism

e. g. Hobbes, see 192; Comte, see 194   See also 149 Realism

147 Pantheism   Monism

e. g. Spinoza, see 199   See also 212 Natural theology

148 Eclecticism

e. g. Cousin, see 194

149 Other filosofic systems

See 211 Rationalism, skepticism; 214 Fatalism

150 Psychology

For alternativ scheme see 159.9   For related topics, see Mental in Relativ index following Tables

151   Intellect   Capacity for knowing
        Genius

152   Sensation   Sense perceptions
        Passiv or receptiv faculty

153   Understanding   Depth psychology
        Activ or thinking faculty

154   Memory   Reproductiv power
155   Imagination   Creativ power
156   Intuitiv faculty   Innate reason
        For reasoning, the act of deriving conclusions from premises, see 153

157   Sensibility   Emotions   Affections
158   Instincts   Appetites   Conation

159   Volition   Wil

159.9 Psychology   (Alternativ scheme)

The following tables for Psychology may be used insted of 130–139 and 150–159 by those preferring a scheme based on current lines of thought

.901   Filosofy   Theories   Laws
        Mind and body

.91 Physiologic psychology   Mental physiology and hygiene
        New thought

.92 Mental development and capacity
        Consciousness, intelligence, intellect, etc.

.922   Mental caracteristics
        See alo 159.91 Mental physiology

    7   Childstudy   Paidology

.923   Psychology of types   Individual psychology
        Personality, temperaments, idiosyncrasies

.924   Genius

.925   Physiognomy   Frenology   Grafology   Palmistry
        Expression of mentality thru the body

.93 Sensation   Sense perception
        Receptiv functions

.94 Executiv functions

.942   Emotions   Sensibility   Affections

.943   Conation and movement   Motor functions
        Drives, instincts, appetites

.947   Volition   Wil

159.95 Higher mental processes

.953   Memory and lerning   Reproductiv power

.954   Imagination   Creativ power

.955   Thought and thinking   Understanding

.956   Intuition   Innate reason

        For reasoning, the act of deriving conclusions from premises, see 159.955

.96   Special mental conditions

        Psychic fenomena

.961   Psychic research

        Occultism, witchcraft, magic; astrology; telepathy, clairvoyance; spiritism

.962   Hypnotism   Mesmerism   Animal magnetism

.963   Sleep and wakefulness   Dreams   Somnambulism

.964   Depth psychology   Psychoanalysis

.97   Abnormal psychology

        Mental derangements, psychiatry

159.9 Psychology (alternativ scheme)

Index

Aberration, mental	159.97	Cardiff giant humbugs	159.961
Abnormal children childstudy	159.9227	Catalepsy	159.97
psychology	159.97	**Characteristics, mental**	**159.922**
Absent-mindedness	159.95	Charlatanry	159.961
Abstraction	159.955	Charms	159.961
Acclimatization	159.922	Children, abnormal childstudy	159.9227
Affections	159.942	Childstudy	159.9227
Age	159.922	Chirognomy	159.925
Alienism	159.97	Chiromancy	159.925
Ancestry	159.922	Chirosofy	159.925
Anglo-Saxon race caracteristics	159.922	Choice, freedom of	159.947
Animal electricity	159.962	Clairvoyance	159.961
magnetism	159.962	Cleptomania	159.97
Anthropology	159.901	Color sense	159.93
Apparitions	159.961	Conation	159.943
Appetites	159.943	Concept	159.955
Association	159.953	Conjuring	159.961
Astrology	159.961	Consciousness	159.92
		Creativ power	159.954
		Criminals, juvenil childstudy	159.9227
Black art	159.961		
Body and mind	159.901	Deduction	159.955
Boy problem	159.9227	Delineation of children	159.9227
Brain mental derangements	159.97	Delusions	159.961
physiology	159.91	Demonology	159.961
		Depth psychology	159.964
Cabalistic art	159.961	Derangement, mental	159.97
Capacity for knowing	**159.92**	Determinism	159.947
Caracteristics, mental	**159.922**	Devils witchcraft	159.961

Topics in blackface type ar subdivided in the Tables

Dipsomania	159.97
Diseases, mental	159.97
Divination	159.961
Dreams	159.963
Drives	159.943
Ear	159.93
Ecstatics	159.97
Electricity, animal	159.962
Electro-biology	159.962
physiology	159.962
Emotions	159.942
Enthusiasm	159.942
Environment	159.922
Errors, popular	159.961
Evil eye	159.961
Executiv functions	**159.94**
Exorcism	159.961
Expression, facial physiognomy	159.925
Eyes	159.93
Faculty, intuitiv	159.956
Fancy	159.954
Fantoms	159.961
Fear	159.942
Feeble-minded childstudy	159.9227
mental derangements	159.97
Feelings	159.942
Filoprogenitivness frenology	159.925
Fools	159.97
Fortune-telling	159.961
Free wil	159.947
Frenology	159.925
Genius	159.924
hereditary	159.922
Geomancy	159.961
Ghosts	159.961
Giant, Cardiff humbugs	159.961
Graphology	159.925
Habit	159.943
Hallucinations	159.961
Hand chiromancy	159.925
Haunted houses	159.961
Hearing	159.93
Hed frenology	159.925
Hereditary genius	159.924
Heredity, mental	159.922
Horoscope	159.961
Human body and mind	159.901
faculties, mental	**159.9**
nature	**159.922**
Humbugs	159.961
Hygiene, mental	159.91
Hypnotism	159.962
Hypochondria	159.97
Hysterics	159.97
Ideas, innate	159.956
Idiocy	159.97
Idiosyncrasies, mental	159.923
Illusions	159.961
Imagination	159.954
Imbecility	159.97
Imposture	159.961
Incantations	159.961
Indeterminism	159.947
Individual psychology	159.923
Induction	159.955
Infancy, psychology of	159.9227
Innate ideas	159.956
Insanity	159.97
Instinct, human	159.943
Intellect	159.92
Intellectual filosofy	**159.9**
Intelligence, human	159.92
Intuition	159.956
Judgment	159.955
Kleptomania	159.97
Laughter	159.942
Learning	159.953
Levitation	159.961
Liberty of wil	159.947
Lunacy	159.97
Lycanthropy	159.97
Madness	159.97
Magic, natural	159.961
Magnetism, animal	159.962
Man mental caracteristics	**159.922**
psychology	**159.9**
Mania	159.97
Mediums	159.961
Melancholy	159.97
Memory mental derangements	159.953
psychology	159.953
Mental capacity	**159.92**
of women	159.922
caracteristics	**159.922**
derangements	159.97
development childstudy	159.9227
faculties	**159.9**
filosofy	**159.9**
fotografs	159.925
heredity	159.922
physiology and hygiene	159.91
Mesmerism	159.962
Mind	**159.9**
and body	159.901
reading	159.962

Topics in blackface type ar subdivided in the Tables

Mnemonic derangements	159.953
Mnemonics	159.953
Monomania	159.97
Motor functions	159.943
Movement	159.943
Muscle-reading	159.961
Muscular sense	159.93
Mysteries	159.961
Natural magic	159.961
Necromancers	159.961
Negro race mentality	159.922
New thought	159.91
Notion	159.955
Observation	159.93
Obsession	159.961
Occult sciences	159.961
Odic force	159.962
Olfaction	159.93
Omens	159.961
Oracles	159.961
Overwork, mental	159.91
Paidology	159.9227
Palmistry	159.925
Pathology mental	159.97
Perception	159.93
Personality	159.923
Phantoms	159.961
Phrenology	159.925
Physical conditions	159.922
Physiognomy	159.925
Physiologic psychology	159.91
Physiology mental	159.91
Pleasure	159.942
Popular delusions	159.961
Portents	159.961
Predictions	159.961
Presages	159.961
Prognostications	159.961
Psychiatry	159.97
Psychic fenomena	**159.96**
medicin	159.97
research	159.961
Psychoanalysis	159.964
Psychology	**159.9**
Psychomancy	159.961
Quackery	159.961
Race influence on mind	159.922
Reason, innate	159.956
Reasoning	159.955
Receptiv functions	159.93
Reflection	159.955
Reproductiv power	159.953
Research, psychic	159.961
Satan and Satanism	159.961
Science, mental	**159.9**
Sciences, occult	159.961
Sea serpent delusions	159.961
Second sight	159.961
Sensation	159.93
Sense	159.93
Sensibility	159.942
Sexes mental caracteristics	159.922
Sibyllin books	159.961
Sight	159.93
Sleep	159.963
Sleepwalking	159.963
Smel	159.93
Somnambulism	159.963
Sorcery	159.961
Specters	159.961
Spiritism	159.961
Spiritual heredity	159.922
Spiritualism, modern	159.961
Suggestion hypnotism	159.962
Supernaturalism	159.961
Superstitions	159.961
Susceptibility	159.942
Sympathy	159.942
Table tipping	159.961
Talent	**159.92**
Talismans	159.961
Taste	159.93
Telepathy	159.961
Temperaments	159.923
Tests, psychologic	159.92
Thinking	159.955
Thought	159.955
transference	159.961
Touch	159.93
Trance	159.962
Types psychology of	159.923
Understanding	159.955
Vaticination	159.961
Vision	159.93
Visions and dreams	159.963
Volition	159.947
Voodooism	159.961
Wakefulness	159.963
Warnings	159.961
Wil	159.947
Witchcraft	159.961

Topics in blackface type ar subdivided in the Tables

160 Logic   Dialectics

See also 153 (or alternativ number 159.955) Reasoning power.   For Logic of chance, see 519 Probabilities

161 Inductiv

162 Deductiv

163 Assent   Faith

See also 234 Doctrin of salvation

164 Symbolic   Algebraic

Logical machines

Logical topics

165 Sources of error   Fallacies

166 Syllogism   Enthymeme

167 Hypotheses

168 Argument and persuasion

169 Analogy   Correspondence

See also 219 Natural theology

170 Ethics, theoretic and applied

Many topics in applied ethics occur also in law, specially in 343 Criminal law. See also 377 Ethical education

171 Theories   Filosofy of ethics

172 State ethics

.4   International ethics   Peace and war

See also 341 International law

173 Family ethics

Duties of husbands and wives, parents, children, masters and servants

174 Professional and business ethics

Including speculation, mammonism, avaris; gambling; honor, honesty, dishonesty

175 Ethics of amusements

For Amusements, see 790

176 Sexual ethics

Including immorality in art and literature

177 Social ethics   Caste

178 Temperance   Stimulants and narcotics

See also 613 Hygiene; 331.8 Laboring classes

179 Other ethical topics

.2   Cruelty

Societies for preventing cruelty to children and also general humane societies covering work for both children and animals. See also Infanticide in ethics 173, in customs 392; 331.3 Labor of children

.3   Cruelty to animals

.4   Vivisection

180 Ancient filosofers

Sections 180–199 ar for the history of filosofy in special countries and for the discussion of the filosofic systems of individual authors and for their works not clearly belonging elsewhere. Mill's *Logic* is 160 not 192, and Hegel's *Filosofy of history* is 901 not 193, but their complete filosofic works belong here. Collected lives of filosofers ar clast 921, and individual lives ar placed in the alfabetic series of biografy

181   Oriental

Here ar clast *all* Oriental filosofers, including medieval and modern

182   Early Greek

183   Sofistic and Socratic

184   Platonic   Older Academy

185   Aristotelian   Paripatetic   Lyceum

186   Pyrrhonist   New Platonist

187   Epicurean: Epicurus   Lucretius

188   Stoic

189   Early Christian and medieval

See note under 181

190 Modern filosofers

See notes under 140 and 180

191   American

192   British

193   German

194   French

195   Italian

196   Spanish

197   Slavic

198   Scandinavian

199   Other modern

See note under 181

Religion

200 Religion in general

201 Filosofy, theories; 202 Compends, etc. like 101–109
Class history, reports, etc. of Bible, Tract, etc. societies in 206, but put their publications with subject. Class theologic seminaries in 207. See also 377 Religious and secular education

210 Natural theology

Concerns evidence in nature exclusiv of revelation, also Christian or skeptic discussion of specific topics (211–214, 216–218). For general defense of Christian theology, see 239 Apologetiçs

211 Deism and atheism

Skepticism. Infidelity. Rationalism, etc.
Atheism denies existence of God. Deism accepts existence, but denies revelation and rejects Christianity. Theism believes in a god supernaturally reveald, e. g. Judaism, Mohammedanism, Buddhism, etc. Arguments from nature in support of any of these views go here
See also 231 Christian theism; 273 Heresies; 149 Agnosticism

212 Pantheism Theosofy

See 147 Pantheism; 129 Origin of soul

213 Creation Evolution

From religious viewpoint; attempts to harmonize *Genesis* and geology. See also metaphysics, 113 Cosmology; and natural science, 575 Evolution

214 Providence Theodicy

See 231 for Christian view

215 Religion and science

Antagonism or reconciliation between science and Bible religion. Arguments of scientists against scientists. Bridgewater treatises. For theologic defense, see 239. For creation, see 213

216 Good Evil Depravity

See also 149 Pessimism; 233 Sin

217 Prayer

Tests of efficacy of prayer. See also 264 Ritual; 248 Personal religion

218 Future life Immortality Eternity

See also 237 Future state; 128 The soul

219 Analogies Correspondences

See also 169 Logic

220 Bible General works

For similar works limited to Old or New Testament, or individual books, see specific hed below

.1 Canon Inspiration Profecy
.2 Concordances Analyses
.3 Dictionaries Cyclopedias
.4 Original texts and early versions Codices
.5 Versions of Bible Polyglots

These ar translations from original Hebrew and Greek. Translations from other early texts, e. g. an English translation of the Syriac, go in 220.4

.6 Hermeneutics Exegesis Symbolism Typology
.7 Commentaries on whole Bible, and annotated editions

For notes, etc. on parts of the Bible, see the most specific hed in 221–229

.8 Special topics
e. g. Biblical astronomy, botany, etc.

.9 Biblical geografy and history

221   Old Testament: texts, introductions, etc.

222   Historical books: Genesis to Esther
223   Poetic books: Job to Song of Solomon
224   Profetic books: Isaiah to Malachi

225   New Testament: texts, introductions, etc.

226   Gospels and Acts
227   Epistles
228   Apocalypse

229   Apocryfa

230   Doctrinal   Dogmatics   Theology

General doctrinal works may be subdivided by churches like 280–289. See also 252. Class here polemics either offensiv or defensiv, when distinctly doctrinal; but class history of a sect in 280, even if largely controversial and of a limited period. Class controversy about a special doctrin with its subject; e. g. controversy on the atonement 232

231   God   Unity   Trinity
232   Christology   Lives of Christ
233   Man
234   Salvation   Soteriology
235   Angels   Devils   Satan
236   Escatology   Last things
237   Future state   Immortality

     See also 218 Natural theology

238   Creeds   Confessions   Covenants   Catechisms
239   Apologetics   Evidences of Christianity

240   Devotional   Practical

241   Didactic

     Specifying the Christian's duty to do and to avoid. For catechisms, see 238

242   Meditativ   Contemplativ

     Consolatory. See also 248 Personal religion

243   Hortatory   Evangelistic

     Urging sinners to Christian repentance

244   Miscellany   Religious novels

     Sundayschool books, allegories, etc. But class Bunyan's *Pilgrim's progress* in fiction, because of his literary prominence

245   Hymnology   Religious poetry

     Hymns without music; hymns with music, see 783. See also 223 Psalms; 264 Public worship

246   Ecclesiology   Symbolism   Religious art

     246–247 cover religious bearings. For art side, see 700

247   Sacred furniture   Vestments   Vessels   Ornaments, etc.
248   Personal religion   Asceticism

     See also 273 Heresies

249   Family devotions

     For public worship, see 264

250 Homiletic   Pastoral   Parochial

251   Homiletics   Preaching

> See also 264 Public worship

252   Sermons

> Sermons on specific topics ar more useful, like other pamflets, clast with the topics, e. g. a sermon on family devotions in 249, not 252; on strikes in 331.89

253   Pastoral life, evangelistic   Celibacy

> See also 176 Sexual ethics; 248 Asceticism; 348 Celibacy, in canon law

254   Church finance   Cleric support

255   Brotherhoods   Sisterhoods

> Use of orders in parish work. See also 271 Monastic orders; 267 Religious societies

256   Societies for parish work: gilds, sodalities

> Local societies. Discussion of desirability of such work. For general societies, see 206 and 267

257   Parochial schools   Libraries, etc.

> See 377 Religious and secular education; ·027.8 Libraries

258   Parish care of sick, fallen, etc.

> See also 176 Sexual ethics

259   Other ministrations and work

260 Church   Institutions and work

261   The church

> Its influence on morals, civilization, etc. Relation to social questions, laboring classes, etc.

262   Ecclesiastic polity, church government

> Ministry, apostolic succession; parish, see; authority, private judgment, etc. See also 348 Canon law

263   Sabbath   Lord's day   Sunday

264   Public worship   Divine servis   Ritual

> See also 246 Ecclesiology; 247 Sacred furniture

265   Sacraments   Ordinances

266   Missions   Home and foren

> Missions of a special sect in several countries ar clast here. Missions in special countries or places covering the work of several sects go under the geograficly divided Religious history 274–279. The mission of a single sect in a special country or place may be clast with Missions in 266, or preferably with Religious history 274–279

267   Associations

> General societies demanding of members activ personal work. For local societies, see 256. For Bible, tract, and] similar general societies, see 206. For monastic orders, see 271, and for their use in parish work, see 255

   .3   Y M C A (Young Men's Christian ass'n)
   .5   Y W C A (Young Women's Christian ass'n)

268   Sunday schools   Religious education

269   Revivals   Retreats   Parish missions

270 General history of Christian church

For religious history of special countries, either general or for special periods, see country divisions, 274–279; e. g. English reformation, 274.2

271 Religious orders   Monasteries

Including monasticism and monastic foundations. See also 255 Use of brotherhoods in parish work; 377 Religious and secular education; 726 Religious architecture

271 .9   Sisterhoods

272   Persecutions

By Roman and by Anglican church, by puritans, etc.
See also special sects, 280; and history of special countries, 940–999

273   Heresies: gnostic, Sabellian, Arian, Pelagian, Molinist, agnostic, etc.

For the history of special doctrins, see 230–239 Doctrinal theology

274   General church history of Europe

.1	Scotland	Ireland	.6	Spain Portugal
.2	England	Wales	.7	Russia
.3	Germany	Austria	.8	Norway, Sweden and Denmark
	Czechoslovakia, Poland, Hungary			
.4	France		.9	Other European countries
.5	Italy			For countries included, see 949

275   General church history of Asia

.1	China		.6	Turkey in Asia
.2	Japan		.7	Siberia
.3	Arabia		.8	Afghanistan Turkestan
.4	India			Baluchistan
.5	Persia		.9	Farther India
				For countries included, see 959

276   General church history of Africa

.1	North Africa		.6	North central Africa
.2	Egypt		.7	South central Africa
.3	Abyssinia		.8	South Africa
.4	Morocco		.9	Madagascar Mauritius
.5	Algeria			

277   General church history of North America

.1	Canada British America
.2	Mexico Central America West Indies
.3	United States
.4	Northeastern or North Atlantic states, New England
.5	Southeastern or South Atlantic states
.6	South central or Gulf states
.7	North central or Lake states
.8	Western or Mountain states
.9	Pacific states

For the exact states covered by these general designations, see 974–979

278   General church history of South America

.1	Brazil		.6	Colombia Panama
.2	Argentina	*Patagonia		Ecuador
.3	Chile		.7	Venezuela
.4	Bolivia		.8	Guiana
.5	Peru		.9	Paraguay Uruguay

279   General church history of Oceania   Polar regions

.1	Malaysia Philippines		.6	Polynesia Hawaii
.2	Sunda		.7	Isolated ilands
.3	Australasia New Zealand		.8	Arctic regions Greenland
.4	Australia		.9	Antarctic regions
.5	New Guinea			

280   Christian church and sects
See also 270 Religious history

281   Primitiv and oriental churches
Eastern or Greco-Russian

282   Western or Roman catholic church

283   Anglican and American P E church

284   Continental protestant sects   Protestantism
Lutheran, Waldenses, Huguenots, Moravian

285   Presbyterian   Reformd   Congregational
Puritanism

286   Baptist   Immersionist

287   Methodist

288   Unitarian
See also 273 Heresies

289   Other Christian sects

290   Non-Christian religions
Including comparativ religion and general histories of religion where an equal or minor place is given to Christianity

291   Comparativ and general mythology

292   Greek and Roman mythology

293   Teutonic and northern mythology

294   Brahmanism   Buddhism
For other Indic religions, see 299. See also 891 Sanskrit literature; 177 Caste

295   Parseeism   Zend Avesta
For other Iranic religions, see 299. See also 891 Zend literature

296   Judaism   Jews
For other Semitic religions, see 299

297   Mohammedanism

298

299   Other nonchristian religions

Social sciences

300 Social sciences   Sociology in general

301 Filosofy (see 901 Filosofy of history), theories; 302 Compends, outlines, like 101, 102, etc. In 308 put collected works of statesmen; e. g. works of Adams, Jefferson, etc. 301–309 all hav Sociology in general as their subject, but it is treated in these various forms. A periodical on education is 370, not 305, which is only for periodicals on sociology in general. In sociology, most works in these forms ar limited to one division; e. g. to political economy, education, law, etc.

309   History of social science

.1   Social surveys

Better clast by general libraries in 913–919

310 Statistics

311   Theory, methods   Science of statistics

312   Population: progress   Vital statistics: births, deths, mortality, longevity

See also 614 Public helth

313   Special topics

Statistics of any special matter ar put with the subject, e. g. of Domestic animals in 636, of Shorthand in 653, of French novels in 843, of Theaters in 792, etc. The statistics of New York city would be 317, but the statistics of Medicin in New York would be put with 610 Medicin, i. e. topic outranks locality

Statistics of

314 Europe	317 North America
315 Asia	318 South America
316 Africa	319 Oceania

320 Political science

Theory of state and government. See also 350

321   Form of state

For discussion of form of state, what *may* be; for what *is*, see 342 Constitutional law and 353–354 United States and foren governments

322   Church and state

See also 172 State ethics; 261 The church

323   Internal relations with groups and individuals

Free speech, Liberty of the press; for Morals of the press, see 179; also, 070 Newspapers

.6   Citizenship

324   Suffrage

325   Colonies and immigration

Foren population in

.4	Europe	.7	North America
.5	Asia	.71	Canada
.6	Africa	.73	United States
.67	South Central Africa	.8	South America
.68	South Africa	.9	Oceania

326   Slavery
      See also 973.7 Civil war

327   Foren relations
      Diplomacy, consular servis

328   Legislation, lawmaking
      Legislativ bodies and annals

  .1   Parliamentary law

329   Political parties   Party conventions

330 Economics   Political economy

331   Labor and wages   Capital

  .1   Relations of capital to labor
        Industrial arbitration. Disciplin: deductions, stoppage, fines

  .2   Remuneration for work
        Wages, hire, pay, salary, fees

  .3   Labor of children
        See also 179.2 Cruelty to children

  .4   Labor of women
        See also 396 Employments of women

  .5   Work at reduced wages

  .6   Pauper labor   Cheap foren labor   Chinese
        See also 339 Pauperism; 362.5 Asylums

  .7   Skild and unskild labor

  .8   Laboring classes

  .87   Organization of labor

  .88   Trade unions and other labor societies
          See also 338 Gilds

  .89   Strikes
          Combinations of workmen   Retaliation by employers

332   Private finance: banks, money, credit, interest
      Stocks, bonds, investments

333   Land: ownership, rights and rent
      Conservation of natural resources
      See also 338 Production; 347 Realty; and 630 Agriculture

334   Cooperation

335   Socialism   Communism   Bolshevism

336   Public finance

  .2   Taxation

  .3   Loans   Public securities

337   Protection and free trade

  .9   Reciprocity

338   Production   Manufacture   Prices

339   Consumption of welth   Pauperism
      Conservation; restrictions on use or waste of materials and national resources
      See also Pauper, Pauperism, Welth, in Relativ index following Tables

340 Law

Most periodicals belong in Private law 347

Public law

341 International law

Including arbitration, Leag of Nations, treaties, etc.

342 Constitutional law and history

For administrativ law, see 350

343 Criminal law

344 Martial law

Private law

345 U S statutes and cases

346 British statutes and cases

Includes all reports in English language except U. S. reports

347 Treatises   General works

Put law of special topics with the subject; e. g. Insurance law, 368

348 Canon law

349 Foren law

350 Administration

Including military and naval science

351 Administration of central government

.6   Civil servis, civil servis reform, etc.

352 Local government   Town   City   County

See also 379 Public schools; 020 Libraries

353 United States and state government

See also 342 Constitutional law and history

354 Organization of central government   Foren states

See also 342 Constitutional law and history

355 Army   Military science

See also 623 Military engineering; 629.1 Aeronautics
Military organization, strategy, tactics, etc. For War department of U. S. or history
of regular army regiments, see 353; for Civil war regiments, see 973.7

.2   Military resources

Preparedness, recruitment, voluntary and compulsory enlistment, etc.

356 Infantry

357 Cavalry

358 Artillery, engineers, etc.

359 Naval science

See 623.8 Naval engineering

360 Welfare and social associations and institutions

Since the activities of bodies best known as 'Charities and corrections' societies cover several numbers, general works on this topic go in 360; e. g. *Proceedings* of national conference on social work

361   Charitable

362   Hospitals, asylums, and allied societies

.1   Sick and wounded   Incurables   Eye and ear infirmaries Lying-in hospitals   Dispensaries

.2   Insane
    For other relations, see Insane, Insanity in Relativ index

.3   Idiotic
    For other relations, see Idiocy, Idiots in Relativ index

.4   Blind   Def   Dum
    See also 371.9 Education

.5   Paupers
    For other relations, see Pauperism, Paupers in Relativ index

.6   Aged   Infirm   Bereft
    Mothers pensions.   Aid in cases of deth

.7   Children   Orfans   Foundlings
    Child welfare.   See also ethics, 179.2 Cruelty

363   Political: Tammany, Primrose leag, Ku Klux, etc.

364   Reformatory: schools, discharged convicts, criminal classes

365   Prisons   Disciplin

366   Secret societies   Masons, Rosicrucians, etc.
    See also 371.8 Coilege secret societies

367   Social clubs

368   Insurance
    See also 334 Cooperation

369   Other: e. g. Cincinnati

.1   Hereditary and patriotic societies (American)
.4   Young peoples' societies
.42   Boys   .46   Girls
.43   Boy scouts   .47   Campfire girls

370 Education

Disciplin in broad sense

.1   Theory, filosofy   Meaning   Aim
    Including science of education and general methodology. Not limited to any curriculum, school or class of schools. For specific methods, pedagogics, see 371

.7   Study of education   Institutions and organizations for training teachers
    Means and methods, including normal schools, institutes, etc. For need of training, kind and amount, see 371.1

371 Teachers   Methods   Disciplin

Practical methods. See 370.1 for theories of education. The following divisions concern instruction of all grades

.1   Teachers: professors, masters, instructors

See also 370.7 Training of teachers

.2   School organization   School records

Diary. 'Logbook.' For government of students, disciplin, see 371.5. For government supervision, see 379.1

.3   Methods of instruction and study

Discussion of pedagogic value of various methods. For methods of teaching specific subjects, see those subjects; for their educational value, see 375 Curriculum; e. g. teaching of science, 507, place of science in curriculum, 375.5

.4   Systems of education

Discussion of vocational or industrial training in schools. For Fröbel's system, see 372.2 Kindergarten; for trade schools, see 607

.5   Government   Disciplin   Authority

Including rewards, prizes, interschool literary contests, etc.

.6   School premises and equipment

.7   School hygiene   Overstudy   Fatigue

Including sanitary and medical inspection, school meals, championship games, etc.

.8   Student life and customs

Various aspects of student life and student activities outside regular courses of study

.9   Education of special classes

General questions; kind and methods of education for the physically, mentally or morally defectiv, exceptionals, Indians, etc. For institutions, see 362, 364. For study of abnormal children, see 136.7 (or alternativ number 159.9227) Childstudy

372   Elementary education

.2   Kindergarten

See also 371.4 Pestalozzian system, for theory and early history. Put Fröbel's work and development of his system here

373   Secondary   Academic   Preparatory

Class here discussions of general theories, methods, etc. pertaining specifically to secondary education, regardless of source of support. Class here also all private or endowd secondary schools for boys or both sexes; all public (taxsupported) secondary schools for boys or both sexes may be clast here or in 379.4–.9, all elementary schools (regardless of support) in 372, all schools and colleges solely for women in 376, and all colleges for men or for coeducation in 378. Class methods and questions peculiar to monastic, diocesan and parochial schools in 377, but class the schools themselves in 372, 373, 378, etc. according to their grades
For specific topics, see 371

.4   European schools

Eton, Harrow, Rugby, etc.

.7   American schools

Phillips academy (Andover or Exeter), Lawrenceville, etc.

**374   Home education   Self education and culture
Adult education**

Cultural, personal aspect of education
The term Home education covers the broad field of adult self education thru private reading, study clubs and reading circles, summer, vacation, evening, and correspondence schools, lecture courses and other forms of extension teaching, and other agencies for extending more widely opportunities and facilities for education outside the usual teaching institutions
For relations of this work to libraries, the natural centers for such activities, see 021.
See also 378.1 University extension

With or without personal guidance

374.1 Solitary study   Private reading   Conversation

Advantages to be derived from reading. Study alone with or without aid of reading lists, syllabuses, etc.

See 028 for preparation of guides, policy, methods, etc.

For vocational guidance, see 371.4

.2 Associated study   Clubs

Including debating societies, community centers, etc.

With personal guidance

.4 Correspondence teaching   Manuscript aids

Including methods of correspondence teaching

.5 Lectures

.6 Extension courses   Lecture study

.8 Continuation schools

Summer, winter, vacation, night (adult) etc. German auxiliary schools

.9 Central organizations, state departments, institutes

N Y state library extension division, Brooklyn institute, Cooper institute, Chautauqua, etc.

375 Curriculum

Educational value or place in curriculum of

.1	Filosofy, logic, ethics	6	Useful arts, trades
.2	Religion, theology	.7	Fine arts
.3	Social sciences	.8	Literature
.4	Filology, languages	.9	History, geografy,
.5	Pure science		antiquities

376 Education of women

See also 396 Woman's position and treatment

.7 Coeducation   Segregation   Separation

Discussion of collegiate education of women in separate institutions or those for both sexes, whether in the same or separate classes. See 378 for coeducational institutions, 376.8 for separately organized colleges, either affiliated like Barnard and Radcliffe or independent like Vassar, Smith, etc.

Class here by attraction general discussion of coeducation of sexes in college and secondary school

.8 Colleges for women

Degreeconferring colleges go here. Arrange material of each college by 'Table for school and college publications' following 378.9. All other schools for women go in 376

377 Religious, ethical, and secular education

378 Colleges and universities

With power of conferring degrees; also junior colleges

.1 Organization   Location   Scope

Classes, colleges, graduate departments, etc.   Freedom of teaching

.2 Academic degrees and costume   College colors

For state control of medical degrees, see 614.2

.3 Endowment of research   Fellowships   Scholarships   Student aid

378.4–.9 Colleges and universities in special countries

.4 Europe .8 South America
.5 Asia .9 Oceania: New Zealand, Aus-
.6 Africa tralia, etc.
.7 North America, United States
.71 Canada

Table for school and college publications

A Charter and statutes
B Trustees Regents Resolutions, reports, etc.
C Administration President, chancellor Reports, etc.
D Finances Tresurer's reports
E History Foundation, growth, etc.
F Biografy Necrology
G General catalogs Triennials, etc.
H Annual catalogs Attendance, registers, etc.
I Handbooks Circulars of information
J Bulletins Official periodicals
K Commencements, inaugurals, etc. Baccalaureate and other addresses
L Programs Tickets Memorabilia
M Faculty (as a body) Publications Regulations Certificates
for admission
N Lectures Class manuals Examination questions
O Student theses Orations, essays, etc.
P Student catalogs Society annuals, etc.
Q Student periodicals
R Student societies, including periodicals
S Student miscellany Songs Class day, etc.
T Alumni Societies, committees, etc.
U Classes Histories, records, etc.
V Pictures Class albums
W Bildings and grounds Descriptions, maps, etc.
Z Schools: divinity, law, medical, etc.

Better clast with subject; e. g. Divinity schools 207

379 Public schools Relation of state to education

.1 Public school system
Funds, laws, supervision, etc.

.2 Illiteracy Instruction of illiterates Compulsory education

.4–.9 Public education in special countries
Subdivided like 378.4–.9

380 Commerce Communication

Public utilities. The technical side of these questions goes mostly in 650 Useful arts.
Here belong discussions of social and political relations; e. g. government control of railways, telegraf, etc.

381 Domestic trade

382 Foren trade Consular reports
Trade between mother country and colony

383 Postal servis

384 Telegraf Cable Telefone
See also 621.3 for construction and 654 for operation

385 Railroad and express
Government ownership or control. Interstate commerce commission
See also 656 Railroading

386 Waterways   Inland navigation
See also useful arts, 656 Transport

387 Ocean and air transport
History of shipping. Ship subsidies.   See also useful arts, 656 Transport

388 Local transit: city and interurban   Highways
See also 625 Engineering

389 Weights and mesures   Metrology
See also 658 Business manuals

390 Customs   Costumes   Popular life
These heds ar for discussions by topics. Customs, etc. of any special country go in
913–919. Books on a special topic in a special country go here, as the grouping by
topics is the more important; e. g. Marriage in Japan is 392, but Japanese customs,
915.2. For customs of primitiv man, see 571

391 Costume and care of person
See 646 Clothing; 613 Hygiene

392 Birth, home, and sex customs

393 Treatment of the ded
See 614.6 Public helth

394 Public and social customs
Including fairs; chivalry, tournaments; dueling, suicide

395 Etiquet
Codes of social procedure and behavior. For social ethics, see 177

396 Woman's position and treatment
For costumes, see 391; biografy, 920.7
If a special library about women is wisht, 396 is the best place for it; but it would
be unwise to bring everything about women here, e. g. to remove 618 Diseases of
women, from the rest of medicin. Books on woman in general go in 396

397 Gipsies   Nomads   Outcast races
People without nationalities who do not coalesce with the ruling people among whom
they liv. This includes Gipsy language, which, tho now regarded as a modern Sanskrit dialect, has no place in the linguistic groups of 400, as the Gipsy people hav no
place in the geografic divisions of history

398 Folklore   Proverbs, etc.
See also 291–293 Mythology
This section is for material needed in studying folklore. Mere stories for children,
unless having a value to students of folklore, go in fiction, or in juvenil

.2 Legends, tales, traditions
Legends of Charlemagne, Faust, Renard the Fox, etc. But poems, dramas, etc.
based on these legends class in literature

.3 Folklore, traditional beliefs and customs, popular superstitions
Origin and explanation of Christmas, New Year, Easter, etc. beliefs and practises

.4 Fairies, elvs, ogers, monsters, etc.
Bogies, gnomes, dragons, vampires, werewolvs

399 Customs of war
Wepons. War dances. Treatment of captivs. Scalping. Mutilation. Burning.
Cannibalism

Filology

400   Filology in general

The general works put under 400–419 deal almost entirely with Indo-European languages. They ar put here because they cover most of the divisions of this class, and in practis ar most convenient here. Under 439, 479, and 489 ar clast books limited to the Teutonic, Romance or Hellenic groups, and under 491 ar clast only works dealing mainly with the Indo-European languages there specified

401 Filosofy, origin of language; 402 Compends, outlines, like 101, 102, etc.   Class universal language, e. g. Volapük, Esperanto, in 408

410   Comparativ

410–419 includes comparativ works in general and also those on the Indo-European group in general, but general and comparativ works on Teutonic group ar 439; on Romance group, 479; on Hellenic group, 489.   Put everything about an individual language with that language

411   Orthografy   Orthoepy   Alfabets

412   Etymology   Derivation

413   Dictionaries   Lexicografy

414   Fonology   Visible speech

415   Grammar   Morfology   Syntax

416   Prosody

417   Inscriptions   Paleografy

Rare early manuscripts ar put in 091; inscriptions of an individual language ar clast with its orthografy; Latin inscriptions, 471; Greek inscriptions, 481, etc.

418   Texts

419   Hieroglyfics   Sign language

See also 493 Egyptian hieroglyfics

420   English filology

421   Orthografy

See also this hed treated in general grammars clast under 425

422   Etymology   Derivation

422 is limited to derivation.   For inflection, also calld etymology, see 425

423   Dictionaries   Idioms

Put a dictionary of 2 languages with the less known language.   Under 423 put only English-English dictionaries.   Put an English-French dictionary with French, 443; a French-Latin dictionary with Latin, 473.   If in several languages, put with 413, or with least known.   This plan brings together under each of the less known, all the dictionaries for translating either into or from that language.   Some prefer to put each dictionary under the first language; i. e. that by which it is alfabeted.   This gives under *each* language, regardless of its familiarity, *all* dictionaries for translating *from* it, but none for translating *into* it.   These must be sought under the language from which the translation is to be made.   For a cosmopolitan library this plan is simplest and best; but in an English library, the first plan, with only English dictionaries in 423, and both *in* and *out* dictionaries together under little known tongues, is more convenient.   References in either case show what may be found in the other place

424   Synonyms   Homonyms

425   Grammar

425 includes general works, covering also orthografy and prosody

426   Prosody

See also the hed prosody, in general grammars, 425

427   Dialects   Early forms   Slang

428   School books   Texts for learning the language

> Including only books for *learning* the language, with grammatic or filologic notes, etc. For other works see the literature of the language, 820

429   Anglo-Saxon
430   German

> 431 Orthografy; 432 Etymology, derivation, like 421, 422, etc.

439   Other Teutonic   Teutonic group

> Low German, Dutch; Icelandic, Swedish, Danish, Norwegian

440   French

> 441 Orthografy; 442 Etymology, derivation, like 421, 422, etc. Old French is 447

449   Provençal, Catalan

450   Italian

> 451 Orthografy; 452 Etymology, like 421, 422, etc.

459   Wallachian   Rumanian   Romansh

460   Spanish

> 461 Orthografy; 462 Etymology, like 421, 422, etc.

469   Portuguese   Galician

470   Latin

> 471 Orthografy; 472 Etymology, like 421, 422, etc

479   Other Italic   Medieval and modern Latin   Romance group

480   Greek

> 481 Orthografy; 482 Etymology, like 421, 422, etc.

489   Other Hellenic   Modern Greek   Hellenic group

> Works on Latin and Greek together, unless very clearly most useful with Latin, go with Greek, which here as elsewhere is made to include general works on the ancient classics

490   Other languages

491   Indo-European languages in general

> The Gipsy language is placed for convenience with 397 Gipsies

.6   Keltic: Irish   .8   Polish, Bohemian, Serbian

.7   Russian   Ruthenian   and other Slavic

492   Semitic: Hebrew, Yiddish, Arabic

493   Hamitic: Egyptian

> See 419 Hieroglyfics

494   Scythian   Ural-Altaic   Turanian

> Dravidian. Tamil. Finnish. Turkish. Magyar or Hungarian

495   Eastern Asiatic: Chinese, Japanese

496   African

> Excluding 493 Hamitic, 492 Semitic, etc. included in families above

497   North American

498   South American

499   Malay-Polynesian and other

Pure science

500 Science in general

501–509 all hav *Science in general* as their subject, but it is treated in these various forms. A periodical on *chemistry* goes in 540, not in 505, which is only for periodicals on science in general

501	Filosofy Theories Utility
502	Compends Outlines Ancient and medieval science
503	Dictionaries Cyclopedias
504	Essays Lectures Addresses
505	Periodicals Magazines Reviews
506	Societies Transactions Reports
507	Education: teaching and studying Museums

See also 370

508   Polygrafy   Collected works   Extracts, etc.

Scientific travels

.3	General scientific travels and surveys	.6	Africa
.4	Europe	.7	North America
.5	Asia	.8	South America
		.9	Oceania

509   History of science

510 Mathematics

511   Arithmetic

See also 372 Elementary education

512   Algebra

513   Geometry

Descriptiv geometry is 515. See also 744 Mathematical drawing

514   Trigonometry

515   Descriptiv geometry and projections

See also 744 Mathematical drawing

516   Analytic geometry

517   Calculus

519   Probabilities

520 Astronomy

.1   Astrology

521   Theoretic astronomy

Mathematical investigation of celestial motions, specially of solar system. **Motions** of individual bodies ar clast in 523

522   Practical and sferic

523 Descriptiv astronomy

.1 Universe
Nebular hypothesis, plurality of worlds, etc.

.3 Moon
.4 Planets
Including theories as to conditions on planets; e. g. life on Mars

.7 Sun
.8 Stars

524 Maps, observations, tables
For keeping all astronomic maps and observations together, when so desired; or they may be gatherd under 522 with the observatory history and reports. Special maps or observations, e. g. on sun or moon, ar better in 523

525 Earth
526 Geodesy and surveying
527 Navigation
528 Efemerides   Nautic almanacs
529 Cronology   Horology   Calendars   Almanacs

530 Physics

531 Mecanics
532 Liquids   Hydrostatics   Hydraulics
533 Gases   Pneumatics
Theory of aerostatics and aerodynamics. For aeronautics, see 629.1

534 Sound   Acoustics
535 Radiation   Light   Optics   Color
536 Heat: temperature, calorimetry
537 Electricity
See also 621.3 Electric engineering

538 Magnetism
For animal magnetism or mesmerism, etc. see 134

539 Molecular physics

540 Chemistry

.1 Early theories, alchemy, phlogiston

541 Theoretic   Physical
Modern chemic theories. General properties of bodies from chemic point of view. Composition. Constitution, atomic theory. Elements and compounds. Affinity. Formulas. Nomenclature. Foto, thermo, electro and radio chemistry

542 Practical and experimental chemistry
543 Analysis
Of special materials. See also 614.3 Adulterations

544 Qualitativ analysis
545 Quantitativ analysis   Synthesis
546 Inorganic chemistry
547 Organic chemistry

548   Crystallografy
General.   Class fenomena of a special mineral in 549

549   Mineralogy

550   Geology

551   Physical and dynamic geology
Including physical geografy: volcanoes, earthquakes, glaciers, icebergs, coral reefs, etc.   For cosmic geografy, see 523

.5   Meteorology   Climate

552   Lithology   Petrografy   Petrology
Various kinds of rocks: igneous, metamorfic, sedimentary, meteorites.   Rock decay

553   Economic geology
See also 622 Mining engineering
While history of other mineral products goes here, history of metals is more useful in 669 Metallurgy

554   Geology of Europe

.1	Scotland Ireland	.6	Spain Portugal
.2	England Wales	.7	Russia
.3	Germany Austria	.8	Norway, Sweden and
	Czechoslovakia, Poland, Hungary		Denmark
.4	France	.9	Other European countries
.5	Italy		For countries included see 949

555   Geology of Asia

.1	China	.6	Turkey in Asia
.2	Japan	.7	Siberia
.3	Arabia	.8	Afghanistan Turkestan
.4	India		Baluchistan
.5	Persia	.9	Farther India
			For countries included, see 959

556   Geology of Africa

.1	North Africa	.6	North central Africa
.2	Egypt	.7	South central Africa
.3	Abyssinia	.8	South Africa
.4	Morocco	.9	Madagascar Mauritius
.5	Algeria		

557   Geology of North America

.1   Canada
.2   Mexico   Central America   West Indies
.3   United States
.4   Northeastern or North Atlantic states   New England
.5   Southeastern or South Atlantic states
.6   South central or Gulf states
.7   North central or Lake states
.8   Western or Mountain states
.9   Pacific states
For the exact states coverd by these general designations, see 974–979

558 Geology of South America

.1	Brazil		.6	Colombia	Panama
.2	Argentina	Patagonia		Ecuador	
.3	Chile		.7	Venezuela	
.4	Bolivia		.8	Guiana	
.5	Peru		.9	Paraguay	Uruguay

559 Geology of Oceania   Polar regions

.1	Malaysia	Philippines	.6	Polynesia	Hawaii
.2	Sunda		.7	Isolated ilands	
.3	Australasia	New Zealand	.8	Arctic regions	
.4	Australia		.9	Antarctic regions	
.5	New Guinea				

560 Paleontology
For scope of heds below, see same names in 592–599

561 Plants

562 Invertebrates

563 Protozoa   Radiates
564 Mollusks
565 Articulates

566 Vertebrates

567 Fishes   Batrachia
568 Reptils   Birds
569 Mammals

570 Biology   Archeology

571 Prehistoric archeology
Stone, bronze and iron ages.   Utensils, ornaments; dwellings, mounds, monuments
For customs, see 390.   For archeology of special countries, see 913

572 Ethnology   Anthropology
Races: unity, diversity, migrations, etc.   See also 136 (or alternativ number 159.922)
Mental race caracteristicts

573 Natural history of man   Somatology
Antiquity, color, craniology, dwarfs and giants, etc.

574 Physiologic and structural biology   Natural history

575 Evolution
See also 213 Creation; 215 Religion and science; 239 Apologetics
Including natural and sexual selection, degeneration, origin of species and sexes

576 Origin and beginnings of life

577 Properties of living matter
Difference between organic and inorganic, ded and living matter, plants and animals.
Vital force, deth, etc.

578 Microscopy
See also 535 Optics

579 Collectors manuals
Collecting. preparing, arranging and preserving specimens

580 Botany

581   Physiologic and structural botany

.9   Geografic

        Use only for general works; e. g. Gray's *Manual*. The ' Flora of North America ' is put 581.9; but ' North American cryptogams' is clast 586 with a reference from 581.9, and North American phanerogamia goes with 581.9 because it so nearly covers the subject

        General works covering both Phanerogamia and Cryptogamia ar put under 580, as books on Vertebrates and Invertebrates ar put under 590

582   Phanerogamia, flowering plants

        See also 715 Trees

583   Dicotyledones

584   Monocotyledones

        Orchids, palms, lilies, sedges, grasses

585   Gymnospermae: conifers, evergreens

586   Cryptogamia, flowerless plants

587   Pteridofyta: ferns

588   Bryofyta: mosses

589   Thallofyta

        Lichens, fungi, seaweeds, yeast, bacteria

590 Zoology

591   Physiologic zoology

.5   Habits and behavior

        Including popular books; animal stories, except fiction

.9   Geografic distribution of animals

592   Invertebrates

593   Protozoans   Radiates

        Sponges, jelly fish, starfish, urchins, etc.

594   Mollusks

        Oysters, clams, snails, nautilus, cuttlefish, etc.

595   Articulates

        Worms, crabs, lobsters, centipedes, spiders, insects, etc.

.7   Insects

596   Vertebrates

597   Fishes   Batrachians: frogs, salamanders, etc.

598   Birds   Reptils

        Class here books on birds alone or on birds and reptils treated together; but put reptils alone in 598.1

.1   Reptils

599   Mammals   Mammalia

        Chiefly quadrupeds, whales, apes, man

Useful arts   Applied science

600 Useful arts in general
601 thru 605 like 101, 102, etc. *Spon's mechanics' own book* in 602

606   Societies: transactions, reports   Fairs, exhibitions
Special exhibitions go with their topics. This is general only

607   Education: schools of technology

608   Patents   Inventions

609   History of useful arts
For its history, see each special department

610 Medicin

611   Anatomy   Histology
For malformations, see 617 Surgery. See also 591 Physiologic zoology

612   Physiology
For vital fenomena in general, see 577 Properties of living matter. See also 591 Physiology of animals

613   Personal hygiene
Care of helth; prophylaxis; individual helth; laws of helth

.2   Dietetics
Food for special ages, conditions, occupations, etc.

.7   Gymnastics and athletics   Recreation and sleep

.9   Hygiene of offspring: heredity, eugenics
See also 575 Evolution

614   Public helth
Public hygiene and sanitation. State and preventiv medicin. See also 628 Sanitary engineering; 352 Local administration

.1   Registration and vital statistics
Births, deths, morbidity, marriage

.2   State control of medicin
Medical education and degrees; registration and license; sale of poisons; medical police

.3   Adulterations   Inspection of articles liable to affect public helth
Public analysts. State laboratories. For chemic analysis, see 543

.4   Contagious and infectious diseases: general
Causes and origin; geografic distribution; modes of propagation and communication; prevention and restriction. Epidemics, plagues

.5   Contagious and infectious diseases: special
These heds ar for public helth discussions only. For treatment, etc. see 616 Pathology

.6   Disposal of the ded
See customs, 393 Treatment of the ded

.7   Hygiene of the air and ground   Nuisances

.8   Protection of human life from accidents, etc.

.9   Hygiene of animals   Veterinary sanitation

615   Materia medica and therapeutics
616   Pathology   Diseases   Treatment
617   Surgery
618   Diseases of women and children   Obstetrics
619   Comparativ medicin   Veterinary

620   Engineering

.1   Strength of materials

621   Mecanical engineering

.1   Steam engineering

.2   Hydraulic engins or motors

      Industrial use of water as motiv power, including machines run by water under pressure produced by accumulators and also constructions and appliances for distributing and regulating supply of water to motors

      For hydraulic engineering (dam, breakwater, etc.) see 627; for pumps, see 621.6; for reservoirs, aqueducts, etc. see 628; for theory of mecanics of liquids, see 532

.3   Electric engineering
.4   Heat, air and gas engins
.5   Pneumatic machinery   Mecanical refrigeration

      Comprest air.   Ice making

.6   Blowing and pumping engins: fire engins

622   Mining engineering
623   Military and naval engineering

      For military and naval science, maneuvers, strategy and tactics, see 355-359

.8   Naval engineering   Shipbilding

624   Bridges and roofs
625   Railroad and road engineering

      See also 624 Bridges

626   Canal engineering
627   River, harbor and general hydraulic engineering
628   Sanitary engineering   Waterworks

      House drainage, ventilation, heating, lighting

629   Other branches of engineering

.1   Aeronautics   Aircraft
.2   Motor vehicles, automobiles

      Mecanically propeld and motor vehicles for highways: bicycles, motor cycles, etc. For highway vehicles for separate tractors (animal or mecanical) see 684

630   Agriculture

.1   Rural life
.5   Periodicals
.6   Societies
.61   Official organizations; departments
.62   Associations not under government control
.7   Study and teaching

      Schools, experiment stations, etc.

631   Farm, farmsted   Soil   Fertilizers

      Machinery, farm operations, reclamation (drainage, irrigation)

632   Hindrances: blights, pests, insects

633   Field crops: grains, grasses, fibers, etc.

634   Fruits   Orchards   Vinyards
  .9   Forestry
    See also 715 Landscape gardening

635   Garden crops: kitchen and market gardening
    See 716 for Flower gardens

636   Domestic animals
    See also 619 Veterinary medicin; 599 Zoology

  .1   Horse
  .2   Cattle   Greater ruminants
    Including bison, deer, camel, yak, etc.

  .3   Sheep, goats   Smaller ruminants
  .4   Swine
  .5   Poultry
    Including pigeons, peacocks, fezants

  .6   Birds: cage and ornamental
  .7   Dogs
  .8   Cats
  .9   Other: rabbits, guinea pigs, etc.

637   Dairy and dairy products

638   Useful invertebrates
    Bees, silkworms, resin- and dye-producing invertebrates

639   Hunting, trapping, fish culture, etc.

640   Home economics

641   Food   Cookery
    Food values, costs, markets. For dietetics, food for special conditions (the very young, aged, il, etc.) see 613.2

  .5   Cook books

642   Serving   Table   Entertaining

643   Shelter: house, home

644   Heat   Light   Ventilation
    From householder's point of view. See also 628 Engineering and 697 Bilding

645   Furniture, carpets, upholstery   Decoration
    See also 729 Architectural decoration; 740 Decorativ arts

646   Clothing   Toilet
    See also 613 Hygiene; 391 Costume and care of person

647   Household organization and administration
    Cost of living; household accounts; servants, wages; collectiv and cooperativ housekeeping, tenements, hotels, clubs, etc.

648   Sanitary precautions: laundry, cleaning

649   Nursery   Sickroom

650 Communication   Business

651   Offis equipment and methods

652   Writing: materials, machines, cifer

653   Abbreviations   Shorthand

654   Telegraf   Telefone   Cables   Signals

> For codes, see 652; for engineering, 621.3

655   Printing   Publishing   Copyright

656   Transport: railroading, etc.

657   Bookkeeping   Accounts

658   Business manuals   Methods   Tables

659   Other topics

.1   Advertising

660 Chemic technology

661   Chemicals

662   Explosivs   Matches   Pyrotechnics, etc.

663   Beverages

> See also 178 Temperance; 614.3 Adulterations

664   Foods

> For adulterations, see 614.3 Public helth. See also 641 Cookery, and 642 Table, serving

665   Oils   Gases   Candles   Lamps

> See also 644

666   Ceramics   Glass, etc.   Bricks, tiles, cements

667   Bleaching, dyeing, etc.   Inks, paints, varnishes

668   Other organic chemic industries

> Soaps, gums, perfumes, fertilizers, etc.

669   **Metallurgy and assaying**

> History of metals goes here, not in 553, 622 nor 671

670 Manufactures

> Specific topics go where of most interest. These heds ar for the *general* subject of metal, wood, etc. manufactures, and for such specific manufactures as ar not of more interest elsewhere. But a specific manufacture is commonly most useful with its own subject; e. g. a steam engin is certainly made of metal, but its manufacture should go under 621.1, not 672. Caracter of the library often decides the place of greatest interest. An agricultural library would prefer the manufacture and everything about wood churns with the dairy, 637, while a manufacturing library might prefer it with other wood manufactures in 674. A general library wil incline to the special subject, as a more minute classification is thus obtaind, and catalog references answer inquiries for all the library has on brass or rubber or paper manufactures. Whether groupt by use or material, if sought from the other standpoint, references show the resources promptly. As a rule the use is the better classification, being more minute and oftener wanted. But if uses ar various the general hed is better; e. g. bels ar for scores of distinct uses, but their manufacture is a unit; but all churns ar for the dairy

671   Articles made of metals

672   Of iron and steel; stoves, cutlery, etc.

673   Of brass and bronz; bels, etc.

> See also 739

674   Lumber, and wood articles
675   Lether, and lether articles
676   Paper, and paper articles
677   Cotton, wool, silk, linen, etc.
678   Rubber, and rubber articles
679   Celluloid and other

680   Mecanic trades   Amateur manuals
681   Watch and instrument making
      Catalogs of miscellaneous instruments.   Class special instruments with their subjects

682   Blacksmithing
683   Lock and gun making
684   Carriage and cabinet making
      Furniture. See also 749 Artistic furniture; 694 Fine joinery, interior finish
      Highway vehicles for separate tractors, either animal or motor. For motor vehicles,
      see 629.2

685   Saddlery   Shoemaking   Glovemaking   Trunks
686   Bookbinding
687   Clothesmaking   Hats
688
689   Other trades

690   Bilding
      For construction according to elements (foundations, walls, roofs, floors, etc.) see
      721 Architectural construction

691   Materials   Preservativ processes
      Waterproofing. See also 620.1 Strength of materials

692   Plans   Specifications, etc.   Bilding laws
693   Masonry   Plastering   Fireproofing
694   Carpentry: joinery, stairbilding
      For cabinet making, see 684

695   Roofing: slating, tiling
      See 721 Roof construction

696   Plumbing   Gas and steam fitting, etc.
697   Heating and ventilation
      See also sanitary engineering, 628; domestic economy, 644

698   Painting   Glazing   Paperhanging
699   Carbilding
      Railway and tramway cars, passenger and freight, with or without motors. For
      highway cars, see 629.2

Fine arts   Recreation

700   Fine arts in general

701 Filosofy, theories, utility, esthetics; 702 Compends, like 101, 102, etc. Put art galleries and museums in 708

710   Landscape gardening

711   Town and city planning

For special cities see 913–919

712   Public parks   Private grounds, lawns

713   Walks   Drives

714   Water: fountains, lakes

715   Trees   Hedges   Shrubs

See also 634.9 Forestry; 582 Phanerogamia

716   Plants   Flowers   Window gardens, ferneries

717   Arbors   Seats   Outlooks

718   Cemeteries   Monuments   Mausoleums

See also 393 Treatment of the ded; 614.6 Public Helth

719   Natural landscapes   Scenery

720   Architecture

721   Architectural construction

For materials and mecanical processes, see 690

722   Ancient and oriental architecture   (Pagan)

See also 571 Prehistoric archeology

723   Medieval (Christian, Mohammedan)

Includes Byzantine, Romanesque, pointed or Gothic

724   Modern

Decline of Gothic and rise of renaissance style, dating from about 1450

725   Public bildings

726   Ecclesiastic and religious

727   Educational and scientific

But class library bildings in 022

728   Residences

729   Architectural design and decoration

Including elevation, plan, accessories and fixt furniture (altars, pulpits, mantels, screens, etc.).   Class here Ruskin's *Stones of Venice*

730 Sculpture
731 Materials and methods
732 Ancient
733   Greek and Roman
734 Medieval
735 Modern
736 Carving: seals, dies, gems, cameos, wood
737 Numismatics: coins, medals
    Artistic and historic side. See also 332   Coins and coinage, as money
738 Pottery   Porcelain
739 Bronzes   Brasses   Bricabrac

740 Drawing   Decoration   Design
741 Freehand   Crayon
    Sketching from nature. Caricatures, cartoons
    Collections on any subject go with that subject with reference from 741

742 Perspectiv
    See also 515 Descriptiv geometry

743 Art anatomy   Life school
744 Mathematical and scientific drawing
    Instructions for architectural and other mathematical drawing, with demonstrations
    (if any) subsidiary. Textbooks with mathematical demonstrations in scientific
    order ar better in 515

745 Ornamental design
    Woven fabrics, carpets, wall paper, etc.

746 Art needlework   Fancy work
747 Interior decoration
    Distemper, fresco, polycrome

748 Staind and iridescent glass
    For leding, see 698

749 Artistic furniture, fireplaces, frames, etc.

750 Painting
751 Materials and methods
752 Color
    See also 535 Optics

753 Epic   Mythic   Idealistic
754 Genre
755 Religious, ecclesiastic
756 Historical: battle scenes
757 Portrait
758 Landscape and marine   Stil life
    Animals, flowers
759 Various schools of painting

760 Engraving
761   Wood
762   Copper and steel
763   Lithografy
764   Cromolithografy
765   Line and stipple
766   Mezzotint and aquatint
767   Etching   Dry point
768   Banknote and machine
769   Collections of engravings

770 Fotografy
771   Materials   Fotografic chemistry
772   Processes
        Silver: daguerreotype, talbotype. Collodion: ambrotype, etc. Dry plate. Color fotografy
773   Gelatin and pigment: woodburytype
      Carbon: lambertype, autotype, etc.
774   Gelatin and printers ink
        Albertype, heliotype, artotype, etc.
775   Fotolithografy, etc.
776   Fotozincografy, etc.
777   Fotoengraving and fotoelectrotyping
778   Special applications
        Moving pictures. See also 522 Astronomy; 578 Microscopy; 792 Fotoplays
779   Collections of fotografs

780 Music
        All heds include both the music itself and everything about it: score, libretto, history, criticism, etc.
781   Theory of music
782   Dramatic music: opera, cantata
783   Sacred music: oratorio, anthem, sacred cantata, church choir
        See 245 Hymnology, sacred poetry for hyms alone; if with tunes they go in 783; 786 Organ; 246 Evangelistic use and eucaristic music; 264 Public worship
784   Vocal music
        Glees, ballads, college and plantation songs, etc.
785   Orchestral music
        For dramatic orchestral music, see 782; sacred, 783
786   Piano and organ
787   Stringd instruments
        Including history, manufacture, instruction, music, etc.
788   Wind instruments
        Including history, manufacture, instruction, music, etc.
789   Percussion and mecanical instruments

790 Amusements

For ethics of amusements, see 175

791 Public entertainment

Concert, panorama, circus, menagerie, summer resort, garden, rink, museum, fair, festival

792 Theater Pantomime Opera

Passion plays. Fotoplays. See also 782 Dramatic music

793 Indoor amusements

Private theatricals, tableaux, charades, dancing

794 Games of skil

Chess, checkers, billiards, bowling, bagatel

795 Games of chance

Cards, dice, backgammon, dominoes

796 Outdoor sports

Children's sports, athletic sports, coasting, skating, skiing, cycling, quoits, croquet, lawn tennis, golf, baseball, football, cricket, polo, boxing, fencing

797 Boating and other water sports Aerostation

Rowing, yachting, swimming

798 Horsemanship and racing

799 Fishing, hunting, target shooting

Literature

800 Literature: general works
801   Filosofy   Theories   Literary esthetics
802   Compends, outlines
803   Dictionaries, cyclopedias
804   Essays, lectures, addresses
805   Periodicals, magazines, reviews
806   Societies: transactions, reports, etc.
807   Study and teaching of literature
808   Rhetoric   Treatises   Oratory   Polygrafy
　.8   Collections
> Those too general to go with any one language, e. g. a book of quotations from many languages

809   History of literature in general
> Including general histories of books and knowledge; e. g. Hallam's *Literature of the middle ages*; also history of poetry, drama, etc. too general to go with any one language

810 American literature
> Includes Canadian English, which may be kept separate by prefixing C; e. g. C 811 Canadian poetry. See also note to 820

811   American poetry
　.08   Collections
812   American drama
813   American fiction
> For treatment of fiction in a popular library, see Introd. p. 10

814   American essays
815   American oratory
> For speakers, see 808.8

816   American letters
817   American satire and humor
818   American miscellany
> Anecdotes, ana, epigrams, quotations, etc. If English, or English and American, they go in 828. If illustrativ of any special subject (e. g. biografy, history, science, art) put with that subject. For riddles, proverbs, see 398. The same rule applies to other languages in 838, 848, etc.

820 English literature
> Canadian literature may be clast as British, if preferd, but separated by prefixing C to 820. See note to 810

821   English poetry
　.08   Collections
822   English drama
　.3   Shakspere

823–828 like 813–818

829 Anglo-Saxon literature
830 German literature
> 831 German poetry; 832 German drama, etc. like 811, 812, etc.

839   Other Teutonic literatures
> Low German, Scandinavian, Gothic

840 French literature
841 French poetry; 842 French drama, like 811, 812, etc.

849 Provençal and Catalan literature

850 Italian literature
851 Italian poetry; 852 Italian drama, etc. like 811, 812, etc.

859 Wallachian literature   Rumanian   Romansh

860 Spanish literature
861 Spanish poetry; 862 Spanish drama, etc. like 811, 812, etc.

869 Portuguese literature   Galician

870 Latin literature
871 Latin poetry in general
Lucretius, Ovid, Phaedrus. See also Dramatic, Epic and Lyric below

872 Latin drama; e. g. Plautus, Terence
873 Latin epic poetry; e. g. Virgil
874 Latin lyric poetry; e. g. Catullus, Horace
875 Latin oratory
Including Cicero's complete works

876 Latin letters; e. g. Cicero, Pliny, Fronto
877 Latin satire and humor; e. g. Martial, Juvenal
878 Latin miscellany
Including Latin historians

879 Medieval and modern Latin

880 Greek literature
Classic literature
881–888 like Latin 871–878; e. g. 883 Homer; 884 Sappho, Pindar, Theocritus

889 Medieval and modern Greek

890 Literature of other languages
891 Other Indo-European
.6   Keltic: Irish
.7   Russian   Ruthenian
.8   Polish, Bohemian, Serbian and other Slavic

892 Semitic: Hebrew, Yiddish, Arabic
893 Hamitic: Egyptian
894 Scythian   Ural-Altaic   Turanian
Dravidian. Tamil. Finnish. Turkish. Hungarian

895 Eastern Asiatic: Chinese, Japanese
896 African
Excluding 892 Semitic, 893 Hamitic, etc. included in families above

897 North American
898 South American
899 Malay-Polynesian and other

History

900 History in general

901–909 all hav History in general as their subject, but it is treated in these various forms. A periodical on English history goes with 942, not 905, which is only for periodicals on history in general. 901 Filosofy, history of civilization; 902 Compends (e. g. Ploetz's *Epitome*) cronologies, charts, outlines, like 101, 102, etc. but use 909 for universal and general modern histories.

For cronology as a science, see 529

910 Geografy and travels

Including topografy, maps, antiquities, descriptions, etc.
For map projection, see 526. See also 310 Statistics; 390 Customs and costumes
For directories, guide books, gazetteers, etc. of special countries or geografic sections, see under those sections, 914–919

.3   Dictionaries, gazetteers
.4   Circumnavigations, ocean travel, shipwrecks and disasters, piratic adventures
.7   Study and teaching of geografy: school map drawing
         For primary teaching of geografy, see 372

911   Historical
Growth and changes in political divisions, etc.

912   Maps, atlases, plans of cities, etc.

913   Antiquities, archeology, of special countries
See also 220.9 Biblical antiquities; 340 Legal antiquities; 571 Prehistoric archeology; 930 Ancient history; 390 Special customs

913.3   Antiquities of ancient countries

.31	China		.36	Kelts
.32	Egypt		.37	Rome Italy
.33	Judea		.38	Greece
.34	India		.39	Other countries
.35	Medo-Persia			

Antiquities of modern countries

913.4	Europe		.7	North America
.5	Asia		.8	South America
.6	Africa		.9	Oceania

914   Travel in Europe

.1   Scotland
.15   Ireland
.16   Ulster
.17   Connaught
.18   Leinster
.19   Munster
.2   England, Great Britain
.21   London
.29   Wales

914 Travel in Europe (*continued*)

.3 Germany and Austria
.31 Prussia and Northern Germany
.36 Austria   Austria-Hungary
.37 Czechoslovakia, Bohemia
.38 Poland
.39 Hungary
.4 France
.5 Italy
.6 Spain
.69 Portugal
.7 Union of Socialist Soviet Republics (Russia)
.8 Norway, Sweden and Denmark
.81 Norway
.82 Oslo (Christiania)   Christiansand
.83 Bergen   Hamar
.84 Throndhjem   Tromso
.85 Sweden
.86 Gothland
.87 Svealand
.88 Norrland
.89 Denmark

914 .9 Other countries of Europe

.91 Iceland   Faroe ilands
.92 Netherlands
.93 Belgium
.94 Switzerland
.95 Greece
.96 Turkey in Europe
.97 Serbia   Montenegro   Bulgaria   Jugoslavia
.98 Rumania: Wallachia, Moldavia
.99 Ilands of Greek archipelago

915 Travel in Asia

.1 China   Chosen (Korea)
.2 Japan
.3 Arabia
.4 India
.5 Iran   Persia
.6 Turkey in Asia
.7 Siberia
.8 Afghanistan   Turkestan   Baluchistan
.9 Farther India

For countries included, see 959

916 Travel in Africa

.1 North Africa
.2 Egypt
.3 Abyssinia
.4 Morocco
.5 Algeria
.6 North central Africa
.7 South central Africa
.8 South Africa
.9 Madagascar   Mauritius

917 Travel in North America

.1   Canada   British America
.2   Mexico
.28   Central America
.29   West Indies: Cuba, Puerto Rico, Jamaica, Bermudas, etc.

.3   United States

.4   Northeastern or North Atlantic   New England
.41   Maine   .46 Connecticut
.42   New Hampshire   .47 New York
.43   Vermont   .48 Pennsylvania
.44   Massachusetts   .49 New Jersey
.45   Rhode Island

.5   Southeastern or South Atlantic
.51   Delaware   .56 North Carolina
.52   Maryland   .57 South Carolina
.53   District of Columbia   .58 Georgia
.54   West Virginia   .59 Florida
.55   Virginia

.6   South central or Gulf
.61   Alabama   .67 Arkansas
.62   Mississippi   .68 Tennessee
.63   Louisiana   .69 Kentucky
.64   Texas
.66   Oklahoma   Indian Ter.

.7   North central or Lake
.71   Ohio   .75 Wisconsin
.72   Indiana   .76 Minnesota
.73   Illinois   .77 Iowa
.74   Michigan   .78 Missouri

.8   Western or Mountain
          Including general works on 'the West'
.81   Kansas   .86 Montana
.82   Nebraska   .87 Wyoming
.83   South Dakota   .88 Colorado
          Including Dakota as a whole
.84   North Dakota   .89 New Mexico

.9   Pacific
.91   Arizona   .95 Oregon
.92   Utah   .96 Idaho
.93   Nevada   .97 Washington
.94   California   .98 Alaska

918 Travel in South America

.1	Brazil		.6	Colombia Panama
.2	Argentina Patagonia			Ecuador
.3	Chile		.7	Venezuela
.4	Bolivia		.8	Guiana
.5	Peru		.9	Paraguay Uruguay

919 Travel in Oceania and Polar regions

.1	Malaysia		.6	Polynesia Hawaii
.14	Philippine ilands		.7	Isolated ilands
.2	Sunda		.8	Arctic regions
.3	Australasia New Zealand			Greenland
.4	Australia		.9	Antarctic regions
.5	New Guinea			

92 Individual biografy

Including autobiografy, diaries, personal narrativs, eulogies and all material relating to a single individual. Assign book number from Cutter or Cutter-Sanborn *Author tables* for name of person written about, so as to bring together on the shelvs all lives of the same person

920 Collectiv biografy

Including general biografic dictionaries and those relating to special countries; e. g. *Who's who in America*; also volumes of short biografies too general for any of the subheds below, e. g. Hale's *Boys' heroes*

.7   Women

General; but Strickland's *Queens of England*, 923

Collectiv by subjects

Collectiv biografy is here group by the main subjects of the Classification

921 Filosofy
Metaphysicians, logicians, moralists, etc.

922 Religion
Ministers, missionaries, church fathers, monks, popes, etc.

923 Sociology
Rulers, statesmen, economists, lawyers, army and navy men, filanthropists, educators, etc.

924 Filology
Lexicografers, grammarians, etc.

925 Science
Astronomers, chemists, geologists, botanists, etc.

926 Useful arts
Physicians, inventors, engineers, manufacturers, printers, etc.

927 Fine arts
Architects, sculptors, painters, musicians, etc.

928 Literature
Writers of poetry, fiction, etc.; essayists, humorists, historians, etc.

929 Genealogy and heraldry

.6	Heraldry
.7	Peerages, precedence, titles of honor Orders of knighthood
.8	Coats of arms, crests
.9	Flags

930 Ancient history To A. D. 476

931 China
932 Egypt
933 Judea
934 India
935 Medo-Persia

Chaldea, Assyria, Nineveh, Media, Babylonia, Persia, Parthia, New Persian or Sassanian kingdom, Mesopotamia, Susiana

936 Kelts
937 Rome   Italy
938 Greece
939 Other countries

Modern history

940 Europe

From fall of the Western empire (Rome) A. D. 476

.1 Medieval Europe   476–1453

For Byzantine empire, see 949.5

.2 Modern Europe   1453–

.27 Napoleonic period 1789–1815
.28 19th century   1815–1914
.3 World war   1914–19

Political and diplomatic history: causes, results

.33 Groups of countries: allies and neutrals
.4 Military history

Including 'Frightfulness,' atrocities as military expedient. But, since the avowd policy of one group of belligerents was 'frightfulness,' it pervades all literature of this war
Land operations wil be subdivided on .41–.43

.44 Air operations
.45 Naval operations
.46 Celebrations, commemorations

Usually better clast with event commemorated

.47 Prisons, hospitals, charities
.48 Personal narrativs, secret servis

When relating to some special battle or event, class with subject

.49 Illustrativ material

For special collections; but most material should be clast with its subject: poetry, drama, etc. with the literatures to which they belong

.5 Later 20th century   1919–

Including works on 20th century as a whole

941 Scotland

.5 Ireland
.6 Ulster
.7 Connaught
.8 Leinster
.9 Munster

942　　England　　Great Britain

Period divisions

.01　Anglo-Saxon　　B. C. 55–A. D. 1066
　　　　Including prehistoric, Roman, British, Danish

.02	Norman	1066–1154
.03	Plantagenet	1154–1399
.04	Lancaster and York	1400–1485
.05	Tudor	1485–1603
.06	Stuart	1603–1714
.07	Hanover	1714–1837
.08	Later Hanoverian　　Windsor	1837–

Geografic divisions

.1　Middlesex　　London

.9　Wales

943　　Germany and Austria

.1　　Prussia and nothern Germany

.6　Austria　　Austria-Hungary

.7　Czechoslovakia, Bohemia, etc.

.8　Poland
　　　　Including history before partition, 1772–95

.9　Hungary, etc.

944　　France

945　　Italy

946　　Spain

.9　Portugal

947　　Union of Socialist Soviet Republics (Russia)

948　　Norway, Sweden, and Denmark

.1　　Norway
.2　　　Oslo (Christiania)　　Christiansand
.3　　　Bergen　　Hamar
.4　　　Throndhjem　　Tromso
.5　　Sweden
.6　　　Gothland
.7　　　Svealand
.8　　　Norrland
.9　　Denmark

949   Other countries of Europe
   .1   Iceland   Faroe ilands
   .2   Netherlands
   .3   Belgium
   .4   Switzerland
   .5   Byzantine empire and modern Greece
   .6   Turkey in Europe
              Including til 1878 the countries following in .7–.9
   .7   Serbia   Montenegro   Bulgaria
   .8   Rumania: Wallachia, Moldavia
   .9   Ilands of Greek archipelago

950   Asia

951   China   Chosen (Korea)
952   Japan
953   Arabia
954   India
955   Iran   Persia
956   Turkey in Asia
         See also 949.6
957   Siberia
958   Afghanistan   Turkestan   Baluchistan
959   Farther India
         Burma, Siam, Cambodia, Cochin-China, Tonkin, Annam, etc.

960   Africa

961   North Africa
         Tunis, Tripoli, Fezzan
962   Egypt
963   Abyssinia
964   Morocco
965   Algeria

966   North central Africa
         Sahara; Sudan; Senegambia, Senegal; Sierra Leone; Upper Guinea; Liberia; Ashanti; Dahomey, Togo; Gold Coast; Nigeria

967   South central Africa
         Lower Guinea, Kamerun; Loango, French Kongo; Portuguese West Africa, Angola, Benguela; Interior; Free State, Kongo basin; Central lake region (Kenya colony or British East Africa, Uganda); Somali; Zanzibar, Tanganyika Territory (German East Africa); Mozambique, Portuguese East Africa

968   South Africa
         Bechuanaland; Transvaal; Zululand; Natal; Orange Free State; Kaffraria; Cape of Good Hope; Southwest Africa Protectorate (German West Africa); Rhodesia, Mashonaland

969   Madagascar   Mauritius

970   North America

.1 Indians, Aborigines   .2 Lives of Indians   .3 Special tribes   .4 Special states   .5 Government relation and treatment   .6 Special subjects: caracter, civilization, agriculture, etc.

> See 371.9 Education; 572 Ethnology; 497 Languages

971   Canada   British America

.01   French régime   1497–1763
> From earliest time til cession to England

.02   End of 7 years war to constitutional act 1791
> Conspiracy of Pontiac 1763–64   Quebec act 1774

.03   1792 to Union act 1841
.04   Union 1841 to Confederation 1867
> Beginning with operation of Union act; Canadian parliament at Ottawa 13 June, 1841. Class clergy reservs agitation in 971.3 Ontario; abolition of seigniories in 971.4 Quebec

.05   Dominion of Canada   1867–
> Canada under British North America act

Geografic divisions

.1   British Columbia
.2   Northwest Territories
> Including former Hudson Bay territory

.21   Yukon
> Klondike region   Dawson (city)

.23   Alberta
.24   Saskatchewan
.27   Manitoba
.3   Ontario
> Formerly also Upper Canada or Canada West. See also 971.4 note.   Class here Clergy reservs
> For St Lawrence river, see 971.4

.4   Quebec   St Lawrence river
> Quebec is from Caudebec (Normandy), home of many of its early settlers
> Class here abolition of seigniories

.5   New Brunswick
.6   Nova Scotia
.7   Prince Edward Island
.8   Newfoundland
.9   Labrador

972   Mexico   Central America

.8   Central America

.9   West Indies: Cuba, Puerto Rico, Jamaica, Bermudas, etc.

973 **United States**

See also 342 Constitutional law and history; 328 Legislativ bodies and annals; 329 Political parties

Period divisions

.1 Discovery   −1607
Norse, Spanish, Dutch, French, English

.2 Colonial   1607–1775
French and Indian wars

.3 Revolution and confederation   1775–89
.4 Constitutional period   1789–1809
For U. S. Constitution, see 342
Federalists and Republicans   See 329
Washington, *1789–97*; John Adams, *1797–1801*; Jefferson, *1801–09*

.5 War of 1812   1809–45
Hartford convention, 1814
Nullification in South Carolina, 1832

Madison, *1809–17*; Monroe, *1817–25*; John Quincy Adams, *1825–29*; Jackson, *1829–37*; Van Buren, *1837–41*; Harrison, *1841*; Tyler, *1841–45*

.6 War with Mexico   1845–61
The Wilmot proviso, 1846
Compromise of 1850
Struggle in Kansas, 1854–59   See also 978.1 Kansas
Polk, *1845–49*; Taylor, *1849–50*; Fillmore, *1850–53*; Pierce, *1853–57*; Buchanan, *1857–61*

.7 Civil war   Abolition of slavery   Lincoln, 1861–65
.8 Later 19th century   1865–1901
Reconstruction.   Civil servis reform.   Spanish war
Johnson, *1865–69*; Grant, *1869–77*; Hayes, *1877–81*; Garfield, *1881*; Arthur, *1881–85*; Cleveland, *1885–89*; Harrison, *1889–93*; Cleveland, *1893–97*; McKinley, *1897–1901*

.9 20th century –   1901–
.91 Early 20th century   1901–
War with Germany 1917–21
Theodore Roosevelt, *1901–09*; Taft, *1909–13*; Wilson, *1913–21*; Harding, *1921–23*; Coolidge, *1923–29*; Hoover, *1929–33*; Franklin Delano Roosevelt, *1933–*

974 **Northeastern or North Atlantic   New England**

.1	Maine	.6	Connecticut
.2	New Hampshire	.7	New York
.3	Vermont	.8	Pennsylvania
.4	Massachusetts	.9	New Jersey
.5	Rhode Island		

975 **Southeastern or South Atlantic**

Including general works on 'the South'

.1	Delaware	.6	North Carolina
.2	Maryland	.7	South Carolina
.3	District of Columbia	.8	Georgia
.4	West Virginia	.9	Florida
.5	Virginia		

976 **South central or Gulf**

.1	Alabama	.6	Oklahoma	Indian Territory
.2	Mississippi	.7	Arkansas	
.3	Louisiana	.8	Tennessee	
.4	Texas	.9	Kentucky	

977 North central or Lake

.1	Ohio	.5	Wisconsin
.2	Indiana	.6	Minnesota
.3	Illinois	.7	Iowa
.4	Michigan	.8	Missouri

978 Western or Mountain
Including general works on 'the West'

.1	Kansas	.6	Montana
.2	Nebraska	.7	Wyoming
.3	South Dakota	.8	Colorado
	Including Dakota as a whole		
.4	North Dakota	.9	New Mexico

979 Pacific

.1	Arizona	.5	Oregon
.2	Utah	.6	Idaho
.3	Nevada	.7	Washington
.4	California	.8	Alaska

980 South America

981 Brazil
982 Argentina   Patagonia
983 Chile
984 Bolivia
985 Peru
986 Colombia   Panama   Ecuador
987 Venezuela
988 Guiana
989 Paraguay   Uruguay

990 Oceania   Polar regions

991 Malaysia
  .4   Philippine ilands
992   Sunda
993 Australasia   New Zealand
994   Australia
995   New Guinea
996 Polynesia   Hawaii
997 Isolated ilands
998 Arctic regions   Greenland
999 Antarctic regions

Relativ Subject Index

HOW TO USE THIS INDEX

Find the subject wanted in its alfabetic place in the index. The number after it is its class number and refers to the place where the topic wil be found, in numeric order of class numbers, on the shelvs, shelf lists, or in the clast catalog, if used. All class numbers ar decimal; e. g. 914.29 travel in Wales, comes before 914.3 travel in Germany, and both of them before 915 travel in Asia. Printed labels on the shelvs or drawer fronts guide redily to the class number sought.

Under this class number wil be found the resources of the library on the subject desired. Other adjoining subjects may often be profitably consulted; e. g. a description of Niagara Falls is wanted and the index refers to 917.47, but much on this topic is likely also to be found in 917.4 (travel in north Atlantic states) and even in 917.3 (travel in United States).

This index contains

in a single alfabet all subjects named in the tables, together with their synonyms and such other topics as ar thought most likely to be needed by libraries using this abridgment.

If nothing is found on the shelvs under a number, it shows that the library does not yet possess any book on that topic.

It does not include

all names of places, minerals, plants, diseases, etc.; but givs only those used in these tables and a farther selection of the most common and useful. It is not a biografic dictionary, and gives **no names of persons** as biografic heds, but only such as appear in connection with some subject like literature or history.

Relativ Subject Index

Abacus	arithmetic	511
Abattoirs	public helth	614.7
	sanitary engineering	628
Abbeys	architecture	726
	history	271
Abbot of misrule	customs	394
Abbots	monastic orders	271
Abbreviations	literary methods	029
	useful arts	653
Abdication	constitutional history	342
	political science	321
Abduction	criminal law	343
Aberration	astronomy	522
	optics	535
	mental disease	616
	insanity	132
Ability, human	theology	233
Abnormal children	child study	136.7
	education	371.9
	psychology	132
Abode of animals	geog. distrib.	591.9
	habits	591.5
Abolition	political science	326
	U. S. history	973.7
Abolitionists	biografy	923
Aborigines	Amer. antiquities	913.7
	Amer. history	970.1
	ethnology	572
	prehistoric archeology	571
Abrasions	surgery	617
Abraxas	gems	736
	gnostics	273
Abridging	literary methods	029
	useful arts	653
Abridgments	English law	346
	U. S. law	345
Abscess	surgery	617
Absent-mindedness		152
Absenteeism	Irish history	941.5
	sociology	333
Absolute, the	ontology	111
Absolution	sacrament	265
Absolutism	political science	321
	predestination	234
Absorption	heat	536
	light	535
	liquids	532
Abstinence	asceticism	248
	temperance	178

Abstracting	literary methods	029
Abstraction	psychology	153
Abyssinia	geology	556.3
	history	963
	language	492
	religious history	276.3
	travel	916.3
Academic degrees and costume		378.2
	education	373
Academies	architecture	727
	female	376
	learned **general societies**	**060**
	private	**373**
	public	**379**
	scientific	506
	of special subject, see subject	
Academy, New		186
	Older Plato	184
Acadia, Nova Scotia	history	971.6
Acalepha	zoology	593
Accession catalogs		018
	dep't library admin.	025.2
Accidence	English language	425
	French "	445
	German "	435
	Greek "	485
	Italian "	455
	Latin "	475
	Spanish "	465
Accident insurance		368
Accidents	medicin	617
	public safety	614.8
	railroad	656
Acclimatization	animals	591.5
	evolution	575
	hygiene	613
	man	573
	mental influences	136
	plants	581
Accomplises	criminal law	343
Accountability	theology	233
Accounts	bookkeeping	657
	library administration	025.1
Accumulation	capital	331
Acetylene	chemic technology	665
Achaian leag	Greek history	938
Achromatism	optics	535
Acids	chemic technology	661
	organic chemistry	547

Topics in blackface type ar subdivided in the Tables

Acids	theoretic chemistry	541
Acoustics	physics	534
Acrobats	amusements	791
Acropolis	architecture	722
	Greek antiquities	913.38
Acrostics	English language	828
Acting	ethics	175
	theater	792
Actinism	fotografy	771
	optics	535
Actinozoa	zoology	593
Actions	legal procedure	347
Actors	biografy	927
Acts and resolvs	Am. statutes	345
	Eng. "	346
of learned societies, general		060
for special subjects, see topic		
legislativ bodies, U. S.		345
Acts of the Apostles		226
Acute diseases		616
Ad valorem duty	protection	337
	taxes	336.2
Adages	English literature	828
	folklore	398
Adams, J:	presidency of	973.4
J: Q.	" "	973.5
Addresses	Amer. lit.	815
class special with subject		
Adhesion	physics	539
Adirondacks	travel	917.47
Adjutant-general's reports, U. S.		353
Administration household		647
	library	025
	of medicins	615
	political sci.	350
Administrativ bildings, architecture		725
	law	350
	reform	351.6
Administrator law		347
Admirals	biografy	923
Admiralty	foren countries	354
Islands	history	993
law		347
Admission	school	371.2
Adobe	masonry	693
Adoption	family law	347
Adult education		374
Adulterations	chemic analysis	543
	" **technology**	660
	public helth	614.3
Adultery	ethics	176
	law	343

Advent	church festivals	264
second	Christology	232
Adventists, second	sect	286
Adventures	biografy	923
	travels, etc.	910
Adversity	pauperism	339
Advertising	commerce	659.1
Advocates, Faculty of		347
lives		923
Advowsons	canon law	348
Ædiles	Roman antiquities	913.37
Æolian harp	music	787
Æolic dialect	Greek language	487
Aerial navigation		629.1
Aerodynamics	engineering	629.1
	physics	533
Aerofytes	lichens	589
	orchids	584
Aerolites	astronomy	523
	geology	552
Aeronautics	engineering	629.1
	physics	533
Aerostatics	engineering	629.1
	physics	533
Æsthetics	fine arts	701
Æthiopia	ancient history	939
see also Abyssinia		
Ætolian leag	Greek history	938
Affections	psychology	157
Affidavits	law	347
Affinity	chemistry	541
	family law	347
Afghanistan	geology	555.8
	history	958
	religious history	275.8
	travel	915.8
Aforisms	English literature	828
	folklore	398
Africa	antiquities	913.6
	botany	581.9
	geology	556
	history	960
	religious history	276
	scientific travels and	
	surveys	508.6
	statistics	316
	travel	916
North	**geology**	556.1
	history	961
	religious history	276.1
	travel	916.1
North Central	geology	556.6

Topics in blackface type ar subdivided in the Tables

Africa, North Central	history	966	
	religious hist.	276.6	
	travel	916.6	
Propria	ancient history	939	
South	geology	556.8	
	history	968	
	religious history	276.8	
	travel	916.8	
South Central	geology	556.7	
	history	967	
	religious hist.	276.7	
	travel	916.7	
African colonization	**sociology**	**325.6**	
languages		496	
	Ethiopic	492	
	Hamitic	493	
literature		896	
methodist church		287	
slave trade		326	
Age	mental caracteristics	136	
	therapeutics	615	
of animals	zoology	591	
man	physiology	612	
	nat. hist. of man	573	
	statistics	312	
pupils		379.1	
the world		550	
voters		324	
Aged, hospitals for		362.6	
Agents, consular		341	
geologic		551	
law		347	
Ages, archeologic		571	
geologic		551	
Agglutination	filology	401	
Agnosticism	filosofy	149	
	natural theology	211	
Agnostics	religious heresy	273	
Agrarian laws	political science	333	
	Roman history	937	
Agreements	ethics	174	
	law	347	
Agricultural classes	pol. econ.	331.7	
colleges		630.7	
colonization		**325**	
experiment stations		630.7	
geology	agriculture	630	
	econ. geol.	553	
implements		631	
law		347	
periodicals		630.5	
pests	agriculture	632	

Agricultural pests	zoology	591	
products	pol. econ.	338	
societies		**630.6**	
system	pol. econ.	330	
Agriculture		**630**	
	cooperativ	334	
	departments of	630.61	
	Indians	970.6	
	rent of land	333	
Aid societies	charitable ass'ns	361	
	cooperation	334	
to the injured		614.8	
Aids to readers	**library economy**	**028**	
•	lib. administration	025.5	
Air analysis	chemistry	543	
Air brakes	railroad engineering	625	
compressors	mec. engineering	621.5	
disinfection	contag. diseases	614.4	
ducts	ventilation	697	
engins	mec. engineering	621.4	
hygiene		613	
	public helth	614.7	
liquid	physics .	533	
meteorology		551.5	
operations	Great war	940.44	
plants	lichens	589	
	orchids	584	
pneumatics		533	
pump		533	
Aix-la-Chapelle	internat. congress	341	
	treaties	341	
Alabama, U. S.	history	976.1	
	travel	917.61	
claims	English history	942.08	
	international law	341	
	United States hist.	973.7	
Alarms, fire	protection of public	614.8	
	signals	654	
Alaska, U. S.	history	979.8	
	travel	917.98	
purchase	U. S. history	973.8	
Albert Nyanza	travel	916.7	
Alberta, Can.	history	971.23	
Albertypes		774	
Albigenses	French history	944	
	persecutions	272	
	sect	284	
Albinism	animals	591	
	dermatology	616	
Alchemy		540.1	
Alcohol	hygiene	613	
	materia medica	615	

Topics in blackface type ar subdivided in the Tables

Alcohol, denatured chem. tech.	661
Alcoholic drinks ethics	178
liquors manufacture	663
Alcoholism diseases	616
Alcohols organic chemistry	547
Alcoran Mohammedanism	297
Alcoves library economy	022.4
Aldermen local government	352
Aldine editions rare printing	094
Ales manufacture	663
Aleutian Islands history	979.8
travel	917.98
Alexandrian filosofy	186
library	027
Alfabet elementary education	372
English orthografy	421
other lang.	431,441, etc.
Alfabetico-clast catalogs	019
Alfabets filology	411
ornamental design	745
Algae	589
Algebra	512
Algebraic logic	164
Algeria, Africa geology	556.5
history	965
religious history	276.5
travel	916.5
Algerine war	965
U. S. history	973.5
Algiers, Africa history	965
travel	916.5
Alhambra architecture	723
history	946
Alien laws	341
Alienism mental path.	132
Aliens international law	341
landholding	333
naturalization	323.6
Alimony law	347
Alkalies chemic technology	661
chemistry	546
Alkalin earths chemistry	546
Alkoran Mohammedanism	297
All fools day customs	394
folklore	398.3
Allhallow eve customs	394
folklore	398.3
All Saints, feast of church festival	264
All Souls, " " " "	264
Alleghany mountains travel	917.5
Allegiance international law	341
naturalization	323.6

Allegiance private law	347
Allegories English literature	828
religious	244
Alliance, Evangelic	206
Alliances international law	341
Alligators zoology	598.1
Alliteration prosody	416
rhetoric	808
Allodium land ownership	333
law	347
Allopathy medicin	615
Allotropism chemistry	541
Allotment system	333
Alloys manufacture	671
physical chemistry	541
Alluvium geology	551
Almanacs, general	529
nautic	528
Almanacs, statistical	**310**
Alms ethics	177
Almshouses	362.5
architecture	725
pauperism	339
Alphabet, see Alfabet	
Alpine plants botany	581.9
travels	914.94
Alps geology	554.9
Altar cloths sacred ornaments	247
Altars ecclesiology	246
Altruism ethics	171
Alumni biografy	**378**
Alwato universal language	408
Amalgamation metallurgy	669
Amalgams manufactures	671
Amateur manuals mec. trades	**680**
theatricals amusements	793
ethics	175
Amazon river travel	918.1
Amazons customs	396
Ambassadors international law	341
political science	327
Amber geology	553
mineralogy	549
Ambrosia antiquities	913.38
mythology	292
Ambrotype	772
Ambulances	614.8
America discovery of	973.1
geografy	**917**
history	**970**
Central geology	557.2
history	972.8

Topics in blackface type ar subdivided in the Tables

America, Central religious hist.   277.2
                 travel   917.28
        North   botany   581.9
                 geology   **557**
                 history   **970**
                 religious history **277**
                 scientific travel   508.7
                 statistics   317
                 travel   **917**
        Russian history   979.8
                 travel   917.98
        South **geology**   **558**
                 history   **980**
                 religious history **278**
                 scientific travel   508.8
                 statistics   318
                 travel   **918**
American antiquities   913.7
        bibliografy   015.7
        colonies   history   973.2
        copyright leag   655
        cyclopedias   031
        essays, collected   041
        filosofy   191
        independence   U. S. hist.   973.3
        Indians   **970.1**
        journalism   071
        languages   No. Amer.   497
                     So. Amer.   498
        literature   **810**
        newspapers, general   071
        painting   759
        party   329
        periodicals, general   051
        political parties   329
        private law   347
        protestant episcopal church   283
        rebellion   history   973.7
        revolution   973.3
        slavery   326
        statutes   law   345
Americana   history   **970**
Americanisms   427
Amharic   language   492
Amiens, peace of   treaties   341
Ammonia   chemic technology   661
           stimulants   615
Ammonium   organic chemistry   547
Ammunition   military engineering   623
Amnesty   international law   341
Amos, book of Bible   224

Amphibians   597
Amphictyonic council   Greek hist.   938
Amphitheater   antiquities   913.37
                architecture   anc.   722
                                mod.   725
Amputation   surgery   617
Amsterdam   history   949.2
             travel   914.92
Amusements   **790**
             ethics   175
             hygiene   613.7
             of laboring classes   331.8
             Sunday   263
Ana   English literature   828
             literature   808.8
Anabaptists sects   284
Anagrams   English literature   828
             pseudonyms   014
Analogy   logic   169
             theology   219
Analysis   arithmetic   511
             botany   581
             chemistry   **543**
             grammar, English   425
             logic   **160**
             microscopy   578
             milk   adulterations   614.3
             mineralogy   549
             qualitativ   chem.   544
             quantitativ   "   545
             soil   hygiene   614.7
             sounds   acoustics   534
             spectrum   astronomy   522
                        chemistry   544
                        optics   535
                water   hygiene   613
Analysts, public   adulterations   614.3
Analytic chemistry   **543**
             geometry   516
             trigonometry   514
Anam, Asia   history   959
              travel   915.9
Anarchism   socialism   335
Anatomy   animals   591
             art   743
             human   611
             laws   614.2
             pathologic   616
             plants   581
Ancestry   evolution   575
             genealogy   929
             psycholgy   136

Topics in blackface type ar subdivided in the Tables

Ancestry	spiritual heredity	233
	traductionism	129
Anchor ice	occurrence in nature	551
Ancient architecture		722
	countries description	913.3
	customs	913.3
	and costume	390
	filosofers' lives	921
	filosofies	180
	geografy description	911
	history	930
	law	349
	maps	912
	music	781
	science	502
	sculpture	732
Ancients, council of		328
Andersonville prison U. S. history		973.7
Andes	description	918
Andora	history	946
Anecdotes, legal		340
	miscel. Eng. lit.	828
	personal *Class with biog.*	
	religious	244
class other special with subject		
Anemometer	meteorology	551.5
Aneroid barometer	physics	533
Anesthetics	therapeutics	615
Angels		235
Anger	ethics	179
Angevin architecture		723
Anglican biografy		922
	brotherhoods	271
	church	283
	creed	238
	missions	266
	persecutions Eng. hist.	942.05
	relig. "	272
	religious history	274.2
	sisterhoods	271.9
Anglicisms	English language	427
Angling		799
Anglo-catholics		283
	Saxon history	942.01
	language	429
	literature	829
	race caracteristics	136
Anglomania	customs	390
Anilin colors	chemic technology	667
Animal chemistry		547
	diseases medicin	619
	electricity	134
Animal food	hygiene	613.2
	hygiene public helth	614.9
	intelligence zoology	591.5
	kingdom	590
	magnetism	134
	parasites diseases	616
	psychology zoology	591.5
	stories zoology	591.5
	trades air pollution	614.7
	worship	291
Animalcules		593
Animals and plants	differences	577
	cruelty to ethics	179.3
	diseases veterinary med.	619
	domestic	**636**
	evolution	575
	geografic distribution	591.9
	insurance	368
	locomotion of	591
	menageries	590
	mind in	591.5
	mythology	291
	paleontology	**560**
	remains of prehist. arch.	571
	traind	791
	training of domestic	636
Animism	metaphysics	128
Anne, Queen, architecture		724
Annealing	manufactures	671
	molecular physics	539
Annexation	internat. law	341
Annihilation	doctrins	237
	natural theology	218
Annuals, statistical		**310**
class special with subject		
Annuities	insurance	368
	mathematics	519
	public finance	336.3
Annunciation, feast of ritual		264
Annunciators	signals	654
Anodynes	therapeutics	615
Anointing	sacraments	265
Anonyms	bibliografy	014
Ansayrii	history	955
Anselm	medieval filosofy	189
Ant	agric. pest	632
	domestic "	648
	insects	595.7
Antagonism of medicins, therapeutics		615
Antarctic current ocean currents		551
	explorations travel	919.9
	ocean oceans	551

Topics in blackface type ar subdivided in the Tables

Antarctic regions	geology	559.9	Ants	agric.	pests	632
	history	999		domestic	"	648
	relig. hist.	279.9		insects		595.7
Antenicene church		281	Antwerp	history		949.3
Anthems	music	783		travel		914.93
	public worship	264	Anvils	blacksmithing		682
	religious poetry	245	Apartment and offis bildings			725
Anthologies	Eng. literature	820		houses	architecture	728
Anthracite	econ. geology	553			dom. economy	647
	fuel	644	Apatite	economic geology		553
	metallurgy	669		fertilizers		631
Anthropofagy	cannibalism	399		mineralogy		549
Anthropoid apes	mammals	599	Apes			599
Anthropology		572	Aphelion	astronomy		521
	mind and body	**130**	Aphorisms	Eng. lit.		828
	nat. hist. of man	573		folklore		398
	relig. doct. of man	233	Apiary	agriculture		638
Anthropometry		573	Apocalypse			228
Anthropomorfism	metaphysics	125	Apocryfa			229
Antiburghers	presbyterians	285	Apocryfal gospels	Bible		229
Antichrist		235	Apogee	moon		523.3
Anticorn law leag	free trade	337		tides		525
Antidotes	materia medica	615	Apollo Belvedere	sculpture		733
Antifederal party		329		worship		292
Antifonal choral servis	music	783	Apologetics			239
	readings pub. worship	264	Apostasy	heresies		273
Antilles	history	972.9	Apostles, acts of			226
	travel	917.29		creed		238
Antimasonry		366		lives	scriptural biog.	225
Antimony	inorganic chemistry	546	Apostolic canons	Apocryfa		229
	ores	553		catholics	sects	289
Antinomianism		273		church		281
Antiquarian societies		**913**		constitutions		281
Antiquarians	biografy	923		epistles		229
Antiquities	Biblical	220.9		fathers		281
	classic	913.38		succession		262
	countries	**913**	Apothecary			615
	customs	**390**	Apothems	English literature		828
	Jewish antiquities	913.33		folklore		398
	history	933	Apparatus	manufacture		681
	religion	296		practical chemistry		542
	legal	340		class special with subject		
	prehistoric archeology	571	Apparitions			133
	class special with subject		Appetites	psychology		158
Antiquity of man		573		temperance		178
Antiseptics	agriculture	632	Apple culture			634
	public helth	614.4	**Applied arts**			**600**
	therapeutics	615		**chemistry**	**useful arts**	**660**
Antislavery	slavery	326		**mecanics**	**engin'g**	**621**
	U. S. history	973.7		science schools		607
Antitrinitarians	heresies	273	Appliqué work			746
	unitarians	288	Appointment of civil servis offisers			351

Topics in blackface type ar subdivided in the Tables

Appointment of teachers education	371.1
Apportionment	representation	328
	taxation	336.2
Apprentises, duties of	ethics	174
Apprentisship	polit. econ.	331.8
Appropriations	public finance	336
Aquariums		590
Aquatint	engraving	766
Aqueducts	canals	626
	Roman antiquities	913.37
	waterworks	628
Aqueous erosion	geology	551
rocks	"	552
Aquinas	medieval filosofy	189
Arabesque decoration	design	745
Arabesques	ornaments	747
Arabia	ancient history	939
	geology	555.3
	modern history	953
	religious history	275.3
	travel	915.3
Arabic architecture		723
filosofy		189
language		492
literature		892
numerals	arithmetic	511
Arabs in Spain	Spanish history	946
Aramaic language		492
Arbitrary power	absolute monarchy	321
Arbitration and award	law	347
	capital and labor	331.1
	international	ethics	172.4
	law	341
Arbor day		715
Arboriculture	forestry	634.9
	landscape gardening	715
Arbors	" "	717
Arcades	architectural design	729
	walls	721
Arcadia	Greek anc. history	938
Archaean age	geology	551
Archaisms	English language	427
Archbishops	ecclesiastic polity	262
	lives	922
Archeology	**anc. description, etc.**	**913**
	Biblical	220.9
	prehistoric	571
Archery		799
Arches	architectural design	729
	constr.	721
	engineering	624
triumfal	Rom. antiq.	913.37

Archimedes screw	physics	532
Archipelago, East Indian		**991**
	Greek	ancient hist.	939
		modern hist.	949.9
Architects, liability of	bilding	692
	biografy	927
Architectural construction		721
	decoration and design	729
	drawing	744
Architecture		**720**
	military engineering	623
	castles	728
	naval engineering	623.8
	plans	692
Archives	*Class with* History, Manuscripts, *or special topics*
Arctic currents		551
	explorations	travel	919.8
	explorers	biografy	923
	ocean	551
	regions	geology	559.8
		history	998
Ardent spirits	manufactures	663
	temperance	178
Areometer	specific gravity	532
Argentina	geology	558.2
	history	982
	religious history	278.2
	statistics	318
	travel	918.2
Argonauts	Greek mythology	292
Argot	French language	447
Argument	logic	168
	from design	apologetics	239
Aria	vocal music	784
Arianism	heresies	273
	unitarianism	288
Aristocracy	polit. science	321
Aristotelian filosofy		185
Arithmetic	mathematics	511
	elementary	education	372
Arithmetic, political	**statistics**	**310**
Arithmometer		510
Arizona, U. S.	history	979.1
	travel	917.91
Arkansas, U. S.	history	976.7
	travel	917.67
Armaments	ordnance	623
Armed neutrality	internat. law	341
Armenia	modern history	956
Armenian architecture		723
	church	281

Topics in blackface type ar subdivided in the Tables

Armenian language		491
literature		891
Armies	Amer. civil war	973.7
	military engineering	623
	military science	**355**
	war customs	399
Arminianism	continental prot. sects	284
	methodism	287
Armistis	international law	341
Armor	war costumes	399
plate	manufactures	672
Armorican language		491.6
Armories	architecture	725
	military engineering	623
Arms, artificial		617
coats of	heraldry	929.8
gunmaking		683
military engineering		623
military science		**355**
war customs		399
Army	foren countries	354
	military science	**355**
lists	foren	354
	United States	353
officials	biografy	923
regulations		**355**
Salvation		267
United States		353
worm	agriculture	632
Arrondissement	French loc. gov't	352
Arrow hed inscriptions		492
heds, stone	prehist. arch.	571
Arrows	archery	799
	war implements	399
Arsacidae	history	935
Arsenals	architecture	725
	military engineering	623
Arsenic	inorganic chemistry	546
	medical jurisprudence	340
	medicin	615
Arson	criminal law	343
Art anatomy	drawing	743
bibliografy		016.7
biografy		927
Art, Christian	**ecclesiology**	**246**
decorativ furniture		749
education		707
fine		**700**
galleries		708
	architecture	727
history		709
industrial	**useful arts**	**600**

Art, interior decoration		747
needlework		746
religious		**246**
rudiments, prehistoric		571
sacred furniture		247
schools		707
studios	architecture	727
woman in		396
Arteries	anatomy	611
	diseases	616
Artesian wels	sanitary engin'g	628
Arthropoda	zoology	595
Arthrostraca	"	595
Arthur, C. A.	presidency	973.8
Arthurian romances		398.2
Articles of confederation U. S. const.		342
thirty-nine	Anglican creed	238
Articulates	paleontology	565
	zoology	**595**
Artificial butter	chemic technology	664
colors	" "	667
eyes		617
flowers	ornamental design	745
fuel	chemic technology	662
ice	manufacture	621.5
lights	chemic technology	665
lims	surgery	617
mineral waters	chem. tech.	663
stone	bilding materials	691
	chemic technology	666
teeth	dentistry	617
Artillery	army dep't	358
	military engin'g	623
Artisans	biografy	926
Artistic furniture		749
Artists	biografy	927
Artotype	fotografy	774
Arts and crafts		**740**
trades		**600**
fine		**700**
	biografy of	927
grafic	**fine arts**	**700**
useful		**600**
	biografy of	926
Arundel marbles	Greek inscrip.	481
Aryan languages		**491**
literatures		**891**
Aryan races	ethnology	572
Asbestos	economic geology	553
Ascensions, balloon	aeronautics	629.1
Asceticism	heresy	273
	personal religion	248

Topics in blackface type ar subdivided in the Tables

Asfalt	economic geology	553
	pavements	625
	roofing	695
Asfaltum	chemic technology	665
Ashangoland	history	967
	travel	916.7
Ashanti	history	966
	travel	916.6
Ashburton treaty	internat. law	341
Ashes	fertilizers	631
Asia	antiquities	913.5
	botany	581.9
	geology	**555**
	history	**950**
	religious history	**275**
	scientific travels	508.5
	statistics	315
	travel	**915**
Minor	ancient history	939
	modern history	956
	travel	915.6
Asiatic cholera	pathology	616
	pub. helth	614.5
languages		**491-495**
	eastern	495
societies	filologic	490
Ass	domestic animals	636.1
	zoology	599
Assassination	criminal law	343
Assassins	lives	923
	Persian history	955
Assault and battery	law	343
Assaults	military engineering	623
Assaying	metallurgy	669
Assembly, legislativ		**328**
Assent	logic	163
Assessment	taxes	336.2
Assignats	French finance	336
Assimilation of food	animals	591
	man	612
	plants	581
Assize, courts of	law	347
Associated press	journalism	070
Association	psychology	153
Associationism	filosofy	149
Associations	bilding private fin.	332
	business cooperation	334
	charitable	361
	gilds	338
	labor	331.88
	religious, nonsect.	**267**
	sociology	**360**
for special object, class with topic		

Assurance		368
Assyria	ancient history	935
	antiquities	913.35
	architecture	722
Assyrian language		492
Asteroids	astronomy	523.4
Astrology	astronomy	520.1
	occultism	133
Astronomers' lives		925
Astronomic almanacs	cronology	529
	fotografy	522
	instruments	522
	maps	524
	observations	524
	spec. observatories	522
	physics	521
Astronomy		**520**
Astrophysics		**523**
Asylum, right of	legal antiquities	340
Asylums	architecture	725
	sociology	**362**
Athanasian creed		238
Atheism	apologetics	239
	natural theol.	211
Atheists	biografy	922
Atheneum libraries		027.2
Athens	ancient history	938
	modern history	949.5
	travel	914.95
Athletic clubs		613.7
sports		**796**
	hygiene	613.7
	school hygiene	371.7
Atlantic ocean	physical geografy	551
	travel	910.4
telegraf	sociology	384
	useful arts	654
Atlantis	antiquities	913.39
	mythology	292
	original home of man	572
Atlases, maps, etc.		912
	celestial astron.	524
	geografy	912
	school furniture	371.6
see also special topics		
Atmosfere	meteorology	551.5
	pneumatics	533
Atmosferic currents		551.5
	electricity	537
	engins pneumatics	533
	pressure pneumatics	533
	railways	625
Atolls	physical geology	551

Topics in blackface type ar subdivided in the Tables

Atomic theory		541
Atomistic filosofy		182
Atoms		541
Atonement	Christology	232
Attendance	church	264
	school	371.5
Attorneys	law	347
	lives	923
Attraction, capillary	liquids	532
	chemic affinity	541
	gravity	531
	magnetism	538
Auburn prison system	sociology	365
Auction catalogs	bibliografy	018
Auctions, book	library econ.	025.2
	law of	347
Audifone	acoustics	534
Auditing		657
Augsburg confession, Lutheranism		284
	reformation	270
Augustine	medieval filosofy	189
Augustinism	doctrins	230
Auricular confession	ordinances	265
Aurora borealis		523
Australasia	**geology**	**559.3**
	history	**993**
	religious history	**279.3**
	travel	**919.3**
Australia	botany	581.9
	geology	559.4
	history	994
	religious history	279.4
	statistics	319
	travel	919.4
Austria	antiquities	913.4
	geology	554.3
	history	943.6
	religious history	274.3
	statistics	314
	travel	914.36
Authenticity of Scripture	Bible	220.1
Author bibliografies, general		011
	individual	012
catalogs	bibliografy	018
Authority	church and ministerial	262
	ethics	171
Authors and publishers		655
anon.	bibliografy	014
bibliografy of individuals		012
	special classes	013
lives		928
rights of	copyright	655

Authors, rights of	law	347
Authorship	literary methods	029
Auto da fé	Spanish inquisition	272
Autobiografy		92
Autocracy	form of state	321
Autografs	book rarities	091
Automatons	mecanical	791
	metaphysics	127
Autotypes		773
Avalanches	physical geology	551
Avars	history	950
Avatars	Brahmanism	294
Average	probabilities	519
Avesta, Zend	language	491
	literature	891
	religion	295
Aviation	amusements	797
	engineering	629.1
	physics	533
Avignon, council of	religious hist.	270
Axle	physics	531
Azoic rocks	stratigrafic geology	551
Azores	history	946
Aztec	architecture	722
	history	972
	language	497
Babism	Moham. sect	297
Babylon	ancient history	935
	architecture	722
	language cuneiform	492
	religion	299
Baccalaureate sermons		252
	colleges	**378**
Bacchanalia	social customs	394
Bacchus	mythology	292
Bachelors	celibacy	176
Backgammon	ethics	175
	games	795
Baconian filosofy		192
	empiricism	144
Bacon-Shakspere controversy		822.3
Bacteria	botany	589
	fermentation	663
	theory of diseases	616
Bactrian, Old	language	491
Badges	heraldry	929.8
Bagatel	amusements	794
Bagpipe		788
Bahamas	history	972.9
	travel	917.29
Baii	criminal law	343

Topics in blackface type ar subdivided in the Tables

Baking	cookery	641		Banners	heraldry	929.9
powder	adulterations	614.3			sacred ornaments	247
	chem. technol.	664		Banquets	social customs	394
Balance	metrology	389		Banting	dietetics	613.2
machines		531		Baptism	sacrament	265
of power	political science	320		Baptismal fonts	sacred furniture	247
trade	commerce	382			regeneration salvation	234
Balances, chemic		542		Baptisms	registers of	929
Baldness	dermatology	616		Baptistery	sacred furniture	247
Balearic Islands	history	946		Baptists		286
Balize	history	972.8			lives	922
	travel	917.28		Bar association		347
Balkan states	**history**	**949.6**		**legal**		**340**
Ball playing	amusements	796			biografy	923
	school hygiene	371.7		Barbados	travels	917.29
Ballads	Danish poetry	839		Barbarians, antiquities		
	English literature	821			see special country	
	folklore	398			**N. American Indians**	**970.1**
	vocal music	784			prehistoric archeology	571
Ballet	amusements	792			**S. American Indians**	**980**
	ethics	175			war customs	399
Ballistics	military engineering	623		Barbarism vs church		261
Ballooning	engineering	629.1		Barbarisms	English language	428
	military	623		**Barbary States**	**history**	**961**
	physics	533		Barbd wire	manufacture	672
Ballot	political science	324		Barbers	customs	391
Balls	dancing	793		Barbizon school	painting	759
	ethics	175		Bards and minstrels	English lit.	821
	projectils	623			other literatures, 831, 841, etc.	
Baltimore	history	975.2		Barebones parliament	English hist.	942.06
	travel	917.52		Barkeepers manuals	chem. tech.	663
Baluchistan	geology	555.8		Barley	agriculture	633
	history	958			brewing	663
	religious history	275.8		Barns	architecture	728
	travel	915.8		Barometer	pneumatics	533
Balustrades	architectural design	729		Barometric leveling	geodesy	526
Bampton lectures		239		Barometry	meteorology	551.5
Bananas	agriculture	634		Baronage	heraldry	929.7
Banditti	biografy	923		Baronetage	"	929.7
	law	343		Barracks	architecture	725
Banishment	criminal law	343		Barrel organs	music	789
Banjo		787		Barricade	military engineering	623
Bank note engraving		768		Barrows	prehist. arch.	571
notes	money	332		Bars	harbor engineering	627
U. S. National	U. S. hist.	973.4		Barter	commerce	380
Bankers	biografy	923		Bartholomew, St	relig. persecution	272
Banking		332		Bartholomew fair	public customs	394
Bankruptcy		347		Base mesuring	geodesy	526
Banks and banking	law	347		Baseball	amusements	796
architecture		725		Bases	theoretic chemistry	541
cooperativ	cooperation	334			walls	721
political economy		332		Bashfulness	ethics	179

Topics in blackface type ar subdivided in the Tables

Basilica	architecture	726
	Roman antiquities	913.37
Basilisk	legends	398.4
	zoology	598.1
Basins	physical geografy	551
Basketry	manufactures	677
	ornamental	745
	prehistoric	571
Basle	history	949.4
	travel	914.94
Bas-relief	sculpture	736
Bastardy	law	347
Bastile	French history	944
	prisons	365
Bath, order of the	heraldry	929.7
Bathing	customs	391
	hygiene	613
Baths	antiquities	913
	architecture	725
	hygiene	613
	practical chemistry	542
	therapeutics	615
Batrachia	paleontology	567
	zoology	597
Bats	"	599
Battalion dril	military tactics	356
Batteries	electric engin'g	621.3
	physics	537
	military engin'g	623
Battering ram	customs of war	399
Battle paintings		756
wager of	legal antiquities	340
Battledoor	outdoor sports	796
Battles	**U S history**	**973**
	World war, 1914-19	**940.4**
land	military science	355
naval	naval "	359
see also hist. of special countries		
Bavaria	history	943
	travel	914.3
Bay windows	architectural design	729
Bayeux tapestry	art needlework	746
Bayonet	military sci.	356
	wepons	399
Beaches, formation of		551
Beacons	navigation	656
	river engineering	627
Beads	archeology	571
	devotional	247
	ornaments	391
Beams	bilding	694
Bear baiting	customs	394

Beards	customs	391
Beasts	zoology	599
of burden	**domestic animals**	**636**
Beatitudes	Gospels	226
Beauties, selections	Eng. lit.	828
Beauty	esthetics	701
personal	"	701
Beaux	social ethics	177
Beaver	animals	599
Bechuanaland	history	968
Bed wagon	aid to injured	614.8
Bedding	dom. econ.	645
Bedouins	Arabian history	953
	travel among	915.3
Beds	furniture	645
	hygiene	613
Bee-keeping	agriculture	638
Beef	food	641
cure	therapeutics	615
production	domes. animals	636.2
Beer	adulterations	614.3
analysis	chem.	543
drinking		178
manufactura		663
Bees	insects	595.7
Beet sugar	chemic technology	664
Beetles	insects	595.7
Beets	garden	635
Beggars	charity	177
	pauperism	339
Behavior		177
Beheading	punishments	343
Behring strait	travels	917.98
Being, nature of	ontology	111
Bel and the dragon	Apocryfa	229
Bel, book and candle	church	262
Belgium	antiquities	913.4
	botany	581.9
	geology	554.9
	history	949.3
	religious history	274.9
	travel	914.93
	zoology	591.9
Belief	salvation	234
	theory of knowledge	121
Bell system	education	371.4
Belles-lettres		**800**
Belligerents, rights of	inter. law	341
Beloochistan, see Baluchistan		
Bel-ringing		789
Bels	manufacture	673
	music	789

Topics in blackface type ar subdivided in the Tables

Bels	signals	654
diving	hydraulic engin'g	627
Belting	mecan. engineering	621
Bench and bar	biografy	923
Benediction		264
Benefactors	biografy	923
Beneficence	ethics	177
Benefises, church	cleric support	254
Benefit of clergy	legal antiquities	340
Benefit societies	insurance	368
Benevolence	ethics	177
Benevolent institutions		**362**
societies		361
	parish work	256
Benguela	nistory	967
Beowulf	Anglo-Saxon poetry	829
Bequests	law	347
Berbers	**description**	**916.1**
Bereft	charities	362.6
Bergen, Norway	history	948.3
	travel	914.83
Bering strait	travels	917.98
Berlin	history	943.1
	travel	914.31
congress	international law	341
decree	" "	341
Bermudas	history	972.9
	travel	917.29
Berne	history	949.4
	travel	914.94
Bertillon system	anthropol.	573
Bessel's functions		517
Bessemer process	metallurgy	669
Best reading		**028**
Beton	artificial stone	666
construction	masonry	693
Betrothal	customs	392
Betterments	law	347
Betting	ethics	175
Beverages	adulterations	614.3
	hygiene	613
	manufacture	663
	temperance	178
Bezique	amusements	795
Bezoar stones	medicin	615
Bhagavat Ghita	Sanskrit literature	891
Bible		**220**
and science	apologetics	239
antiquities		220.9
	Jewish	913.33
classes	Sunday schools	268
cyclopedias		220.3

Bible dictionaries		220.3
geografy	ancient geografy	911
	Biblical	220.9
history	Biblical	220.9
	Jewish history	933
in public schools	education	377
legends of		398
societies		206
Bibliofily		**010**
Bibliografers	biografy	920
Bibliografies, general		011
Bibliografy		**010**
national		**015**
Bibliomania	bibliografy	010
Bicycle	sports	796
motor	engineering	629.2
Bigamy	ethics	173
	law	343
Bigotry	ethics	179
Bil of exchange	banks and banking	332
	law	347
rights	English	342
Bilding	**architecture**	**720**
	useful arts	**690**
associations, cooperativ		334
	loan institutes	332
laws	bilding	692
	protection of life	614.8
stones	econ. geol.	553
Bildings	library admin.	025.9
	architecture	727
economy		**022**
inspection of		614.8
out	architecture	728
public	"	725
	local government	352
Y. M. C. A.		267.3
	architecture	726
Billiards	ethics	175
	games	794
Billon	coins and coinage	332
Bils and notes	law	347
of mortality	statistics	312
sale	law	347
Bimana	mammals	599
Bimetalism	coinage	332
Binding, book	library economy	025.7
	mecanic trades	686
	rare	095
Binocular vision	physiologic optics	535
Binomial theorem	algebra	512
Biogenesis	zoology	591

Topics in blackface type ar subdivided in the Tables

Biografic sermons		920
	homiletics	252
Biografy	bibliografy	016.9
	collectiv	920
	individual	92
	New Testament	225
	of gipsies	397
	Indians	970.2
	slaves	326
	Old Testament	221
	scriptural	220.9
Biology		**570**
Bioplasm		576
Birds		598
	agriculture	632
	cage domestic pets	636.6
	diseases of	619
	flight of migration	591.5
	game sports	799
	paleontology	568
	poultry	636.5
Birth customs		392
	marks	617
	obstetrics	618
	rates public helth	614.1
Birthday customs		392
Births registers of		929
	registration pub. helth	614.1
	statistics	312
Bishops	ecclesiastic polity	262
	lives of	922
Bison	zoology	599
Bithynia	anc. history	939
Bitumen	economic geology	553
Bivalvs	paleontology	564
	zoology	594
Black art	occultism	133
	Forest, Germany travel	914.3
	deth plagues	614.4
	hils, Dakota travel	917.83
	hole, Calcutta	954
	sea travel	914.7
Blacking	chemic technology	667
Blackmail	law	343
Blacksmithing		682
Blasfemy	ethics	179
	law	343
Blast furnace	metallurgy	669
Blasting	explosivs	662
	mining engineering	622
Blazonry	heraldry	929.8
Bleaching	chemic technology	667

Blights	agriculture	632
	bacteria	589
Blind	asylums	362.4
	education	371.9
Blindness		617
Blizzards	meteorology	551.5
Block books		092
Blockade	war	341
Blood	physiology	612
	poisoning diseases	616
	vessels anatomy	611
Bloomer costume		391
Blowing engin		621.6
Blowpipe	apparatus	542
Blowpiping	mineralogy	549
	qualitativ analysis	544
Blue books	lists of offisers	351
	parliamentary	328
	United States	328
	glass therapeutics	615
	laws, Connecticut	345
	prints fotografy	771
Blunders	English language	428
	etiquet	395
Board of helth	city gov't	352
	medicin	614
	sanitary engineering	628
	trade commerce	381
Boarding schools	boys	373
	girls	376
Boards	lumber	674
Boat bilding		623.8
	racing ethics	175
	school hygiene	371.7
Boating	amusements	797
Boats, life	lifesaving servis	614.8
	shipbilding	623.8
Bodily strength	athletics	613.7
Bodleian library		027.7
Body and mind		**130**
	care of hygiene	**613**
	school hygiene	371.7
	mesurements of	573
	natural and spiritual theol.	233
	symmetry art anatomy	743
	training hygiene	613.7
Boeotia	ancient history	938
Boer war		968
Boers	history	968
Bohemia	"	943.7
	travel	914.37
Bohemian brethren	sects	284

Topics in blackface type ar subdivided in the Tables

Bohemian language		491.8
literature		891.8
Bohemianism	customs	394
Bohlen lectures	apologetics	239
Boiler inspection	pub. helth	614.8
Boilers	insurance	368
	steam engineering	621.1
Boiling	heat	536
points	chemistry	541
Boils	diseases	616
Bokhara	history	958
Bolak	universal lang.	408
Bolivia	geology	558.4
	history	984
	religious history	278.4
	travel	918.4
Bolshevism	Russian hist.	947
	sociology	335
Bolting	political parties	329
Bolts	machinery	621
Bombs	military engineering	623
	chemic technology	662
Bonaparte, N.	French hist.	944
Bondage	slavery	326
Bonds and stocks		332
civil trials		347
criminal law		343
insurance of		368
public finance		336.3
Bone caves	prehistoric archeology	571
implements	archeology	571
Bones	diseases of	616
	human anatomy	611
	musical instruments	789
	paleontology	**566**
	physiology	612
	zoology	591
Bonn conference	religious history	284
Bonnets	costume	391
	toilet	646
Book auctions		655
binding	library	025.7
	rare	095
	trade	686
cases	lib. bildings	022.4
catalogs	**bibliografy**	**017–019**
publishers	bibliog.	015
clubs	self culture	374.2
collecting		025.2
holders	offis equipment	651
illustration	inserted plates	096
	typografy	655
Book making	typografy	655
of common prayer		264
ownership	rarities	097
plates	lib. econ.	025.2
rarities		**090**
trade	history	655
worm	library economy	025.8
Bookbuying	lib. administration	025.2
Bookkeeping	accounts	756
	library	025.1
Booklovers circulating library		027.3
Books and reading	**helps**	**028**
bibliografy		**010**
classification of	lib. econ.	025.4
commonplace	" "	029
condemd to be burnd		098
enemies of	library economy	025.8
library economy		**020**
lists of best	library economy	028
of prints		769
prayer		264
preservation of	lib. econ.	025.9
privately printed		094
prohibited		098
restricted	library economy	024
sizes of	" "	025.3
tarif on	" "	021.8
Booksellers catalogs	**bibliografy**	**017–019**
lives	biografy	920
Bookselling	publishing	655
Boomerang	customs of war	399
Bootmaking	trades	685
Booty	international law	341
Bordeaux	history	944
	travel	914.4
Border ballads, Scottish	Eng. poet.	821
ruffians	Kansas history	978.1
Bores	social ethics	177
Borneo	history	991
	travel	919.1
Boron	inorganic chemistry	546
Boro	local gov't	352
Bosnia	history	943.9
Bosporus	travel	914.96
Boss	Amer. politics	329
Boston massacre	U. S. history	973.3
Botanic chemistry		581
gardens	architecture	727
museums	botany	580
Botanists	biografy	925
Botany		**580**
	agricultural	630

Topics in blackface type ar subdivided in the Tables

Botany	fossil	561		Brazil	statistics	318
	geografic distribution	581.9			travel	918.1
	medical	615		Breach of promis	law	347
	structural	581		Bread, *see* Bred		
Bottom of ocean	physical geografy	551		Breakwaters	harbor engineering	627
	zoology	591.9		Breathing	animals	591
Boulders	physical geology	551			man	612
Boundaries	law	347		Bred	adulterations	614.3
	national foren relations	327			cookery	641
	intern. law	341		Bredstufs	production	338
	U. S. hist.	**973**		Breechloading guns		683
Bounties	army	355.2		Breeding	agriculture	636
	protection	337			zoology	591.5
	U. S. army	353		Brehon laws	Irish law	349
	wage scales	331.2		Brethren, United	sects	284
Bounty mutiny, Pitcairn iland		997		Breton language		491.6
Bourbons	French history	944			literature	891.6
Bourgeoisie	soc. classes	323		Breviaries		264
Bourse	stock exchange	332		Brewd beverages	adulterations	614.3
Bowling	amusements	794			chem. technol.	663
Boxer uprising	Chinese hist.	951		Breweries	architecture	725
Boxing	athletics	796		Brewing		663
Boy problem	childstudy	136.7			air pollution	614.7
scouts	societies	369.43		Bribery	criminal law	343
Boycotting	laboring classes	331.89			electoral fraud	324
Boyle lectures	apologetics	239			legislativ abuses	328
Boys' religious societies		267		Bricabrac		739
societies	**sociology**	**369.42**		Brick clays	economic geology	553
Brachiopoda	paleontology	564		construction	masonry	693
	zoology	594		Bricks	bilding material	691
Brachygrafy	shorthand	653			manufacture	666
Brahmanism		294		Bridal customs		392
Brahmo Somaj	Indian religion	294		Bridge-bilding		624
Brain	anatomy	611		Bridges	administration	351
	diseases	616			engineering	624
	mental derangements	132			local government	352
	mental physiology	131			military engineering	623
	physiology	612		Bridgewater treatises		215
Brakes	railroad engineering	625		Brief longhand	abbreviations	653
Branch libraries	library economy	022		Brigandage	criminal law	343
Brandy	manufacture	663		Brigands	biografy	923
	stimulant	615		Bright's disease of the kidneys		616
	temperance	178		Briticisms	filology	427
Brass instruments	music	788		**British America**	**history**	**971**
manufacture		673			travel	917.1
Brasses, monumental	ecclesiology	247		army		354
	sculpture	739		barrows	prehist. arch.	571
Bravery	ethics	179		Burma	history	959
Brazil	botany	581.9			travel	915.9
	geology	558.1		colonies	polit. sci.	325
	history	981		Columbia	history	971.1
	religious history	278.1			travel	917.1

Topics in blackface type ar subdivided in the Tables

British constitution		342
empire	**history**	**942**
	travel	**914.2**
filosofers		192
Guiana	history	988
	travel	918.8
India	history	954
	travel	915.4
museum		069
	library	027.5
navy		354
régime	**Canada hist.**	**971**
statutes		346
Britons	**history**	**942**
Brittany, France	history	944
	travel	914.4
Broad church	Anglican church	283
Broadsword exercise	military sci.	355
Brokerage	law	347
Bromids	hypnotics	615
Bronchi	anatomy	611
Bronchitis	diseases	616
Bronze age	prehist. archeology	571
manufactures		673
Bronzes	fine arts	739
Brook farm	socialism	335
Brooklyn, N. Y.	history	974.7
	travel	917.47
Brooms	domestic economy	648
Brothels	ethics	176
Brotherhoods	monks	271
	parish work	255
Brownies	folklore	398.4
Brownists	congregationalists	285
Brunswick, house of	English hist.	942.07
Brussels	travel	914.93
Brutes, immortality of	zoology	591.5
Bryofyta	botany	588
Bryology	"	588
Bryozoa	molluscoidea	594
Bubble, Mississippi	French finance	336
South sea	stocks	332
Bubonic plague	pub. helth	614.4
Buccaneers	adventures, etc.	910.4
	law	343
Buchanan, J.	presidency U. S. hist.	973.6
Buckshot war	Penn. hist.	974.8
Bucolic poetry	English literature	821
Buddhism		294
Buddhist architecture		722
Budget	public finance	336
Buenos Aires	history	982
Buenos Aires	travel	918.2
Buffalo	zoology	599
Bugle	wind instrument	788
Bugs	rhynchota	595.7
Buhlwork		749
Bul fights	amusements	791
	ethics	175
Bulgaria	history	949.7
	language	491.8
	travel	914.97
Bulletins	library admin.	025.1
	publications	**027**
Bullion	coins and coinage	332
Buls and bears	stock exchange	332
Irish	English humor	827
papal	eccles. polity	262
	Roman church	282
Bundesrat	German empire	354
Bundling	customs	392
Bunker hil monument		718
	history	973.3
Bunsen pump	pneumatics	533
Buoys	harbor engineering	627
	protection of life	614.8
Bureaucracy	administration	351
Burglar alarms	signals	654
Burglary	criminal law	343
Burial	cemeteries	718
	church rituals	265
	customs	393
	public helth	614.6
	societies cooperation	334
Burking	criminal law	343
Burlesque	English literature	827
Burma	history	959
Burmese architecture		722
Burning glass	optics	535
the ded	customs	393
Burnings	customs of war	399
	student life	371.8
Burns and scalds	surgery	617
Burying grounds	cemeteries	718
	public helth	614.6
Business arithmetic		511
bildings	architecture	725
cooperation		334
education		650
ethics		174
law		347
manuals		658
methods		658
sociology		380

Topics in blackface type ar subdivided in the Tables

Business useful arts	650
Butter adulterations	614.3
artificial chem. technology	664
Butterflies fossils	565
pests	632
zoology	595.7
Buttermaking	637
Buttermilk adulterations	614.3
Buttons manufacture	679
Byzantine architecture	723
art	709
ecclesiology	246
empire history	949.5
Cab manufactures	684
Cabalistic art occultism	133
Cabinet council, English	354
making	684
officers U. S. gov't	353
work joinery	694
Cable roads city transit	388
road engineering	625
telegrafic business	654
engineering	621.3
sociology	384
Cables manufactures	677
wire "	677
Cabs city transit	388
manufactures	684
Cadets military schools	355
Caedmon Anglo-Saxon poetry	829
Caesar Latin literature	878
Caesars lives	923
Roman history	937
Cafés architecture	725
Cage birds domestic pets	636.6
Cairns prehistoric archeology	571
Calcium inorganic chemistry	546
light chemic technology	665
Calculators mathematics	510
offis equipment	651
Calculus diseases	616
mathematics	517
of direction analyt. geom.	516
Caledonia history	941
Calendar	529
ecclesiastic, Anglican	264
Calendering paper manufacture	676
textil fabrics	677
Calico manufactures	677
printing chemic tech.	667
California, U. S. history	979.4

California, U. S. travel	917.94
Califs Mohammedanism	297
Caligrafs writing machines	652
Caligrafy manuscripts	091
writing	652
Calisthenics hygiene	613.7
school hygiene	371.7
Calmucks history	950
Caloric physics	536
engins engin'g	621.4
Calorimeter	536
Calsomining	698
Calvinism sects	284
vs free wil dogmatics	234
Calvinistic confession	238
Calvinists' lives	922
Cambistry metrology	389
money	332
Cambodian architecture	722
Cambria, Wales history	942.9
Cambrian age geology	551
Cambridge confession	238
Camel domestic animals	636.2
zoology	599
Cameos	736
Camera fotografy	771
lucida microscopy	578
optics	535
obscura "	535
fotografy	771
Cameralistic science	**336**
Cameronians sects	285
Camp life hygiene	613
meetings	269
Campains political	329
Campbellism sects	286
Campfire girls societies	369.47
Camping out	796
Camps, disinfection pub. helth	614.4
Canada botany	581.9
geology	557.1
history	**971**
immigration	325.71
religious history	277.1
statistics	317
travel	917.1
Canal engineering	626
transit sociology	386
transport	656
Canary birds care of	636.6
zoology	598
iles history	946

Topics in blackface type ar subdivided in the Tables

Candles	chemic technology	665
Candor	ethics	177
Candy	adulterations	614.3
	making	641
Cane, sugar	agriculture	633
	botany	584
Cannel coal	economic geology	553
Cannibalism	customs of war	399
Canning of food	chem. tech.	664
Cannon	military engineering	623
Canoes and canoeing		797
Canon	law	348
	music	781
	of Scripture	220.1
Canons	ecclesiastic polity	262
Cañons	phys. geog.	551
	of Colorado river descr.	917.91
Cantata	dramatic music	782
	sacred music	783
Canticles	Bible	223
Canvas roofing	bilding	695
Canvassing	bookselling	655
Canyons, see cañons		
Caoutchouc	organic chemistry	547
	rubber manufacture	678
Capacity for knowing	**psychology**	**151**
Cape Breton	history	971.6
	travel	917.1
of Good Hope	history	968
	travel	916.8
Capillary attraction in plants		581
	of liquids	532
Capital and labor		**331**
	punishment law	343
Capitalists' lives		923
Capitation-tax		336.2
Capitols	architecture	725
Caps, percussion	chemic tech.	662
Captivities among the Indians		970.3
Captivity	prison disciplin	365
Captivs	international law	341
	war customs	399
Captures	international law	341
Car bilding		699
Caracter	**ethics**	**170**
	self culture	374
	of reading	028
Caracteristics, mental		**136**
Caravans	transport	656
Carbolic acid	disinfection	614.4
	materia medica	615
Carbon	inorganic chemistry	546
Carbon	organic chem.	547
process	fotografy	773
Carbonari	political societies	363
Carbonated waters	hygiene	613
Carbonic acid	toxicology	615
Carboniferous age	geology	551
	fossils	**560**
Card catalog	library admin.	025.3
playing	amusements	795
	ethics	175
system	literary methods	029
Cardiff giant	humbugs	133
Cardinals	ecclesiastic polity	262
	lives	922
	Roman church	282
Care of animals	animal hygiene	614.9
body	**hygiene**	**613**
	school hygiene	371.7
person	customs	391
Caribbean sea	travel	917.29
Caribbee ilands	history	972.9
Caricature	drawing	741
Carillon	music	789
Carlovingian cycle	legends	398.2
Carnivora	mammals	599
Carnivorous plants	botany	581
Carol	sacred music	783
Caroline ilands	history	996
Carpentry		694
Carpets	designing	745
	domestic economy	645
	manufacture	677
Carposporeae	algae and fungi	589
Carriage making		684
Carrier pigeons	domestic birds	636.5
Carriers	law	347
Cars	bilding	699
motor	engineering	629.2
Cartesianism	filosofic systems	144
Carthaginian architecture		722
Cartografy	maps, atlases, etc.	912
Cartoons		741
Cartridges	military science	623
Carving	dining	642
	sculpture	736
Casemates	fortifications	623
Cases	English syntax	425
law	American	345
	English	346
Cashmere	history	954
	travel	915.4
Caspian sea	"	914.7

Topics in blackface type ar subdivided in the Tables

Castanets	musical instrum.	789
Caste	Brahmanism	294
	ethics	177
Casting	foundries	671
Castles	architecture	728
Castor and Pollux	mythology	292
Castrametation	military science	355
Casts	**sculpture**	**730**
Casualties, protec. from	pub. helth	614.8
Casuistry	ethics	171
Cat	domestic animals	636.8
Catacombs	antiquities	913.37
	cemeteries	718
	symbols	246
Catalan language		449
literature		849
Catalepsy	psychology	132
Catalog dep't	library economy	025.3
Catalogers	library staf	023
Cataloging		025.3
Catalogs	**college**	**378**
	library and sale	**017–019**
	of individual authors	012
	subjects	**016**
	star maps	524
	stars	523.8
	trade, book	**015**
	universal	011
Cataracts	eye diseases	617
	physical geografy	551
Catarrh	diseases	616
Catch	vocal music	784
Catechisms		238
Caterer	domestic economy	642
Caterpillars	agricultural pests	632
	systematic zoology	595.7
Cathartics	therapeutics	615
Cathay	history	951
Cathedral canons	eccles. polity	262
servises	musical	783
system	eccles. pol.	262
Cathedrals	architecture	726
Catholic apostolic church		289
church, Roman		282
epistles	Bible	227
Catholicism and protestantism		282
Catholics	biografy	922
Cats	domestic animals	636.8
	diseases of medicin	619
Cattle		636.2
	veterinary hygiene	614.9
	" med.	619
Caucasia	history	947
Caucuses	suffrage	324
Causation	filosofy	122
Cause and effect	filosofy	122
Causes, final	"	124
of contagious diseases		614.4
Cavalry	military science	357
Cavatina	music	784
Cave men	prehistoric archeology	571
temples	Indian architecture	722
Caves	geology	551
	natural dwellings	571
Cayenne iland	history	988
Ceilings	architecture	721
	arch. decoration	729
Celebes	history	991
Celebrations	Great war 1914-19	940.46
Celestial dynamics		521
sfere		522
Celibacy	ethics	176
	hygiene	613
	of clergy	253
Cellular confinement	prisons	365
	punishments	343
Celluloid	manufactures	679
Cellulose	botany	581
Cels	biology	576
	histology botany	581
	zoology	591
Celtic antiquities		913.36
Druids	religion	299
languages		• 491.6
Celts	ancient history	936
stone	archeology	571
Cements	bilding material	691
	economic geol.	553
	manufacture	666
Cemeteries		718
	earth burial	393
	landscape gardening	718
	public helth	614.6
Cemetery chapels	architecture	726
Censers	sacred vessels	247
Censorship of the press		323
Censuses	**statistics**	**310**
Cent-gram-second system	physics	530
Centenarians	physiology	612
Centennial celebrations	see subject	
exhibition, United States		606
Center of gravity	physics	531
Centers, community		374.2
Centipedes	zoology	595

Topics in blackface type ar subdivided in the Tables

Central Africa, North	geology	556.6
	history	966
	relig. hist.	276.6
	travel	916.6
South	geology	556.7
	history	967
	relig. hist.	276.7
	travel	916.7
America	geology	557.2
	history	972.8
	relig. hist.	277.2
	travel	917.28
Asia	history	958
	travel	915.8
park, N. Y.		712

Centralization

administrativ	foren countries	354
	U. S. gov.	353
political science		320
Centrifugal blowers	engineering	621.6
force	physics	531
pumps	engineering	621.6
Centripetal force	physics	531
Cephalopoda	zoology	594
Ceramic products	bilding	691
Ceramics	fine arts	738
	manufacture	666
Cereals	adulterations	614.3
	agriculture	633
	botany	584
trade in	agric. products	338
Cerebral poisons	therapeutics	615
Cerebration, unconscious		153
Cerebrospinal diseases		616
Ceremonies	customs	394
	religious ritual	264
Certainty	knowledge	121
Certificates of teachers		371.1
Cetacea	zoology	599
Ceylon	history	954
	travel	915.4
Chalcografy	engraving	762
Chaldea	ancient history	935
Chaldean architecture		722
filosofy		181
religion		299
Chaldee	language	492
Chalices	sacred vessels	247
Chalk	lithology	552
beds	economic geology	553
Challenger expedition, 1873-76		508.3
Challenges	duels	394

Chalukyan architecture			722
Chamber music			785
Chambers of commerce	reports		381
Chameleon	zoology		598.1
Champagne, France	history		944
Champagne	chemic technology		663
Championship games	**amusem'ts**		**790**
	ethics		175
	school hygiene		371.7
Champlain, lake	history		974.7
	travel		917.47
Chance, games of	amusements		795
	ethics		175
natural theology			214
probabilities			519
vs cause	metaphysics		122
Chancellors	biografy		923
Chancels	ecclesiology		246
Chancery	law		347
reports	American law		345
	English law		346
Chances	mathematics		519
Chandeliers			749
Change of air	hygiene		613
seasons			525
Chant, Gregorian	ecclesiology		246
Chants	sacred music		783
Chapbooks			398
Chapels	architecture		726
Chaplains	ministry		262
Chapter-and-verse division	Bible		220.1
Character, *see* Caracter			
Charades			793
Charcoal	chemic technology		662
	drawing		741
	fuel		644
Charging systems	libraries		025.6
Charitable associations			361
institutions			**362**
Charities and corrections			**360**
Charity	ethics		177
	schools		377
	sisters of		271.9
	sociology		361
Charlatanry			133
Charlemagne, age of	European hist.		940.1
legends			398.2
Charles 1-2	English history		942.06
5	German "		943
	Netherlands history		949.2
	Spanish "		946
Charleston, S. C.	history		975.7

Topics in blackface type ar subdivided in the Tables

Charleston, S. C.   travel   917.57
Charms   occultism   133
Charters of cities   352
Chartism   Eng. constitut. history 342
Chartists   political party   329
Chartografy   maps, atlases, etc. 912
Charts   **astronomy**   **523**
                 history   902
                 maps   912
    of statistics   311
    class special with subject
Chase   hunting   799
Chasing   sculpture   736
Chastity   ethics   176
Chateaux   architecture   728
Chattels   law   347
Chautauqua   self education   374.9
Cheating   ethics   174
                 student life   371.8
Checkers   794
Checks   banks   332
                 commercial law   347
Cheerfulness   ethics   179
Cheers   college   371.8
Cheese   adulterations   614.3
                 dairy   637
Chelonia   reptils   598.1
Chemic affinity   541
    analysis   **543**
    apparatus   542
    elements   chemistry   546
    equations   541
    fire extinguishers   614.8
    industries   **660**
    jurisprudence   law   340
    laboratories   542
    manipulation   542
    nomenclature   541
    physics   541
    technology   **660**
    works   air pollution   614.7
Chemistry   **540**
    agricultural   630
    and natural religion   215
    applied to the arts   **660**
    legal   law   340
    medical   materia med.   615
    of poisons   chem. anal.   543
                 toxicology   615
    soil   631
    physiologic   612
                 zoology   591

Chemists   biografy   925
Chess   amusements   794
                 ethics   175
Chicago, Ill.   history   977.3
                 travel   917.73
Chief justises   biografy   923
Chilblains   skin disorders   616
Child labor   political economy   331.3
                 welfare   362.7
Childbirth   obstetrics   618
Children, abnormal   childstudy 136.7
                         education   371.9
         asylums for   sociology   362.7
         care of   dom. econ. 649
         cruelty to   ethics   179.2
         diseases of   618
         duties of   ethics   173
         education of   **372**
         games of   nursery   649
                         out-door   796
         hospitals for   362.7
         moral care for   377
Children's crusade   European history 940.1
         libraries   027.62
Childstudy   136.7
Chile   botany   581.9
                 geology   558.3
                 history   983
                 religious history   278.3
                 statistics   318
                 travel   918.3
Chiliasm   millennium   236
Chimes of bels   music   789
Chimneys   heating   697
                 masonry   693
China   antiquities   913.31
                 botany   581.9
                 geology   555.1
                 history, ancient   931
                         modern   951
                 religion, Christian 275.1
                 statistics   315
                 travel   915.1
         ware   fine arts   738
                 useful arts   666
Chinese architecture   722
         art   709
         filosofy   181
         immigration   325
         labor   polit. economy   331.6
         language   495
         literature   895

Topics in blackface type ar subdivided in the Tables

Chinese religion		299
Chinook language		497
Chirognomy	palmistry	133
Chirografy	penmanship	652
Chiromancy	palmistry	133
Chiroptera	mammals	599
Chirosofy	palmistry	133
Chivalry	customs	394
age of	Europ. hist.	940.1
Chloral	temperance	178
	therapeutics	615
Chloroform	therapeutics	615
Chlorofyl	botany	581
Chocolate	adulterations	614.3
	manufactures	663
Choctaw language		497
literature		897
Choice, freedom of	metaphysics	123
	psychology	159
of vocation		371.4
Choir	music	783
Cholera	diseases	616
	public helth	614.5
Choral servis	sacred music	783
Chorus	" "	783
	secular "	784
Chosen	history	951
Chrestomathy	English language	428
Christ	⊢ ⊣	232
Christening	baptism	265
	customs	392
Christian apologetics		239
architecture	eccles.	726
	medieval	723
art		**246**
associations		**267**
church		**260–289**
doctrins		**230**
education		377
ethics		171
fathers	relig. hist.	270
fathers' works		281
filosofy, patristic		189
iconografy		**240**
	sculpt.	732
institutions		**260**
life	personal religion	248
names		929
science	church	289
	therapeutics	615
sects		**280**
socialism		335

Christian union		280
unions, young men's		267
Christiania, Norway	history	948.2
	travel	914.82
Christianity	evidences	239
	history	**270–289**
Christians	biografy	922
Christiansand, Norway	history	948.2
	travel	914.82
Christmas	customs	394
festival	sacred music	783
Christology	doctrinal theology	232
Chrom-, Chron- see Crom-, Cron-		
Church		**260–289**
and clergy	law	348
education		377
state	eccles. polity	261
	ethics	172
	persecutions	272
	political science	322
architecture		726
bels	manufactures	673
	music	789
benefises	cleric support	254
biografy		922
decoration ecclesiology		**246**
entertainments		259
finance		254
furniture		247
history		**270–289**
membership	ordinances	265
music		783
needlework		247
of England		283
Rome		282
Scotland	presbyterians	285
property	monastic found.	271
	political science	322
	taxation	336.2
rates	cleric support	254
schools	education	377
	religion	268
Slavonic language		491.8
sociology		322
unity		280
vestments		247
yards	cemeteries	718
see also Religions		
Churches	architecture	726
	burials in pub. helth	614.6
	Christian	**280**
	hygiene	613

Topics in blackface type ar subdivided in the Tables

Churches	unity of	280
Cicero	letters	876
	works	875
Cider	chemic technology	663
Cifer writing		652
Cigarmaking		679
Cilicia	ancient history	939
	modern "	956
	travel	915.6
Cincinnati, O.	history	977.1
	travel	917.71
	Society of	369.1
Cinematics	mecanics	531
Cinerary urns	treatment of ded	393
Cipher writing		652
Circassia	history	947
Circle	German local gov't	352
sailing, great	navigation	527
Circulating libraries		027.3
Circulation and blood	physiology	612
in animals	zoology	591
plants	botany	581
money		332
oceanic	physiografy	551
Circulatory system	anatomy	611
Circumcision	customs	392
Circumnavigations		910.4
Circuses	amusements	791
	ethics	175
Cisterns	rural water supply	628
Cités ouvrières	architecture	728
Cities	administration	352
ancient	**description**	**913.3**
beautification		711
buried	**description**	**913.3**
free	German gov't	354
growth of	administration	352
helth of		614.1
plans of		912
sanitation		628
Citizens, duties of	ethics	172
Citizenship	law	347
	political science	323.6
City governments	administration	352
halls	architecture	725
houses	"	728
mortality	public helth	614.1
planning		711
special cities		**913-919**
transit	sociology	388
Civil authority	local government	352
engineering		**620**

Civil government and the church		322
	ethics	172
	relig.	261
	polit. science	**320**
law	foren	349
liberty	**political science**	**323**
lists		351
pensions	administration	351
procedure	law	347
rights	constitut. law	342
servis	**administration**	**351**
	municipal gov't	352
	officials lives	923
	reform admin.	351.6
	U. S. hist.	973.8
trials		347
war	ethics	172.4
	slavery	326
	U. S. history	973.7
Civility	ethics	177
Civilization and the church		261
	filosofy of	901
	history	901
	primitiv	571
Claims against governments		336
U. S. court of	history	347
	reports	345
Clairvoyance		133
Clans	genealogy	929
	political science	321
	Scottish history	941
Clarinet	wind instruments	788
Class feeling	ethics	177
meetings	public worship	264
reunions	**colleges**	**378**
	student customs	371.8
system	suffrage	324
Classed catalogs	bibliog.	017
Classes, school		371.2
	social polit. science	323
Classic antiquities		913.38
	biografy	920
	education	375.8
filology Greek lang.		**480**
Latin "		**470**
geografy		912
literature, Greek		**880**
Latin		**870**
mythology		292
schools, private	**educ.**	**373**
public	"	**379**
Classics	Greek literature	880

Topics in blackface type ar subdivided in the Tables

Classics Latin literature		870
Classification of animals	zoology	590
	books lib. econ.	025.4
	chemistry	541
	diseases medicin	616
	knowledge filosofy.	112
	languages filology	401
	plants botany	580
	sciences nat. sci.	501
Clast catalogs	bibliografy	017
	library admin.	025.3
Clavichord	musical instruments	786
Clay	chemic technology	666
	petrografy	552
Clays	econ. geology	553
Cleaning	dom. econ	648
Cleanliness	hygiene	613
Clearing house	banking	332
Cleavage	crystallografy	548
	geology	551
Clemency	ethics	179
Clementines	Apocryfa	229
Clenliness	hygiene	613
Cleopatra's needle	monuments	718
Clepsydra	cronology	529
Cleptomania	derangements	132
Clergy, benefit of	legal antiquities	340
	canon law	348
	celibacy of ethics	176
	pastoral theol.	253
	ethics	174
	holy orders	262
	lives of	922
	pastoral work	**250**
Cleric support		254
	taxes	336.2
Cleveland, G.	presidency	973.8
Ohio	history	977.1
	travel	917.71
Clif dwellings	prehistoric arch.	571
Climacterics	physiology	612
	vital statistics	614.1
Climate, effects of	diseases	616
	therapeutics	615
	hygiene	613
	influence on man	573
	meteorology	551.5
	seasons	525
Climatology	contagious diseases	614.4
	physical geografy	551.5
Climbers	birds	598
Clinics	medical education	610

Clippings	literary methods	029
Cloakmaking	trade	687
Clock, sidereal		522
Clockmaking		681
Clocks	artistic furniture	749
	cronology	529
Closet, earth	sanitary engineering	628
water	air pollution	614.7
	sanitary engineering	628
Cloth	manufactures	677
Clothesmaking		687
Clothing	domestic economy	646
	hygiene	613
	of laboring classes	331.8
Clouds	meteorology	551.5
Club foot	surgery	617
houses	architecture	728
libraries		027.2
Clubs, literary,	education	374.2
social		367
Clusters and nebulae	stars	523.8
Cnidaria	zoology	593
Coach bilding	trades	684
Coaching	amusements	798
	business	656
Coal	economic geology	553
	mineralogy	549
	mining	622
fuel	chemic technology	662
	domestic economy	644
	metallurgy	669
gas	domestic lights	644
	heating	697
	illuminating	665
oil	chemic technology	665
	domestic lights	644
	economic geology	553
	mineralogy	549
tar	colors chem. technol.	667
	products " "	668
Coalescence	surgery	617
Coast changes	erosion	551
defense	military engin'g	623
pilot		656
survey, U. S.	geodesy	526
tides		525
Coasting	sports	796
Coats of arms	heraldry	929.8
Cobalt	inorganic chemistry	546
ores	economic geology	553
Coca	hygiene	613
Cocain	therapeutics	615

Topics in blackface type ar subdivided in the Tables

Cochin China, French   history   959
Cochineal   dyeing   667
Cockfighting   ethics   175
                 sports   791
Cocoa   adulterations   614.3
                 manufacture   663
Cocoon   silkworms   638
Cod fishery   business   639
Code Napoleon   French law   349
Codes   American   "   345
Codices   Bible mss   220.4
Codification of law   U. S. law   345
Coeducation   376.7
                 of races   371.9
Coelenterata   zoology   593
Coffee   adulterations   614.3
                 agriculture   633
                 botany   583
                 domestic economy   641
                 hygiene   613
                 stimulants   615
        houses   customs   394
                 temperance   178
Coffer dams   river engineering   627
Coffins   burial customs   393
        perishable   pub. helth   614.6
Cog wheels   mec. engin'g   621
Cognition   metaphysics   126
Cohesion   physics   539
Coils   electricity   537
Coinage   political economy   332
Coins   numismatics   737
Coke   chemic technology   662
                 metallurgy   669
        fuel   domestic econ.   644
Cold baths   hygiene   613
        drinks   "   613
        exposure to   protection of life 614.8
        physics   536
Co'ds   diseases   616
Colenso controversy   Pentateuch   222
Coleoptera   595.7
Colic   diseases   616
Coliseum   Roman antiquities   913.37
Collected biografy   **920**
             sermons   252
             travel   910
          works, see subject
Collecting   biology   579
                 books   lib. econ.   025.2
Collection of taxes   finance   336.2
Collections   art galleries   708

Collections   engravings   769
                 fotografs   779
                 of poetry   Amer. lit.   811.08
                             Eng. lit.   821.08
                             miscel.   808.8
                 useful knowledge   602
                 vocal music   784
             class special with subject
Collectors manuals   biology   579
College cheers   371.8
          degrees   378.2
          libraries   027.7
          regattas   athletics   371.7
          societies   student life   371.8
          songs   784
          Y. M. C. A.   267.3
Colleges   agricultural   630.7
                 and universities   **378**
                 architecture   727
                 business   650
                 for women   376.8
                 hygiene   613
Collegiants   sects   284
Collegiate education   women   376
Collieries   mining engineering   622
Collodion process   fotografy   772
Colombia, S. Amer.   geology   558.6
                      history   986
                      religious hist.   278.6
                      travel   918.6
Colonial history, U. S.   973.2
          law   English statutes   346
          societies   369.1
          system   political science   325
Colonies   "   "   325
          penal   crim. law   343
Colonization   history of Africa   960
                  political science   325
Colonnades   architectural design   729
                 walls   ·   721
Colophons   incunabula   093
Color blindness eye diseases   617
                 fotografy   772
          in man   somatology   573
          plants   botany   581
          of animals zoology   591
          optics   535
          painting   752
          sense   psychology   152 ·
          suffrage   324
Colorado, U. S. history   978.8
                 travel   917.88

Topics in blackface type ar subdivided in the Tables

Colord races   natural hist. of man   573
Colorimetric analysis   chemistry   545
Coloring   dyeing   667
           matters, org. chem.   547
Colors, artificial   chem. tech.   667
       ecclesiology   246
       painting   752
       practical printing   655
       use of   literary methods   029
Colosseum   Roman antiquities   913.37
Colossians   epistles   227
Colossus of Rhodes   monuments   718
Colportage   parochial   259
Columbia, District of, U. S.   history   975.3
           travel   917.53
Columbus day   school observ.   371.3
Colums   architectural construc.   721
               design   729
       carpentry   694
       sculpture   **730**
Combat, judicial   legal antiquities   340
Combinations of capital   pol. econ.   331.1
       labor   "   "   **331.87**
Combinatory analysis   algebra   512
Combustibles, storage   pub. safety   614.8
Combustion   chemistry   541
       heat   536
Comedy   English drama   822
Comets   description   523
       maps, observations   524
       theory   521
Comic journals English literature   827
       music   dramatic   782
       works   English lit.   827
Commanders   biografy   923
Commemorations   Great war 1914-19   940.46
       U. S. history   **973**
Commemorativ sermons   252
Commensalism   zoology   591.5
Commentaries, Bible   220.7
       law   347
Commerce   law   347
       sociology   **380**
       useful arts   **650**
Commercial agencies   credit   332
       arithmetics mathematics   511
       bildings   architecture   725
       law   347
       morals   ethics   174
       panics   political econ.   332
       traveling   commerce   658
Commissions, bilding   692

Common carriers   law   347
       law, American   345
       British   346
       right   copyright   655
       treatises   347
       pleas, court of   347
       prayer   Anglican ritual   264
       schools   **379**
Commonplace books   lit. methods   029
Commons, house of   Eng. legis.   328
       student life   371.8
Commonwelth   English history   942.06
Commonwelths, ideal   polit. sci.   321
Commune, French   local gov't   352
       German   "   "   352
Commune of 1871   French history   944
       political economy   335
Communication   sociology   **380**
       useful arts   **650**
Communion, close   baptists   286
       holy   sacrament   265
       servises   sacred music   783
Communism   political economy   335
Community centers   374.2
       of land   political econ.   333
Compact   ethics   174
Companies   associations   **360**
       joint stock   law   347
Comparativ anatomy   animals   591
       plants   581
       filology   **410**
       legislation   340
       medicin   619
       mythology   ·   **291**
       physiology   zoology   591
       religion   **290**
       theology   dogmatics   **230**
Compass   magnetism   538
       variations   astron.   522
Compends   *Class with subject*
Competition   prices   338
       wages   331.2
Competitiv examinations   civil ser.   351
       schools   371.5
Complex ores   metallurgy   669
       variables   calculus   517
Composers   biografy   927
Composition   music   781
       rhetoric   808
       typesetting   655
       elementary English   428
       with creditors   law   347

Topics in blackface type ar subdivided in the Tables

Compression of gases physics	533
Comprest air engins	621.4
Compromise bil 1850 U. S. history	973.6
ethics	171
Compulsory education	379.2
insurance	331.2
vaccination pub. helth	614.4
Compurgation legal antiquities	340
Computation arithmetic	511
Conation	158
Concept psychology	153
Conception, immaculate Christology	232
Concerts amusements	791
Conchology	594
Conclave, papal eccles. polity	262
Concord filosofy Emerson	191
Concordances, Bible	220.2
class special with subject	
Concordat eccles. polity	262
internat'l law	341
Concrete bilding material	691
construction bilding	693
pavements	625
roofing	695
Concretion geologic agent	551
Concubinage sex customs	392
Concussion injuries	617
Condemd books book rarities	098
Condensation action of heat	536
of vapor pneumatics	533
Condensers chemistry	542
electricity	537
steam engineering	621.1
Condensing pump pneumatics	533
Condenst milk dairy	637
pub. helth	614.3
Condiments adulterations	614.3
chemic technology	664
Condits telegraf	654
ventilation	697
waterworks	628
Conduct of life ethics	**170**
Conductivity of rocks geology	551
Conduits, see Condits	
Confectionery	641
adulterations	614.3
Confederate states, U. S. civ. war	973.7
Confederation, American colonies	973.3
Conference meetings pub. worship	264
Conferences, library	020.6
Confession and absolution	265
Augsburg	238

Confession, auricular sacraments	265
Confessions creeds	238
of faith ritual	264
Confidence practises	174
Confinement crim. law	343
prison disciplin	365
school "	371.5
Confirmation sacraments	265
Conflagrations public safety	614.8
Conflict of duties	171
laws internat'l law	341
Conformity Anglican church	283
Confucianism religion	299
Confucius Chinese filosofy	181
Congelation physics	536
Conglomerate lithology	552
Congo, see Kongo	
Congregation ecclesiastic polity	262
Congregational church	285
orders in ministry	262
singing	783
Congregationalists biografy	922
Congress of nations inter'l law	341
U. S. legis. bodies	328
Congressional papers	328
Conic sections analytic geom.	516
geometry	513
Conicoids analytic geometry	516
Coniferae botany	585
Conjunctions solar system	523
Conjuring sorcery	133
Connaught, Ireland history	941.7
travel	914.17
Connecticut, U. S. history	974.6
travel	917.46
Conquest international law	341
Norman English hist.	942.02
Conscience ethics	171
Consciousness filosofy	126
psychology	**151**
Conscription military science	355.2
Consecration	265
sermons	252
Conservation of energy physics	531
resources national	339
natural	333
Conservatories architecture	728
music	780
plants	716
Consols English finance	336
Consonants language	421
Conspiracies criminal law	343

Topics in blackface type ar subdivided in the Tables

Constables		352
Constance, council of	Hussites	284
	religious hist.	270
Constantinople	history	949.6
	travel	914.96
Constellations	astronomy	523.8
Constitution and bylaws	lib. econ.	023
	day school observ.	371.3
	of matter metaphysics	117
	U. S. history	973.4
Constitutional law		342
	monarchy polit. sci.	321
Construction, architectural		721
	carpentry	694
	masonry	693
Consular reports		382
	systems international law	341
Consuls		327
Consumption, final	pol. econ.	339
	productiv " "	339
Contagious diseases	pathology	616
	pub. helth	614.4–.5
Contemplativ personal religion		248
	theology	242
Contested elections	legis. bodies	328
	suffrage	324
Continental protestant sects		284
travel		**914**
Continents	physical geografy	551
Continuation schools		374.8
Contraband of war	internat. law	341
Contract system	convict labor	331.5
	prisons	365
Contractions	shorthand	653
Contracts	bilding	692
	ethics	174
	law	347
Controversial divinity		**230**
	sermons	252
Contusions	surgery	617
Conundrums	amusements	793
	English literature	828
Convection	heat	536
Convention	ecclesiastic polity	262
	1792-95 French hist.	944
Conventional forms	decoration	729
Conventions	political parties	329
Convents		**271**
	architecture	726
Conventual education of women		376
Conversation	art of	374.1
	ethics	177

Conversion	personal religion	248
	revivals	269
Conveyances	law	347
Convict labor	political economy	331.5
Convicts	criminal law	343
discharged	reformatory ass'n	364
Conviviality	social customs	394
Convocation	ecclesiastic polity	262
Convulsions	diseases	616
Cookbooks	domestic economy	641.5
Cookery	" "	**641**
Coolies	slavery	326
Coolidge, C.	presidency	973.91
Cooper Union	education	374.9
Cooperage	manufactures	674
Cooperation	library economy	021
	literary methods	029
	political economy	334
Cooperativ bilding associations		334
	cataloging lib. admin.	025.3
	insurance	334
Copenhagen	history	948.9
Copepoda	articulates	595
Copernican theory	astronomy	521
Copiers	offis equip.	652
Copper	inorganic chemistry	546
	metallurgy	669
coins	money	332
engraving		762
implements	archeology	571
manufacture		673
ores	economic geology	553
roofing		695
Coptic church	sects	281
	language	493
	literature	893
Copts	history	962
Copy and proof	literary methods	029
books	elementary educ.	372
Copying processes	writing	652
Copyright	international law	341
	law	347
	publishing	655
Coquetry	ethics	177
Coral reefs	geology	551
Corals	zoology	593
Cordage	manufacture	677
Cordials	"	663
Cordilleras, S. A.	description	918
Corea	history	951
Corinthians	epistles	227
Corn	agriculture	633

Topics in blackface type ar subdivided in the Tables

Corn	laws	337
	trade polit. econ.	338
Cornell university		378.7
Cornet	wind instruments	788
Cornices	architec. construc.	721
	design	729
Cornish language		491.6
Corns	dermatology	616
Corona of sun		523.7
Coronation	ceremonies	394
Coroners	local government	352
Corporal punishment school		371.5
Corporate industries		338
Corporation, city administration		352
Corporations		**360**
	business	**380**
	charitable	361
	law of	347
	mining	622
	municipal	352
	railroad	385
Correction, houses of		364
Correlation of forces		531
Correspondence	autobiografy	920
	English literature	826
	letter writing	808
	logic	169
	natural theology	219
	college self-educ.	374.4
	commercial	651
	methods of teaching	374.4
	Swedenborgian	289
Corrosion	physical chemistry	541
Corvée	polit. econ.	331.5
Cosmetics	toilet	646
Cosmic dust	astronomy	523.1
filosofy	**metaphysics**	**113**
time	cronology	529
Cosmogony	**metaphysics**	**113**
	natural theology	213
Cosmografy	phys. geografy	551
Cosmology	**metaphysics**	**113**
	natural theology	213
Cossacks	Russian history	947
Cost	political economy	338
Costa Rica	history	972.8
Costume	academic	378.2
	ecclesiastic	247
	hygiene	613
	military	355
Costumes		391
Cottages	architecture	728

Cotton	agriculture	633
	dyeing chem. technol.	667
	manufactures	677
	trade agric. products	338
Cottonworm	pests	632
Council, ecclesiastic polity		262
Councils	history, religious	270
	local gov't	352
	of state foren gov't	354
Counsel, Christian practical religion		241
Counterfeiting	law	343
	polit. econ.	332
Counterpoint	music	781
Country houses	architecture	728
	life agriculture	630.1
	sociology	323
County government admin.		352
	histories, British	**942**
	U. S.	**974–979**
Courage	ethics	179
Courses	**curriculum**	**375**
	of reading reading and aids	028
Court etiquet	customs	395
	fools "	394
	reports Amer. law	345
	Eng. "	346
Courtesy	ethics	177
Courts	administration	351
	law	347
	authority of	347
	ecclesiastic	262
	juvenil	364
	martial	344
Courtship	ethics	177
Cousins, marriage of law		347
Coutumes	French law	349
Covenant meetings public worship		264
	Scotch creeds	238
Covenanters	religious history	274.1
	Scottish history	941
Covenants	religious creeds	238
Covetousness	ethics	179
Cowardis	ethics	179
Cows	domestic animals	636.2
Crabs	zoology	595
Cranberries		634
Cranes and elevators mil work		621
Craniology	nat. hist. of man	573
Crannoges	prehistoric dwellings	571
Craters	seismology	551
Crayfish	zoology	595
Crayon drawing		741

Topics in blackface type ar subdivided in the Tables

Cream	adulterations	614.3
Creation	evolution	575
	metaphysics	**113**
	natural theology	213
Creativ power	mental faculties	155
Creator	doctrinal theology	231
Crèches	institutions	362.7
Credibility of Scriptures		220.1
Credit	political economy	332
and bonds	insurance	368
mobilier	railroads	385
	U. S. history	973.8
Credo	sacred music	783
Creeds	dogmatic theology	238
	public worship	264
Cremation of the ded	customs	393
	pub. helth	614.6
Crematories	" "	614.6
Creosoting	bilding material	691
Cresting	roofs	721
Crests	heraldry	929.8
Cretaceous era	geology	551
fossils	**paleontology**	**560**
Crevasses	glaciers	551
Crewel work	art needlework	746
Cribbage	games	795
Cribbing	student life	371.8
Cricket	amusements	796
Cries, battle	war customs	399
street	folklore	398
Crime	law	343
and illiteracy	public schools	379.2
suffrage		324
Crimea	history	947
Crimean war	English history	942.08
	Russian "	947
Crimes and punishments	law	343
Criminal classes	reformatory assoc.	364
law		343
international		341
trials	criminal law	343
Criminals, education of		371.9
juvenil	childstudy	136.7
	courts	364
law		343
lives		923
Criminology		364
Crinoidea	zoology	593
Crises, commercial	pol. econ.	332
Criterion	ethics	171
Critical filosofy		142
Criticism	art	701

Criticism	Biblical	220.7
	dramatic	792
	literary	801
	musical	780
	rhetoric	808
Croatia	history	943.9
Croatian language		491.8
literature		891.8
Crocheting		746
Crockery	pottery	738
Crocodiles	zoology	598.1
Crofton system	prisons	365
Cromatic aberration	optics	535
scale	theory of music	781
Cromatics	optics	535
Cromatografy		752
Cromium	economic geology	553
	inorganic chem.	546
Cromlechs	prehistoric archeology	571
Cromofotografy		772
Cromolithografy		764
Cromometry	colorimetry	545
Cromosfere, sun		523.7
Cronic diseases	pathology	616
Cronicles	Bible	222
history	see special subject	
Cronograf	astronomy	522
Cronologies	history	902
Cronology	astronomy	529
	Bible	220.9
Cronometer	astron. instruments	522
	longitude determ.	525
	manufacture	681
Crop farming		633
insurance		368
Croquet		796
Cross	Christian symbols	247
legends concerning		398.2
Crozier	sacred furniture	247
Crucibles	metallurgy	669
	practical chemistry	542
Crucifix	sacred furniture	247
Cruelty	**ethics**	**179.2**
	Great war mil. hist.	940.4
	international law	341
	war customs	399
Cruisers	naval engineering	623.8
Cruising	boating	797
Crusades	European history	940.1
	religious "	270
Crust of the earth	geology	551
Crustacea	paleontology	565

Topics in blackface type ar subdivided in the Tables

Crustacea	zoology	595
Cryptogamia	botany	586
Cryptografic art	religious art	246
Cryptografy	secret writing	652
Crystallin limestone		552
Crystallografy		548
Crystalloids		541
Ctenophora	zoology	593
Cuba	history	972.9
	travel	917.29
Cultivated plants	landscape gard.	716
Culture		301
	and religion	261
	self education	**374**
	vocal	784
Cuneiform inscriptions		492
Cupping	therapeutics	615
Cups	archeology	571
Cures	therapeutics	615
	miraculous theology	231
Curiosa	books	099
Curling	amusements	796
Currency	banking	332
Currents, atmosferic	phys. geog.	551.5
	electric physics	537
	oceanic phys. geog.	551
Curriculum		**375**
Curvature	geology	551
Curvilinear motion	physics	531
Customs and duties	tarif	337
	manners	**390**
	of primitiv man	571
	war	399
	student life	371.8
	taxation	336.2
Cutlery	manufacture	672
Cuttle fish		594
Cutworms	agric. pests	632
Cyanogen	organic chemistry	547
Cyclades	ancient history	939
	modern "	949.9
Cycles, motor	engin'g	629.2
Cycling		796
Cyclones	meteorology	551.5
Cyclopean remains	Greek architec.	722
Cyclopedias, general		**030**
	class special with subject	
Cyfer writing		652
Cymbals	musical instruments	789
Cymric	languages	491.6
	literature	891.6
Cynic filosofy		183

Cypher writing		652
Cypriote architecture		722
Cyprus	ancient history	939
	modern "	956
Cyrenaic filosofy		183
Czechoslovakia	history	943.7
	travel	914.37
Daguerreotype		772
Dairy	agriculture	637
	products adulterations	614.3
Dais	architec. accessories	729
Dakota, U. S.	history	978.3
	travel	917.83
Dalmatia	history	943.6
Daltonism	eye diseases	617
Damascus	ancient history	939
	travel	915.6
Damnation	doctrinal theology	237
Dams	mil. engineering	621.2
	mining "	622
	river "	627
Dance of deth	emblems	246
Dances, war	customs	399
Dancing	amusements	793
	customs	394
	ethics	175
Danes	English history	942.01
Dangerous classes		364
Dangers and accidents	min. eng'g	622
	pub. helth	614.8
	to workmen political econ.	331.8
Daniel	Bible	224
Danish England	English history	942.01
	language	439
	literature	839
Dantzig	history	943.1
Danube river	travel	914.96
Danubian provinces	history	949.6
	travel	914.96
Darien expedition	colonies	325.8
	foren trade	382
	isthmus history	986
	ship canal engineering	626
Darwinism	biology	575
Dates	cronology	902
Dawson, Can.	hist.	971.21
Day of judgment	doctrinal theol.	236
	nurseries	362.7
	schools secondary education	373
	sidereal and solar	529
Days	cronology	529

Topics in blackface type ar subdivided in the Tables

Deacon, Deaconess eccles. polity 262
Dead sea description 915.6
    see also Ded
Deaf, Deafness, *see* Def, Defness
Death, Deaths, *see* Deth, Deths
Debates parliamentary 328
    rhetoric 808
Debating societies self culture 374.2
Debt, *see* Det
Decalog Bible 222
Decay of rocks lithology 552
Decimal system arithmetic 511
    weights and mesures 389
Decision of caracter ethics 170
Declamation rhetoric 808
Declaration of independence, U. S. 973.3
    Savoy creeds 238
    war internat'l law 341
Declarations law 347
Decomposition, chemistry of 541
Decoration, architectural 729
    day schools 371.3
    U. S. history 973.7
    design **740**
    domestic economy 645
    interior 747
    roof architecture 721
Decorations heraldry 929.7
Decorativ art **740**
Decorum ethics 177
Decretals ecclesiastic polity 262
    Roman catholic church 282
Ded, disposal of the pub. helth 614.6
    ministry of sacraments 265
    treatment of customs 393
Dedication church ordinances 265
Deduction psychology 153
Deductiv logic 162
Deeds law 347
Deep boring mining eng. 622
    sea dredging scientific voyages 508.3
    life botany 581.9
    zoology 591.9
Deer domestic animals 636.2
    zoology 599
    stalking sports 799
Def and dum education 371.9
    institutions 362.4
Defacement of books library econ. 024
Defamation law 347
Defense of religion apologetics 239
Defensiv operations military eng. 623

Defness diseases 617
Deformities surgery 617
Degeneration evolution 575
Degrees, academic 378.2
    medical public helth 614.2
Deism natural theology 211
Deists apologetics 239
Deity doctrinal theology 231
Delaware, U. S. history 975.1
    travel 917.51
Delineation of children 136.7
    woman 396
Delinquents institutions 364
Delirium tremens pathology 616
Deliveries and branches lib. econ. 021
Deltas physical geografy 551
Deluge Genesis 222
    geologic agents 551
Delusions occultism 133
Demagogy politics 329
Demand and supply prices 338
    wages 331.2
Demerara history 988
    travel 918.8
Democracy form of state 321
    social 335
Democratic party 329
Demografy statistics 312
Demonetization 332
Demonology dogmatics 235
    witchcraft 133
Demurrage transport 656
Dendrology **botany** **582**
Denmark antiquities 913.4
    botany 581.9
    geology 554.8
    history 948.9
    religious history 274.8
    statistics 314
    travel 914.89
    zoology 591.9
Denominations, Christian **280**
Density gravity 531
    of earth astronomy 525
Dentistry 617
Dentists' registration, state control of 614.2
Denudation geology 551
Deodorization of sewage 628
Deodorizers contagious diseases 614.4
Deontology **170**
Department stores bus. meth. 658
Departments French local gov't 352

Topics in blackface type ar subdivided in the Tables

Departments	library admin.	025
	U. S. government	353
Deposition	geology	551
Depositions	evidence	347
Depravity	natural theology	216
	pessimism	149
total	theology	233
Depressions, trade	commerce	380
	domes. com.	381
	money	332
	production	338
Depth psychology		153
Derangement, mental		132
Derivation of words	comp. filol.	412
	English lang.	422
	other " 432, 442, etc.	
Dermatology	anatomy	611
	animals	591
	pathology	616
	physiology	612
Dermoskeleton	anatomy	591
Derricks	engineering	621
Dervishes		297
Descartes	French filosofy	194
Descent	genealogy	929
of man	evolution	575
rules of	law	347
Description	**travel**	**910**
Descriptiv astronomy		**523**
	geometry	515
Deserts	physical geografy	551.5
Design, architectural		729
	arguments from doc. theol.	239
	nat. "	211
arts of		**740**
	metaphysics	124
Designing	decoration	745
Desks	offis equipment	651
Desmidiaceae	algae	589
Despotism	form of state	321
Det	ethics	174
	local government	352
public	pol. econ.	336.3
Detectivs		352
Determinants	algebra	512
Determinations, astron.	geodesy	526
Determinism	doctrinal theology	234
	psychology	159
Deth and resurrection		236
biology		577
dance of	emblems	246
penalty	criminal law	343

Deth, physiology		612
rates	public helth	614.1
theology		236
Deths	public helth	614.1
	registers of	929
	registration of, official	352
	statistics	312
Detritus	geology	552
Dets, state and national		336
Dettor and creditor	law	347
Deuteronomy	Bible	222
Deutsch, Platt	language	439
	literature	839
Developing interest in libraries		021
	method of teaching	371.3
Development, intellectual, and church		261
	nutrition	591
	physiology	612
	theory apologetics	239
	evolution	575
Deviation of compass	magnetism	538
Devil, personal	theology	235
worship		291
Devils	dogmatics	235
	witchcraft	133
Devonian age	geology	551
fossils	**paleontology**	**560**
Devotional exercises	prayer	264
	sermons	252
theology		**240**
Dew	meteorology	551.5
Diabolism	doctrin	235
Diabolo	game	796
Dialectics	**logic**	**160**
Dialects	English language	427
	other lang.	437, 447, etc.
Dialogs	entertainments	793
Dials	cronology	529
Dialysis	qualitativ analysis	544
Diamagnetism	physics	538
Diameter of earth		525
Diamonds	economic geology	553
	mineralogy	549
Diaries	**biografy**	**92**
Diatessaron	harmonies of gospels	226
Diathermancy	heat	536
Dice	ethics	175
	games	795
Dicotyledones	botany	583
Dictation machines		651
Dictatorship		321
Dictionaries	English language	423

Topics in blackface type ar subdivided in the Tables

Dictionaries   other lang.   433, 443, etc.
    of quotations   Eng. lit. 828
    class special with subject
Dictionary catalogs   bibliografy   019
       library admin.   025.3
Didactic theology   241
Didactics   **education**   **371**
Die sinking   736
Diet circle   German local gov't   352
Dietetics   hygiene   613.2
Differential calculus   517
Differentiation   evolution   575
Diffraction   acoustics   534
    optics   535
Diftheria   diseases   616
    public helth   614.5
Digestion, aids to   therapeutics   615
     animals   591
     man   612
     plants   581
Digestiv system   anatomy   611
Digests   American law   345
    English   "   346
Dignities   heraldry   929.7
Dikes   geology   551
    river and harbor eng.   627
Dilation   gases   533
Diligence   ethics   179
Diluvial deposits   geology   551
Dimension, fourth   geometry   513
Dimensions of earth   525
     sun   523.7
Dimorfism   crystallografy   548
Dining   domestic economy   642
Dinners   "   "   642
Diocesan schools   education   377
Diocese   ecclesiastic polity   262
Dioptrics   optics   535
Dip of rocks   geology   551
Diphtheria   diseases   616
    public helth   614.5
Diplomacy   327
    international law   341
Diplomas   school organization   371.2
Diplomatics   English language   421
    paleografy   417
Dipsomania   mental derangements   132
    temperance   178
Diptera   insects   595.7
Direct taxation   political economy   336.2
Directories   **914-919**
    class special with subject

Directors   library government   023
Disabilities, political   suffrage   324
Disasters at sea   adventures   910.4
     navigation   656
Discharge of water   engineering   627
Disciples of Christ   sects   286
Disciplin, civil servis   351
    ecclesiastic polity   262
    education   371.5
    mental   education   370.1
    military   military science   355
    prison   365
Disciplinary power   administration   351
Discount   banking   332
Discounts   library bookbuying   025.2
Discourses   theology   252
    class special with subject
Discoverers   biografy   923
Discoveries   **geografy**   **910**
    science   509
    useful arts   608
Discussion, freedom of   polit. sci.   323
Disease germs   medicin   616
Diseases   pathology   616
    public helth   614.4-.5
    animals   veterinary med.   619
     zoology   591
    mental, medicin   616
     psychology   132
    of children   medicin   618
     ear   surgery   617
     eye   "   617
    plants   agriculture   632
     botany   581
     teeth   dentistry   617
     women   pathology   618
Disfranchisement   suffrage   324
Dishes   pottery   738
Disinfection   contagious diseases   614.4
Disintegration   geol. agents   551
Dislocations   geology   551
    surgery   617
Dispensaries   farmacy   615
    institutions   362
Dispensatories   materia medica   615
Dispersion   optics   535
Displacement of molecules   physics   539
Display   social ethics   177
Disputations   religion   204
    class special with subject
Dissection   anatomy, animal   591
     human   611

Topics in blackface type ar subdivided in the Tables

Dissection   ethics   179
         laws   state control of   614.2
Dissenters   English religious hist. 274.2
Dissipation   ethics   178
Distance of earth from sun   525
                moon   523.3
                stars   523.8
Distances, mesurement   surveying   526
Distemper   fine arts   751
                useful arts   698
Distild beverages   adulterations   614.3
                       chem. tech.   663
Distillation   chemic technology   668
                practical chemistry   542
Distortions, congenital   surgery   617
Distribution of animals   591.9
                capital   331
                plants   581.9
                products   polit. econ. 338
                time   cronology   529
Distributiv cooperation   334
District of Columbia, U. S. history   975.3
                       travel   917.53
Dithyrambics   Greek lyrics   884
Divination   occultism   133
Divine attributes   doctrinal theol.   231
         healing   265
         law   231
         Providence   natural theol.   214
         right of kings   pol. sci.   321
         servis   public worship   264
Diving bels   pneumatics   533
         submarine   engineering   627
Divining rod   mining   622
Divinity schools   architecture   727
                theology   207
         theology   **230**
Divorce   ethics   173
                law   347
                public helth   614.1
Dobruja   history   949.8
Docks   harbor engineering   627
                shipbilding   623.8
Dockyards   harbor engineering   627
Doctors   biografy   926
Doctrins   heresies   273
                theology   **230**
Documents, public   328
                library economy   025.8
Dog fighting   ethics   175
         tax   political economy   336.2
Dogma   **230**

Dogmas   religious history   273
Dogmatics   **230**
Dogs, diseases of   comparativ med.   619
         domestic animals   636.7
Dolmens   prehist. arch.   571
Domain, eminent   law   347
         state   public finance   336
Domes   architectural construc.   721
                       design   729
                observatories astron.   522
Domesday book   Eng. finance   336
                       history   942.02
Domestic animals   **636**
         architecture   728
         duties   ethics   173
         economy   **640**
         medicin   616
         relations   law   347
                       political sci. **323**
         sanitation   628
         servis   647
         trade   381
         worship   249
Domestication   evolution   575
Domicil   law   347
Dominoes   games   795
Donatists   sects   281
Donkeys   domestic animals   636.1
Doors   arch. construction   721
                       design   729
Doric order   architecture   729
Dormer windows   arch. construction   721
                       design   729
Dormitories   architecture   727
                student life   371.8
Dort confession   238
         synod of   284
Douay Bible   Eng. version   220.5
Double bass   stringd instruments   787
         flowers   floriculture   716
                       morfology   581
         refraction   optics   535
         standard   money   332
         stars   astronomy   523.8
Doubt   metaphysics   121
Dout   metaphysics   121
Dower   law   347
Drafts   games   794
Dragon flies   insects   595.7
Drainage   agriculture   631
                hydraulic engineering   627
                mining   "   622

Topics in blackface type ar subdivided in the Tables

Drainage	public helth	614.7
	sanitary engineering	628
Drama	American literature	812
	other "	822, 832, etc.
	ethics	175
	sacred	244
	see also Miracle plays	
Dramas	Amer. civil war	973.7
Dramatic amusements		792
	art theater	792
	biografy actors	927
	authors	928
	composition	808
	music	782
	orchestral music	785
Dramatists	biografy	928
Draughts	games	794
Dravidian architecture		722
	language	494
	literature	894
Drawing		**740**
	elementary education	372
	room amusements	793
	topografic	526
	see also special applications	
Drawings, architectural		729
	bilding	692
	engineering	620
	linear	741
	prehistoric archeology	571
Dream books	folklore	398
Dreams		135
Dred Scott decision	slavery	326
Dredging	engineering	627
	scientific voyages	508.3
Dresden	travel	914.3
Dress	costume	391
	ecclesiastic	247
	ethics	177
	fashion	646
Dressmaking		646
Drift remains	prehist. archeol.	571
Drifting and tunnelling	mining	622
Dril	military science	355
Drilling	mec. engineering	621
	mining "	622
Drink	chem. analysis	543
Drinking, social	ethics	178
	usages customs	394
Drinks	hygiene	613
	intoxicating ethics	178
Drives	landscape gardening	713

Drives	psychology	158
Driving	recreations	798
Drouths	meteorology	551.5
Drowning	protection of life	614.8
Drugs		615
	adulterations	614.3
	analytic chemistry	543
	economic botany	581
	intoxicating ethics	178
Druids		299
Drummond light		665
Drunkenness	criminal law	343
Druses	religion	297
Dry docks	engineering	627
	goods trade production	338
	plate process fotografy	772
	point engraving	767
	rot bilding	691
Dualism	ontology	111
	Parseeism	295
	Parsee heresies	273
Ducks	poultry	636.5
Ducts, air	ventilation	697
Dueling	ancient law	340
	criminal "	343
	customs	394
	ethics	179
	student life	371.8
Dum	asylums	362.4
	education of	371.9
	bels gymnastics	613.7
Dunes		551
Dunkers	baptists	286
Duns Scotus	mediev. filos.	189
Duodecimals	arithmetic	511
Duplicates, sale of	library econ.	025.2
Duplicating machine	offis equip.	652
Durbar	social customs	394
Dust	air pollution	614.7
	cosmic descriptiv astronomy	523
	inhalation of hygiene	613
	prevention of, in factories	628
Dutch East Indies	history	991
	Guiana "	988
	travel	918.8
	language	439
	literature	839
	painting	759
	reformed church	284
	in America	285
	republic history	949.2
Duties and customs	tarif	**337**

Topics in blackface type ar subdivided in the Tables

Duties, ethics   **170**
    remitted   library aid   021.8
    stamp   political econ.   336.2
Duty   religion   233
    free importation for colleges   337
Dwarfs   biology   573
Dwelling houses   architecture   728
      sanitation   628
Dwellings   prehistoric   571
Dyaks   travel   919.1
Dye-producing invertebrates   638
Dyeing   chem. technology   667
Dyes, anilin   "   "   667
Dykes   engineering   627
    geology   551
Dynamic electricity   537
    engineering   **621**
    geology   551
Dynamics   531
    celestial   521
    electro   537
Dynamite   chemic technology   662
    storage   pub. safety   614.8
Dynamo-machines   engineering   621.3
Dynamometer   531
Dynamos   electric engin'g   621.3
    electrodynamics   537

Ear   anatomy   611
    def and dum asylums   362.4
    diseases   surgery   617
    hospitals   362.1
    physics   534
    physiology   612
    psychology   152
Early Christian architecture   723
    filosofy   189
    Christians   history   270
    education, elementary   **372**
    English text society   820
    forms of English language   427
      other languages, 437, 447, etc
    Greek filosofy   182
    institutions   pol. science   321
    printed books   093
    rising   hygiene   613.7
Earth   astronomy   525
    burial of ded   customs   393
      pub. helth   614.6
    closet system   sanitation   628
    figure of   526
    physical geology   551

Earthenware   chemic technology   666
Earthquakes   551
Earth's attraction of moon   523.3
    figure   526
Earthwork
    foundations   architec.   721
      engin'g   624
Earthworks   fortifications   623
Easements   law   347
East and West, religious schism   270
    India company   382
    Indian archipelago   history **991**
      architecture   722
      languages   491
    Indies   history   954
      Dutch   history   991
    river bridge   engineering   624
Easter   church calendar   264
    cronology   529
    music   783
Eastern churches   281
    empire   949.5
    question   Turkish history   949.6
    states, U. S.   history   **974**
Eating   customs   394
    hygiene   613.2
Eccentricity in manners   ethics   177
    of orbit of earth   525
Eccentrics, lives of   920
    machinery   621
Ecclesiastes   Bible   223
Ecclesiastic antiquities   209
    architecture   726
    art   ecclesiology   **246**
    biografy   922
    calendar   cronology   529
    ceremonies   customs   394
    costume   247
    councils   262
    fasts   personal relig.   248
      public worship   264
    feasts   264
    furniture   ecclesiol.   247
    history   **270**
    Latin, modern   filol.   479
    law   canon law   348
    legends   209
      special with topic
    music   783
    polity   262
    statistics   209
    trials   262

Topics in blackface type ar subdivided in the Tables

Ecclesiastics	biografy	922
Ecclesiology	church	261
	symbolism	**246**
Echinoderms	paleontology	563
	zoology	593
Eclectic filosofy		148
	medicin	615
Eclipses, finding longitude by		525
	of moon	523.3
	sun	523.7
	theory	521
Ecliptic	earth	525
	solar system	523
Economic botany		581
	chemistry	**660**
	geology	553
	zoology	591
Economics	political economy	**330**
Economy, domestic		**640**
	ethics	174
	library	**020**
	political	**330**
Ecstasy	religion	248
Ecstatics	mental derangements	132
Ecuador	geology	558.6
	history	986
	religious history	278.6
	travel	918.6
Ecumenic council	eccles. polity	262
	religious hist.	270
Eden	original home of man	572
Edict of Nantes	Huguenot hist.	284
Ediles	Roman antiquities	913.37
Editions, choice of	lib. econ.	028
Editorial work	journalism	070
Education		**370**
	and the church relig.	261
	sociol.	377
	in relation to labor	331.8
	industrial systems	371.4
	useful arts	607
	of voters	324
	systems of	371.4
	special, see subject	
Educational bildings	architect.	727
	ethics	171
	reports, public	**379**
Educator, library as		021
Educators	biografy	923
Efemerides		528
Effect and cause	metaphysics	122
Efficiency	bus. meth.	658
Effigies, monumental		718
Effluvium nuisances	san. engin'g	628
Egina marbles	anc. sculpture	733
Egoism	ethics	171
Egs	oology	598
	poultry	636.5
Egypt	antiquities	913.32
	architecture ancient	722
	medieval	723
	botany	581.9
	geology	556.2
	hieroglyfics	493
	history, ancient	932
	modern	962
	language, old	493
	literature	893
	mythology	299
	obelisks monuments	718
	pyramids antiquities	913.32
	religion	299
	travel	916.2
Egyptian filosofers		181
	Sudan history	962
	travel	916.2
Egyptology	antiquities	913.32
Eight-hour law		331.8
Einstein theory	astron.	521
	physics	530
Elasticity	physics	539
Elders	ecclesiastic polity	262
Eleatic Greek filosofers		182
Election	doctrinal theology	234
	frauds, U. S.	324
Elections	political science	324
	city administration	352
Electiv franchise		324
	system education	375
Electoral commission suffrage		324
	U. S. history	973.8
	frauds	324
	system polit. science	321
Electric apparatus inspection		614.8
	engineering	621.3
	fenomena physics	537
	heating bilding	697
	light libraries	022
	mec. eng.	621.3
	physics	537
	mesuring of temperature	536
	muscular fenom. physiol.	612
	railways engineering	621.3
	shock surgery	617

Topics in blackface type ar subdivided in the Tables

Electric signals   654
        storms   meteorology   551.5
                      physics   538
        telegraf   communication   654
                      engineering   621.3
Electricity   537
                accidents from   614.8
                animal   psychology   134
                therapeutics   615
Electro-biology   animal magnetism 134
        blasting   mining   622
        chemistry   541
        cronograf   astronomy   522
        dynamics   physics   537
        magnetism   "   538
        metallurgy   "   537
        motors   engineering   621.3
                     science   537
        physiology biology   577
                     mesmerism   134
Electrolysis   quantitativ analysis   545
Electrometers   engineering   621.3
                physics   537
Electroplating   manufactures   671
Electrostatics   physics   537
Electrotherapy   medicin   615
Electrotyping   printing   655
Eleemosynary institutions   362
Elegiac poetry English lit.   821
                Greek   "   884
                Latin   "   874
Elementary education   372
                forms   arch. design   729
                readers   Eng. language   428
                theory of music   781
Elements, chemic   chem. tech.   661
                chemistry   546
Elephants   domestic animals   636.9
                zoology   599
Eleusinian mysteries   Greek antiq.   913.38
                              mythol.   292
Elevated ground   hygiene   613
        railroad   city transit   388
                   engineering   625
        temperature   hygiene   613
        ways   public helth   614.7
Elevation   architec. design   729
Elevations   meteorology   551.5
Elevators   mec. engineering   621
Elgin marbles   733
Elian filosofers   Greek filos.   183
Elixir of life   alchemy   540.1

Elizabethan persecutions   history   272
Elliptic functions   calculus   517
Elocution   808
            vocal culture   784
Eloquence   808
            American oratory   815
Elvs   folklore   398.4
Elzevir editions   rare printing   094
Emanation   metaphysics   129
Emancipation of slaves   326
                    U. S. history   973.7
                    woman   396
Embalming of the ded   customs   393
                    pub. helth   614.6
Embankments river engineering   627
Embargo   martial law   344
        of 1808-12   U. S. history   973.4
Embassadors   international law   341
                political science   327
Emblems   ecclesiology   246
Embossing, book   library economy   025.2
Embroidery   746
Embryology   animals   591
                botany   581
Emergencies   surgery   617
Emery wheels   621
Emetics   therapeutics   615
Emigration   political science   325
Emotions   psychology   157
Emperors   biografy   923
Empire, Eastern   history   949.5
Empiric filosofy   144
Empiricism in medicin   quackery   614.2
Employers and employd, ethics   174
                    polit. econ.   331.1
Employment agencies   "   "   331.1
                hygiene   613
                of time   ethics   179
                women   customs   396
                labor   331.4
Empresses   biografy   923
Emulation   ethics   179
Enamel   chem. technology   666
              painting   751
Encaustic painting   751
Encyclic letters   eccles. polity   262
Encyclopedias, general   030
            class special with subject
Encyclopedists   biografy   920
Endemic diseases   616
Endemics   medical geografy   614.4
Endless punishment   theology   237

Topics in blackface type ar subdivided in the Tables

Endowd libraries		027.4
schools education		**373**
	vs public schools	379
Endowment of research univ.		378.3
Energy, conservation of		531
Engineering		**620**
	industrial	658
	municipal	352
	topografic	526
Engineers biografy		926
Engins		**621**
England, antiquities		913.4
	bank of	332
	church	283
	colleges educ.	378.4
	constitution	342
	fauna	591.9
	flora	581.9
	filosofers biografy	921
	filosofy	192
	geology	554.2
	government	354
	history	**942**
	language	**420**
	law	346
	libraries	027
	literature	**820**
	painting	759
	religious history	274.2
	sculpture	735
	slavery	326
	statistics	314
	travel	**914.2**
	universities	378.4
English composition		808
	cyclopedias	032
	essays, collected	042
	filology	**420**
	journalism	072
	literature	**820**
	newspapers	072
	periodicals, general	052
	private law	347
	socialism	335
	societies, general	062
Engravers biografy		927
	occupational hygiene	613
Engraving		**760**
	of seals and gems	736
Engravings, catalogs of		016.7
	collections of	769
Enigmas amusements		793

Enigmas English literature		828
Enlistment army		355.2
Enoch, Book of		229
Enrolment school organization		371.2
Ensigns flags		929.9
Ensilage agriculture		633
Entail law		347
Entertaining collections Eng. lit.		828
Entertainments, licenses for		352
	public	791
Enthusiasm psychology		157
	religious	269
Enthymeme logic		166
Entomology zoology		595.7
Entomostraca "		595
Entozoa parasitic diseases		616
	zoology	595
Enunciation elocution		808
Environment evolution		575
	influence of anthrop.	573
	therap.	615
	mental caracteristics	136
Envy ethics		179
Eocene fossils paleontology		**560**
	period geology	551
Eolian harp music		787
Eolic dialect		487
Eolithic age prehist. arch.		571
Ephemerides		528
Ephesians Bible		227
Epic dramatic music		782
	painting	753
	poetry English literature	821
	Greek	883
	Latin	873
Epicurean filosofy		187
Epidemics diseases		616
	public helth	614.4–.5
Epigenesis spontan. generation		576
Epigrams English literature		828
Epiphany church festival		264
Epirus ancient history		938
Episcopacy sects		283
Episcopal charges sermons		252
	church	283
	orders ministry	262
Episcopalians biografy		922
Episcopate ministry		262
Episties Amer. literature		816
	Bible	227
	church ritual	264
Epistolografy		808

Topics in blackface type ar subdivided in the Tables

Epitafs	genealogy	929
	monuments	718
Epizoa	economic zoology	591
Epizootic diseases	veterinary med.	619
Equador	history	986
	travel	918.6
Equality	social ethics	177
Equation-machine	astron.	522
of center	orbits	521
time	cronology	529
personal	astron.	522
Equations, algebraic		512
	chemic	541
	trigonometric	514
Equator, inclination of	seasons	525
Equatorial belt	earth	525
	telescope astronomy	522
Equestrian exercise		798
Equilibrium	astronomic laws	521
	of liquids physics	532
Equinoxes	astronomy	525
Equipment of armies		355
	navies	359
Equity	law	347
Equivalence	theoretic chemistry	541
	of force physics	531
Equivocation	ethics	177
Eretrian filosofers		183
Erosion	geology	551
Erotica	ethics	176
Error, sources of	logic	165
Errors, grammatic	Eng. language	428
of observation	probabilities	519
popular		133
Erse language		491.6
Eruptions	volcanoes	551
Escatology		236
Esdras	Bible	229
Eskimos	history	998
Esperanto	language	408
Esquimaux	history	998
Essayists	biografy	928
Essays	American literature	814
	other " 824, 834,etc.	
	general collections	**040**
	class special with subjct	
Essence	metaphysics	121
Essences	chem. tech.	668
Essenes	Jewish religion	296
Establisht church, Anglican		283
Estates	law	347
	social classes	323

Estates of the relm		328
Esther	Apocryfa	229
	Bible	222
Esthetics	fine arts	701
	literature	801
Etchers	biografy	927
Etching		767
Eternity	natural theology	218
Ether	temperance	178
	therapeutics	615
Ethers	chemic technology	668
	organic chemistry	547
Ethical culture societies		170
education		377
Ethics		**170**
of copyright		655
Ethiopia	ancient history	939
	modern "	963
Ethiopic language		492
Ethnic religions		**290**
Ethnografy		572
Ethnology		572
Etiology	medicin	616
Etiquet	customs	395
	ethics	177
Etruscan architecture		722
language		477
Etymologies	English language	422
	French "	442
	other languages 432, 452, etc.	
Etymology, comparativ	filology	412
inflection	Eng. lang.	425
Eucharist	sacrament	265
Eucharistic music	religious art	246
vessels	sacred furniture	247
Euchre	amusements	795
Euclidian geometry		513
Eudiometer	experimental chem.	542
Eudiometry	quantativ anal.	545
Eufuism	rhetoric	808
Eugenics	hygiene	613.9
Eulerian integrals	calculus	517
Eulogies	**biografy**	**920**
	sermons	252
Euphuism	rhetoric	808
Europe	antiquities	913.4
	fauna	591.9
	flora	581.9
	geology	**554**
	history	**940**
	religious history	**274**
	scientific travels	508.4

Topics in blackface type ar subdivided in the Tables

Europe	statistics	314
	travel	914
European politics	parties	329
Evaluation of books		028
Evangelic alliance	religion	206
Evangelist ministry		262
Evangelistic art		246
	music ecclesiology	246
	sacred music	783
	work pastoral theol.	253
	writings practical "	243
Evaporation	meteorology	551.5
	physics	536
	practical chemistry	542
	steam engineering	621.1
Evening prayer	Anglican ritual	264
	family devotions	249
	personal "	248
schools	public educ.	379.1
	self "	374.8
Evergreens	coniferae	585
Evidence	law	347
	logic	163
Evidences	Bible	220.1
	of Christianity	239
Evil	nat. theol.	216
	origin of	216
	pessimism	149
	sin	233
	theodicy	231
eye	occultism	133
spirits		235
Evolution	algebra	512
	arithmetic	511
	biology	575
	ethics	171
	natural theology	213
	religion and science	215
Ex libris	book rarities	097
Examination, civil servis		351
	for academic degrees	378.2
	of teachers education	371.1
	papers Eng. filol.	428
	post mortem pathology	616
	school education	371.2
Examining boards	medical licenses	614.2
Excavation	mining	622
Excavations	**antiquities**	913
Excess of food	hygiene	613.2
Exchange, bils of	law	347
	money	332
	international money	332
Exchange of duplicates	lib. admin.	025.2
	specimens biology	579
	stock	332
	tables business	658
Exchequer	administration, foren	354
	U. S.	353
	finance	336
Excise laws		336.2
Excommunication	eccles. polity	262
	ordinances	265
Excrementa	sewerage	628
Excreta, disinfection	pub. helth	614.4
Excretion	physiologic zoology	591
Excretions, organic	physiology	612
Execution	criminal law	343
Executiv department	const. law	342
	lib. adminis.	025.1
	functions psychology	157
Executors	law	347
Exegesis	Bible	220.6
Exemplaria typografica	**rarities**	090
Exercise	hygiene	613.7
	therapeutics	615
Exertion, excessiv, effects of		616
Exhalation of vapor	physiology	612
	zoology	591
Exhaustion, effects of	diseases	616
Exhibition halls	architecture	725
Exhibitions, bilding		690
	international	606
	of art	708
	industry	606
	school	371.2
	class special with subject	
Exhortations	public worship	264
Exile	punishments	343
	social ethics	177
Exodus	Bible	222
Exorcism		133
Exotics	horticulture	716
Expansion	heat	536
Expatriation		341
Expenditure, public	**finance**	336
Experiments, chemic		542
	class special with subject	
Exploitation	mining	622
Explorations		910
	scientific	508.3
Explorers' lives		923
Explosions, history of		614.8
	of fire damp mining	622
	protection of life	614.8

Topics in blackface type ar subdivided in the Tables

Explosivs	chem. tech.	662
	mining dangers	622
	protection of life	614.8
Export duties, U. S.	tarif	336.2
Exports		382
	free trade	337
Expositions	useful arts	606
Exposure of children	customs	392
ded	"	393
to cold	protection of life	614.8
Express companies	sociology	385
	useful arts	656
Expression, facial	art anatomy	743
	physiognomy	138
musical		780
Extatics	mental derangements	132
Extemporaneous speaking		808
Extempore prayer	public worship	264
Extension courses	education	374.6
of libraries		021
teaching		374.6
university		378.1
Extinct animals	**paleontology**	**560**
plants		561
Extinction of fire	pub. safety	614.8
species		575
Extra fingers or toes	deformities	617
Extraction	mining	622
of teeth	dentistry	617
Extracts	English literature	828
class special with subject		
Extradition	international law	341
Extreme unction	sacraments	265
Eyes	anatomy	611
	asylums for blind	362.4
	diagnosis	616
	hospitals	362.1
	optics	535
	physiology	612
	protection in factories	628
	psychology	152
artificial	surgery	617
care of	hygiene	613
	school hyg.	371.7
diseases of	surgery	617
Ezekiel	Bible	224
Ezra	"	222
Fables	English literature	828
Fabrics, textil	manufactures	677
Façades	architecture	729
Face	anatomy	611
Face	surgery	617
Facetiae	English literature	827
Factories	architecture	725
	cooperativ pol. econ.	334
	sanitation in	628
	useful arts	**670**
Factors and brokers	law	347
Factory, inspection	polit. econ.	331.8
laws	" "	338
management	bus. meth.	658
system	**labor and wages**	**331**
wastes	sanitary engin'g	628
Faculty, intuitiv	psychology	156
Fagging	student life	371.8
Fahlbands	economic geology	553
Faience ware	pottery	738
Failures, trade		332
Fairies		398.4
Fairs, agricultural		630.6
amusements		791
commercial		381
industrial		606
social customs		394
Fairy tales	Amer. literature	813
	folk-lore	398.4
	mythology	**291**
Faith, confessions of	creeds	238
	pub. worship	264
cure	religion	265
	therapeutics	615
doctrinal theology		234
logic of assent		163
Falconry	amusements	799
Falkland ilands	history	997
	naval battle	940.45
	travel	919.7
Fall of man	doctrinal theology	233
Fallacies	logic	165
Fallen, parish care of		258
Falling bodies, laws	physics	531
Falsehood	social ethics	177
Fame	" "	177
Family devotions		249
ethics		173
genealogies		929
histories		929
law		347
libraries		027.1
medicin		616
political science		321
relations	customs	392
Famin	diseases	616

Topics in blackface type ar subdivided in the Tables |

Famin	hygiene	613.2
Fanaticism	religion	248
Fancy	psychology	155
Fancywork		746
Fans	blowing engins	621.6
	mining engineering	622
	toilet	391
	ventilation	697
Fantasia	music	786
Fantoms	occultism	133
Faradization	electric medicin	615
Farces	amusements	792
	English drama	822
Farmacal drugs	adulterations	614.3
Farmaceutic chemistry		615
Farmacists	registration	614.2
Farmacopoeias	mat. med.	615
Farmacy	materia med.	615
Farmers-general	finance	336
Farmers' occupation	hygiene	613
Farmhouses	architecture	728
Farming	**agriculture**	**630**
Farms	agriculture	631
sewage	sanitary eng.	628
Faro	amusements	795
	ethics	175
Faroe ilands	history	949.1
	travel	914.91
Faroese language		439
literature		839
Farriery	horse shoeing	682
	vet. medicin	619
Farther India	geology	555.9
	history	959
	religious history	275.9
	travel	915.9
Fascination	animals	591.5
Fashion	**customs**	**390**
magazines	dom. econ.	646
Fashionable education, women		376
Fastening tools	mech. engineering	621
Fasti, Roman		529
Fasting	asceticism	248
	hygiene	613.2
	temperance	178
Fasts	church	264
Fata Morgana	mirage	535
Fatalism	natural theol.	214
Fathers	duties	173
of the church	hist.	270
	lives	922
	works	281

Fats	adulterations	614.3
	chemic technology	665
	organic chemistry	547
	physiology	612
Faults	structural geology	551
theory of	mining eng.	622
Fauna	zoology	591.9
Faust, legend of	folklore	398.2
Favorits, royal	biografy	923
Fear	psychology	157
Feasts	church	264
	social customs	394
Feathers	birds	598
	comparativ anatomy	591
Fecundity	physiology	612
Federal government	polit. science	321
party	American politics	329
Federalism	political science	321
Federalists	U. S. history	973.4
Feeble-minded, asylums for		362.3
	childstudy	136.7
	education of	371.9
	mental derangement	132
Feeding of animals	animal hygiene	614.9
Feejee ilands	history	996
	travel	919.6
Feelings	emotions	157
Fees	political economy	331.2
Feet	costumes	391
	English prosody	426
	human anatomy	611
	weights and mesures	389
artificial	surgery	617
Fellenberg's system	educ.	371.4
Fellowship, church		265
Fellowships	colleges	378.3
Felons	criminal law	343
Felt	roofing	695
Female education		**376**
	employments	396
labor	polit. economy	331.4
sex	duties	173
	suffrage	324
Fences	law	347
Fencing	amusements	796
Fenianism	Irish history	941.5
	polit. assoc.	363
Fenomena, nutritiv	physiology	612
vital	biology	577
Fermentation	chem. tech.	663
	yeast, etc.	589
Fermented beverages	adultera.	614.3

Topics in blackface type ar subdivided in the Tables

Fermented beverages	chem. tech.	663
Ferments	materia medica	615
Ferneries		716
Ferns	botany	587
	paleontology	561
Ferries	transport	656
Ferrotype	fotografy	772
Fertilization	botany	581
	zoology	591
Fertilizers	agriculture	631
	air pollution	614.7
	manufacture	668
	from sewage	628
Festivals	amusements	791
	cathedral music	783
	church	264
	of song music	784
Fethers	birds	598
	comp. anat.	591
Fetichism		291
Feudal institutions		321
	tenure law	347
Feudalism, age of European hist.		940.1
	political science	321
Fever	animal heat	612
Fevers	diseases	616
Fibrous materials agriculture		633
	manufacture	677
Fiction	American literature	813
	other " 823, 833, etc.	
	reading of	028
	writing	808
Fictitious caracters, dict. of		803
	imprints bibliografy	014
	rarities	098
	names pseudonyms	014
	titles of books	098
Fidelity	ethics	177
Fief		321
Field books	engineering	620
	crops	633
	fortifications	623
	operations geodesy	526
	sports	796
Fife	musical instruments	788
Fighting	ethics	175
Figs	agriculture	634
Figure, human, in art art anatomy		743
	of earth astronomy	525
	geodesy	526
	windows arch. dec.	729
Figureheds	carving	736

Figures of hevenly bodies astron.		521
	prosody Eng. language	426
	other " 436, 446, etc.	
	rhetoric	808
Fiji ilands	history	996
Filanthropists' lives		923
Filanthropy	ethics	177
Files	literary methods	029
	offis equipment	651
Filial duty	ethics	173
Filibustering	piracy	910.4
Filibusters	criminal law	343
	Cuban history	972.9
Filicinae	botany	587
Filing machines mecanical eng.		621
Filioque controversy theology		231
Fillmore, M. presidency		973.6
Filologists	biografy	924
Filology		**400**
	bibliografy of	016.4
	classic	**470-489**
Filoprogenitivness frenology		139
	zoology	591.5
Filosofer's stone alchemy		540.1
Filosofers	biografy	921
Filosofic apparatus		530
	classification of knowledge	112
	instrument making	681
	magazines	105
	systems	**140**
Filosofy		**100**
	bibliografy of	016.1
	biografy of	921
	natural	**530**
	of special topics, see subject	
Filth diseases pathology		616
	public helth	614.5
Filtration	hygiene	613
	practical chem.	542
	sanitary eng.	628
Final causes metaphysics		124
Finance, private		332
	public	**336**
Finances local government		352
Financial admin. civil servis		351
	crises pol. economy	332
	institutions pol. economy	332
Financiers' lives		923
Finding latitude or longitude		525
	at sea	527
	meridian line astronomy	522
	time	529

Topics in blackface type ar subdivided in the Tables

Finding time at sea		527
Fine arts		**700**
	bibliografy of	016.7
	biografy of	927
Fines	library economy	024
Finger alfabet, def and dum		371.9
	rings costumes	391
Fingers, extra	deformities	617
Finishing	painting	698
Finite and infinit	metaphysics	125
Finland	history	947
Finnish language		494
	literature	894
Finno-Hungarian language		494
Fire alarm stations	architecture	725
alarms	signals	654
arms	manufacture	683
	mil. engin'g	623
balls	meteors	523
chemistry		541
clays	economic geology	553
departments	administration	352
engins	mecanical engin'g	621.6
	protection of life	614.8
escapes and exits		614.8
extinction	local government	352
	protection of life	614.8
insurance		368
physics		536
works	chemic tech.	662
worshipers		295
Fireplaces, artistic		749
Fireproofing	bilding	693
Fires	library	022
	local government	352
	mines	622
	protection of life	614.8
First cause	metaphysics	122
editions	rarities	094
lessons in English language		428
Fish air pollution		614.7
as food	hygiene	613.2
commission		639
culture		639
inspection	pub. helth	614.3
preservation	chem. tech.	664
Fisheries	business	639
	ownership	333
	production	338
Fishermen's occupation	hygiene	613
Fishes	paleontology	567
	zoology	597
Fishing	business	639
	sports	799
Fittings, library		022.9
Fiume	history	943.9
Fixt furniture	arch. dec.	729
location	lib. economy	025.8
Fixtures	law	347
	library	022.9
Flagellants	monastic order	271
Flagellation	religious asceticism	248
Flageolet	musical instruments	788
Flags	heraldry	929.9
Flamboyant architecture, Gothic		723
Flames	physics	536
Flanders	history	949.3
Flats	architecture	728
	housekeeping	647
Flattery	ethics	177
Flax	agriculture	633
	manufacture	677
Fleets	naval science	359
	shipbilding	623.8
Flemish language		439
	literature	839
	painting	759
Flies	insects	595.7
	pests	632
	public helth	614.4
artificial	fishing	799
house	dom. econ.	648
Flight of birds	migration	591.5
Flint	stone age	571
Floating batteries	naval engin'g	623
bodies	physics	532
det	finance	336.3
Flogging in navy		359
	punishments law	343
	school	371.5
Flooding of mines		622
Floods	meteorology	551.5
	protection against	627
Floors and flooring	architecture	721
mosaic	arch. decoration	729
Flor and Blancheflor	legends	398.2
Flora, geografic		581.9
Floriculture	landscape gardening	716
Florida, U. S.	history	975.9
	travel	917.59
	war 1835–42 U. S. hist.	973.5
Flour manufacture		679
Flow of streams	meteorology	551.5
Flower garden	landscape garden'g	716

Topics in blackface type ar subdivided in the Tables

Flowering plants	botany	582
Flowerless plants	"	586
Flowers	botany	582
	gardening	716
	language of	716
	national	929.8
Flues, smoke	heating	697
Fluids, physics		532
	preservativ biol. specimens	579
Fluorescence	light	535
Flute	musical instruments	788
Flutina	music	786
Fluxes	metallurgy	669
Fluxions	calculus	517
Fly, *see* Flies		
Flying	animal locomotion	591
machines	aeronautics	629.1
	pneumatics	533
Fog signals	commerce	654
Folds	geology	551
Foliage	botany	581
Folklore	sociology	398.3
Folksong	folklore	398
	music	784
Fonetic shorthand		653
spelling	Eng. lang.	421
Fonics	elementary educ.	372
Fonograf	acoustics	534
	music	789
Fonografy		653
Fonology		414
Fonoscribing	shorthand	653
Font	sacred furniture	247
Food, acquisition	physiol. zool.	591
adulterations	public helth	614.3
chemic analysis		543
	technology	664
cures	therapeutics	615
digestion and nutrition		612
	zoology	591
domestic economy		641
hygiene		613.2
of animals		591.5
plants		581
preservation of		664
Fools	biografy	920
	customs	394
	mental derangements	132
Foot	English prosody	426
	human anatomy	611
	mesures	389
prints, fossil	paleontology	566

Football	amusements	796
Foraminifera	zoology	593
Force and energy	statics	531
electric	engineering	621.3
	physics	537
intermolecular	physics	539
lines of	magnetism	538.
	metaphysics	118
of water	river engin'g	627
pump	pneumatics	533
transmission	mil work	621
	physics	531
Foreclosure	law	347
Foreign, *see* Foren		
Foreknowledge of God	theol.	231
Foren banks		332
bodies, presence of	diseases	616
	surgery	617
elements	Eng. language	422
enlistment		355.2
labor	political economy	331.6
law		349
missions		266
relations	internat. law	341
	polit. science	327
states	administration	354
trade		382
Forensic chemistry	law	340
medicin	"	340
Foreordination	theology	234
Forest trees	botany	582
Forestry	agriculture	634.9
	landscape gard.	715
Forests	meteorology	551.5
	ownership	333
Forge-bellows		533
Forgemen's occupation	hygiene	613
Forgery	law	343
	of academic degrees	378.2
	political economy	332
Forgivness of sin	theology	234
Forks, tuning	acoustics	534
Form	music	781
	ontology	111
books	law	347
of state	pol. sci.	321
Formation of caracter		374
Formosa	history	951
Forms, elementary	arch. design	729
Formularies	materia medica	615
Fortifications	military engin'g	623
Fortune-telling		133

Topics in blackface type ar subdivided in the Tables

Fosfates econ. geology	553	
as fertilizers agricul.	631	
Fosforescence	535	
Fosforescent animals	591.5	
Fosforus inorganic chemistry	546	
materia medica	615	
compounds air pollution	614.7	
Fossil man antiquity of man	573	
paleontology	569	
resins economic geology	553	
Fossils	**560**	
Fotochemistry	541	
Foto-electrotyping	777	
Foto-engraving	777	
Fotografic chemistry	771	
Fotografs collections of	779	
of moving animals art anat.	743	
zoology	591	
hevenly bodies	**523**	
Fotografy	**770**	
astronomy	522	
optics	535	
Fotolithografy	775	
Fotometric observations stars	523.8	
Fotometrics optics	535	
Fotometry astronomy	522	
Fotoplays amusements	792	
censorship	175	
fotografy	778	
scenario writing	808	
Fotozincografy	776	
Foucault's pendulum	525	
Foulahs Sudan, travels	916.6	
Foundations arch. construction	721	
pier bridge engin'g	624	
Founding of libraries	021	
Foundling asylums sociology	362.7	
Foundries metal manufactures	671	
Fountains landscape gard.	714	
Fourierism communism	335	
Fowling sport	799	
Fowls domestic animals	636.5	
Fox-hunting amusements	799	
Fractures surgery	617	
Frames artistic furniture	749	
Framing carpentry	694	
France antiquities	913.4	
botany	581.9	
geology	554.4	
history	944	
language	**440**	
laws	349	

France literature	**840**	
religious history	274.4	
travel	914.4	
zoology	591.9	
Franchise, electiv polit. sci.	324	
Franking privilege post-offis	383	
Franks history	943	
Frauds, art "	709	
literary "	809	
Fraudulent elections	324	
Fraunhofer's lines spectroscope	535	
Freckles dermatology	616	
Free agency doctrinal theol.	234	
church of Scotland sects	285	
hand drawing	741	
love ethics	173	
news and reading rooms	027.9	
public libraries	027.4	
religion	211	
school system education	**379**	
soil party political party	329	
U. S. history	973.6	
speech polit. science	323	
thinkers biografy	922	
thought ecclestiastic polity	262	
rationalism	211	
trade and protection	**337**	
use of libraries	024	
wil metaphysics	123	
psychology	159	
theology	234	
Freebooters criminal law	343	
Freedmen education	371.9	
slavery	326	
Freedmen's bureau	361	
Freedom and emancipation slavery	326	
U. S. hist.	973.7	
metaphysics	123	
of man doct. theol.	233	
political liberties	323	
religious eccles. polity	262	
salvation	234	
Freehold land societies	334	
law	347	
Freemasonry	366	
Freezing physics	536	
artificial ice machines	621.5	
Freight transport	656	
French and Indian wars U. S. hist.	973.2	
church	282	
cyclopedias	034	
essays, collected	044	

Topics in blackface type ar subdivided in the Tables

French filosofers	biografy	921
	filosofy	194
Guiana	history	988
	travel	918.8
horn	wind instruments	788
journalism		074
Kongo	history	967
language		**440**
literature		**840**
newspapers		074
old	language	447
opera	dramatic music	782
painting		759
periodicals, general		054
polish	chem. tech.	667
protestants	persecutions	272
revolution		944
Romanesque architecture		723
roofs	arch. construc.	721
sculpture		735
societies, general		064
spoliations	U. S. history	973.4
Frenologists' lives		920
Frenology		139
Fresco painting	bilding	698
	interior decoration	747
	painting	**750**
	sacred ornament	247
Fresh-air mission		361
Freshets	meteorology	551.5
Fretwork		747
Friars	monastic orders	271
Friction	mec. engineering	621
	physics	531
Friendly ilands	history	996
	societies	334
Friends, society of	sects	289
Friendship	ethics	177
Friesland	history	949.2
	travel	914.92
Friezes	architect. decoration	729
Frisian language		439
	literature	839
Fröbel's system	education	372.2
Frogs	zoology	597
Frost action	geology	551
bites	skin disorders	616
blight	agriculture	632
meteorology		551.5
Fructification	botany	581
Fruit culture		634
drinks	adulterations	614.3

Fruits and seeds	agriculture	634
	organografy	581
inspec. of	pub. helth	614.3
preservation of	chem. tech.	664
Fuel	chem. technology	662
	domestic economy	644
	metallurgy	669
	steam engineering	621.1
Fugitiv slave law	U. S. slavery	326
Fugitivs from justis	extradition	341
Fugue	music	786
Fulminating powders	chem. tech.	662
Fumes, prevention of, in factories		628
Fumigating apparatus	pub. helth	614.4
Functions, calculus of		517
	symmetric, algebra	512
	trigonometric	514
Funding system	public finance	336.3
Funds, public		**336**
Funeral rites	customs	393
	religious ordinance	265
sermons		252
Fungi	botany	589
pests	agric.	632
vegetables	"	635
Fur-trade	political econ.	338
Furnaces	house warming	697
	metallurgy	669
	steam engineering	621.1
Furniture	domestic economy	645
	library economy	022.9
	manufacture	684
	offis equipment	651
artistic		749
ecclesiastic		247
fixt	arch. decorat.	729
Furs	clothing	646
Fuses	explosivs	662
Fusion-point	physics	536
Future events	probabilities	519
judgment	doct. theology	236
life	natural theology	218
state	doctrinal theol.	237
G. A. R.	associations	369.1
Gabbro	plutonic rocks	552
Gables	arch. construction	721
	design	729
Gadhelic language		491.6
Gadsden purchase	U. S. history	973.6
Gaelic language		491.6
Gaging	arithmetic	511

Topics in blackface type ar subdivided in the Tables

Gaging	mesures	389
Galatians	Bible	227
Gales	meteorology	551.5
Galician language		469
literature		869
Gall flies	agric. pests	632
Gallantry	ethics	177
Galleries and libraries		021
art		708
architecture		727
library bildings		022
Galleys	criminal law	343
Gallican church		282
Gallows	criminal law	343
Galls	pests	632
Galvanic manipulation	chemistry	542
Galvanism	physics	537
Galvanoplasty	manufactures	671
Gambling	ethics	174
	of amusements	175
	law	343
Game laws	hunting	799
Games	**amusements**	**790**
	customs	394
	ethics	175
champ'nship	school hygiene	371.7
children's	dom. econ.	649
Greek		913.38
kindergarten		372.2
Roman		913.37
school		371.7
Garbage	sanitation	628
Garden crops		635
tools		631
Gardening, flower		716
kitchen		635
landscape		**712**
window		716
Gardens, botanic		580
public		712
school		372
zoologic		590
Garfield, J. A.	presidency	973.8
Garter, order of	heraldry	929.7
Gas engins	engineering	621.4
	physics	536
fitting		696
fuel		662
heating		697
illuminating	public helth	614.7
light	domestic economy	644
library	"	022
Gas manipulation	practical chem.	542
manufacture		665
natural	economic geology	553
sewer	air pollution	614.7
	sanitary engin.	628
suffocation by	protect. of life	614.8
works	air pollution	614.7
Gases	" "	614.7
	chem. tech.	665
	effect on books	025.8
	in mines	622
	pneumatics	533
	qualitativ analysis	544
	quantitativ analysis	545
Gasoline engins		621.4
vehicles		629.2
Gastronomy	cookery	641
Gastropoda	zoology	594
Gates	arch. construction	721
Gaul	history	944
Gautama	Buddhism	294
Gazetteers		910.3
special country, see country		**914–919**
Gearing	mil engineering	621
Gehenna	doctrinal theology	237
Geissler's tubes	electricity	537
Gelatin processes	fotografy	773
Gem engraving		736
Gemara	Judaism	296
Gems	carving	736
	economic geology	553
	mineralogy	549
Genealogy		**929**
General council	eccles. polity	262
councils	religious history	270
Generalization, logic		161
Generals, lives of		923
Generation	botany	581
	zoology	591
spontaneous		576
steam		621.1
Genesis	Bible	222
Geneva confession	creeds	238
history		949.4
travel		914.94
tribunal	international law	341
Genii	folklore	398.4
Genius		151
hereditary		136
Genre painting		754
Gentlemen	courtesy	177
Gentleness	ethics	179

Topics in blackface type ar subdivided in the Tables

Geodesy		526
Geognosy		**551**
Geografic coordinates		525
discovery, history of		910
distribution, animals		591.9
fossils		560
plants		581.9
names		929
Geografy, ancient		912
Biblical		220.9
descriptiv		**910**
elementary	education	372
historic		911
physical		551
Geologic reports		**550**
surveys		**554–559**
Geologists	biografy	925
Geology		**550**
agricultural		631
and religion	apologetics	239
	nat. theol.	215
applied	mining eng.	622
Geomancy	divination	133
Geometric drawing	math. drawing	744
forms	arch. decoration	729
Geometricians	biografy	925
Geometry		513
analytic		516
descriptiv		515
Geomorfology	geol.	551
Geomorfy		525
Georgia, U. S.	history	975.8
	travel	917.58
Germ theory	biology	576
of disease	bacteria	589
	pathology	616
German	dances	793
catholic church	sects	282
cyclopedias		033
empire		**943**
essays, collected		043
filosofers	biografy	921
filosofy		193
journalism		073
language		**430**
low		439
middle high		437
old "		437
literature		**830**
low		839
mythology		293
opera	music	782
German painting		759
periodicals, general		053
reformation	relig. hist.	274.3
	secular hist.	943
reformd church		284
sculpture		735
socialism		335
societies, general		063
Germany	antiquities	913.4
	botany	581.9
	geology	554.3
	government	354
	history	**943**
	laws	349
	religious history	274.3
	statistics	314
	travel	**914.3**
Germination	botany	581
Gesta Romanorum	mod. Lat. lit.	879
Gestures	oratory	808
Geysers	physical geology	551
Ghebers	Parseeism	295
Ghibelines	Italian history	945
Ghost, Holy	dogmatics	231
	knights	929.7
Ghosts	occultism	133
Giant, Cardiff	humbugs	133
Giant's causeway	descrip.	914.1
Giants	natural history of man	573
Gibraltar	history	946
Gilding		671
Gilds	parish work	256
	polit. economy	338
Gilead	travel	915.6
Gin	chemic technology	663
Gipsies		397
Gipsy language		397
moth	agric. pests	632
Girders	bridge engineering	624
Girls, counsels to	ethics	173
education		**376**
religious societies		267
societies	**sociology**	**369.46**
Girondists, France	history	944
Glacial period		551
Glaciers		551
Gladiators	customs	394
Glass	bilding	691
	manufacture	666
	ornamental	748
	prehistoric	571
	roofs architecture	721

Topics in blackface type ar subdivided in the Tables

Glass, staind, design architecture	729
Glazing	bilding	698
Glees	vocal music	784
Globes	school apparatus	371.6
use of	astronomy	522
Globular projection		515
Gloria in excelsis	sacred music	783
Glossaries	English dialects	427
	dictionaries	423
class special with subject		
Gloves	clothing	646
	costume	391
	lether, manufacture	685
	woven, "	685
Glucose	chem. technology	664
Glue	" "	668
making	air pollution	614.7
Gluttony	temperance ethics	178
Glycerin	chemic technology	668
Glyfografy	engraving	762
Glyptics	carving	736
Gnats	agric. pests	632
	animal parasites	616
	zoology	595.7
Gneiss	lithology	552
Gnomes	folklore	398.4
maxims	Eng. lit.	828
Gnomic poetry	Greek literature	881
Gnomonic projection	descr. geom.	515
Gnosticism	filosofy	189
Gnostics	heresy	273
Goats		636.3
Gobelin tapestry	art needlework	746
Goblins	folklore	398.4
God	doctrins	231
Gods	**ethnic religions**	**290**
	mythology	**291**
Goiter	pathology	616
Gold	chemistry	546
	manufactures	671
	metallurgy	669
	political economy	332
Coast, Africa	history	966
ores	econ. geology	553
Golden Fleece, knights of		929.7
Goldsmithing	fine arts	739
	useful arts	671
Golf	amusements	796
Goniometry	crystallografy	548
Good	natural theol.	216
Friday	church calendar	264
	music	783

Good Templars	temperance	178
Goodness	ethics	179
Goose, Mother	folklore	398
Gorilla	zoology	599
Gospels	Bible	226
	church ritual	264
pseudo	Apocryfa	229
Gossip	ethics	177
Gotama	Buddhism	294
Gothic architecture		723
ecclesiology		246
language		439
literature		839
revival, architecture		724
Gothland, Sweden	history	948.6
	travel	914.86
Goths	history	943
Gouache painting		751
Governess	private education	373
Government	**central admin.**	**351**
	family ethics	173
	foren countries	354
	library economy	023
	local administration	352
	political science	**320**
	U. S. and state admin.	353
bildings	architec.	725
church		262
divine		231
forms of		321
libraries		027.5
loans	finance	336.3
publishing		655
school	education	371.5
Governors	biografy	923
Grace	doctrinal theology	234
	esthetics	701
Graces	mythology	292
Graded degrees, academic		378.2
Grades	schools	371.2
Grading	engineering	625
Graeco-Russian church		281
Graffiti	Latin inscriptions	471
Grafic arts, fine arts		**700**
statics		531
Grafite	economic geology	553
Grafology	psychology	137
Grafting	fruit culture	631
Grail, Holy	legends	398.2
Grain	agriculture	633
Coast, Africa	hist.	966
trade	dom. trade	381

Topics in blackface type ar subdivided in the Tables

Graining	housepainting	698	**Great war 1914–19**	**hist.**	940.3–.4
Grains	agriculture	633	Grecian bend	fashions	391
Grammar, comparativ		415	Greco-Russian church		281
	elemen. education	372	Greece	ancient history	938
	schools	public schools	379.1	modern	administration	354
	universal	compar. filol.	415		botany	581.9
Grammars	English language	425		geology	·554.9
	other	"	435, 445, etc.		history	949.5
Grand army of the repub. association		369.1		travel	914.95
	U. S. hist.	973.7	Greek antiquities		913.38
opera		782		archipelago	ancient hist.	939
Grangers		630.62		modern "	949.9
Granit	bilding stone	553		travel	914.99
	rock	552		architecture	722
Grant, U. S.	presidency	973.8		art, history of	709
Grants, land	public finance	336		church	281
	to schools	379.1		**classics**	**880**
Grape culture		634		dialects	487
sugar	manufacture	664		**filosofy**	**180**
Graphic arts	**fine arts**	**700**		fire	customs of war	399
statics		531		independence	mod. history	949.5
Graphite	economic geology	553		**language**	**480**
Graphology	psychology	137		modern	489
Grasses	agriculture	633		**literature**	**880**
	botany	584		modern	889
	ornamental	716		mythology	292
Grasshoppers	pests	632		orders of architecture	729
	zoology	595.7		paleografy	inscriptions	481
Gratitude	ethics	179		revival	architecture	724
Grave mounds	prehist. archeol.	571		sculpture	733
stones	monuments	718	Green mts, Vt.	description	917.43
yards		718	Greenback party		329
Gravel	disease	616	Greenbacks	paper money	332
	petrografy	552		U. S. finance	336
Graves	cemeteries	718	Greenhouses		716
Gravimetric analysis	chemistry	545		architecture	728
Gravitation	celestial dynamics	521	Greenland	history	998
	theories	531	Greensand	petrografy	552
Gravity, experiments	geodesy	526	Gregariousness of animals		591.5
physics		531	Gregorian calendar		529
specific		532		chant	ecclesiology	246
Grease	chemic technology	665		sacred music	783
Great Britain	antiquities	913.4	Grilles	arch. construction	721
	church hist.	274.2	Grimm's law	comparativ filology	412
	colonies	325	Grinders' occupation	hygiene	613
	commerce	382	Grinding	flour mils	679
	det of	finance	336	machines	mec. engin'g	621
	history	**942**	Grip	pathology	616
	parliament	328		public helth	614.5
	politics	329	Groceries	adulterations	614.3
Salt lake	travel	917.92	Grocers' occupation	hygiene	613
schism		270	Groind vaults	architecture	721

Topics in blackface type ar subdivided in the Tables

Grottos physical geografy 551
Ground air hygiene 613
    public helth 614.7
  water physical geog. 551
Grounds, private 712
Groves landscape gardening 715
Growth biology 574, 577
    botany 581
    of cities adminis. 352
      statistics 312
    physiology 612
    zoology 591
Guano agriculture 631
    economic geology 553
Guardianship law 347
Guatemala history 972.8
Guelfs Italian history 945
Guerilla warfare international law 341
Guerillas U. S. civ. war 973.7
Guiana, South America geology 558.8
    history 988
    relig. hist. 278.8
    travel 918.8
Guidance, vocational 371.4
Guide books 910
Guides, railroad 656
Guilds, business political economy 338
    parish work 256
Guillotin law 343
Guinea, Lower, Africa history 967
  New, Oceania history 995
  Upper, Africa " 966
Guitar music 787
Gulf states, U. S. history 976
  stream physical geografy 551
Gums and resins chem. tech. 668
  fossil economic geology 553
Gun cotton explosivs 662
  making 683
Gunnery military engineering 623
Gunning sports 799
Gunpowder chemic tech. 662
  public safety 614.8
Guns military engineering 623
Gunter's scale math. instrum. 510
Gutta percha rubber manufacture 678
Gymnasia German schools 379.4
Gymnasiums architecture 725
Gymnastics curativ 615
  hygiene 613.7
  school hygiene 371.7
  vocal elocution 808

Gymnastics vocal vocal music 784
Gymnosofists filosofy 181
Gymnospermae botany 585
Gynecology diseases of women 618
Gypsies 397
Gypsum agriculture 631
  economic geology 553
  lithology 552
Gypsy Romany language 397
Habakkuk Bible 224
Habeas corpus law 347
Habit psychology 158
Habitations, animal zoology 591.5
  human hygiene 613
Habits customs 390
  of animals zoology 591.5
  children dom. econ. 649
  laboring classes pol. econ. 331.8
  plants physiol. bot. 581
Hades ancient mythology 292
  doctrinal theology 236
Haggai Bible 224
Hague, The history 949.2
  travel 914.92
  tribunal 341
Hahnemann's theory therapeutics 615
Hail storms meteorology 551.5
Hair anatomy 611
  diseases of 616
  dressing customs 391
    toilet 646
  physiology 612
Half-way covenant 285
Halids organic chemistry 547
Hall marks plate 736
Halloweve customs 394
Halls architecture 725
  public hygiene 613
  society student life 371.8
Hallucinations 133
Halogen group chemistry 546
Haloids organic chemistry 547
Halos optics 535
Hamar, Norway history 948.3
  travel 914.83
Hamitic language 493
  literature 893
Hammers tools 621
Hand chiromancy 133
  human anatomy 611
  language, def and dum 371.9

Topics in blackface type ar subdivided in the Tables

Hand turning lathes	621	
Handbooks of travel	910	
Handicraft mecanic trades	680	
Handkerchief customs	391	
Hands, artificial surgery	617	
Handwriting	652	
Hanging punishments	343	
Hangings, textil bilding	698	
Hanover, House of English hist.	942.07	
Hanseatic leag history	943	
Happiness ethics	171	
Harbor defenses fortifications	623	
engineering	627	
Harbors, hydrografy of surveying	526	
Hard labor punishments	343	
Harding, W. G. presidency	973.91	
Hardness of molecules physics	539	
Hardware	671	
Harelip surgery	617	
Harems customs	392	
Harmonics analytic geometry	516	
modern "	513	
music	781	
Harmonists sects	289	
Harmonium music	781	
musical instruments	786	
Harmony of colors optics	535	
painting	752	
gospels Bible	226	
Harnessmaking	685	
Harp	787	
Harper's Ferry invasion U.S. hist.	973.6	
Harpsichord	786	
Harrison, B. presidency	973.8	
W. H. "	973.5	
Hart anatomy	611	
Hartford convention U. S. history	973.5	
Harvesting agriculture	631	
Hasheesh ethics	178	
hygiene	613	
Hatmaking	687	
Hatching engraving	762	
artificial poultry	636.5	
Hate ethics	179	
Hats clothing	646	
customs	391	
Haulage mining engineering	622	
Haunted houses	133	
Hawaii annexation to U. S.	973.8	
history	996	
relig. hist.	279.6	
travel	919.6	

Hawaiian language	499	
Hawking sports	799	
trade	639	
Hay agriculture	633	
fever diseases	616	
Haybox cookers	643	
Hayes, R. B. presidency	973.8	
Hayti history	972.9	
travel	917.29	
Haze meteorology	551.5	
Hazing student life	371.8	
Head, *see* Hed		
Headaches diseases	616	
Headstones monuments	718	
mortuary design	247	
Healing cures	615	
divine	265	
Health, *see* Helth		
Hearing acoustics	534	
anatomy	611	
asylums for def	362.4	
diseases	617	
ear hospital	362.1	
physiology	612	
psychology	152	
Heart anatomy	611	
Heat, animal physiology	612	
engins air engins	621.4	
geologic agents	551	
meteorology	551.5	
of earth	525	
hevenly bodies	523	
physics	536	
Heathen art ecclesiology	246	
filosofy vs the church	261	
missions to	266	
religions	290	
salvation of	234	
Heathenism, nonchristian relig.	299	
Heating bilding	697	
domestic econ.	644	
library bldgs	022	
physics	536	
practical chemistry	542	
sanitary engin'g	628	
steam engineering	621.1	
Heaven theology	237	
Hebraic sabbath	263	
Hebrew history, ancient	933	
modern	296	
language	492	
literature	892	

Topics in blackface type ar subdivided in the Tables

Hebrew religion		296
Hebrews	epistles	227
Hebrides	history	941
New	history	993
Hed	anatomy	611
	art anatomy	743
	craniology	573
	frenology	139
	surgery	617
dress	customs	391
Hedakes	diseases	616
Hedgear		646
Hedges	landscape gardening	715
Hedonism	ethics	171
Hedstones	monuments	718
	mortuary design	247
Hegelian filosofy		193
Heirs	law	347
Hel		237
Heliocentric place		521
Heliogravure	fotog.	777
Heliometer	astronomy	522
Heliostat	"	522
Heliotypes		774
Hellebore	poisons	615
Hellenic languages, minor		489
Helminthology	zoology	595
Helps for laboring classes		331.8
Helth affected by soil	pub. helth	614.7
boards of	local gov't	352
	public helth	614
laws	**hygiene**	**613**
lift	therapeutics	615
of students		371.7
public		**614**
resorts	hygiene	613
Helths, drinking of	customs	394
	ethics	178
Hemiptera	insects	595.7
Hemorrhage of lungs	diseases	616
Hemorrhoids	diseases	616
Hemp	agriculture	633
	manufactures	677
Henri Deux ware	pottery	738
Henry 1	English history	942.02
2–3	" "	942.03
4–6	" "	942.04
7–8	" "	942.05
Hens	diseases of	619
	poultry	636.5
Hepaticae	botany	588
Hepatology	physiology	612
Heptarchy	English history	942.01
Heraclitus	Greek filosofy	182
Heraldry		**929.6**
Herb doctors	cures	615
Herbariums		580
Herculaneum	description	913.37
Hereditary diseases	hygiene	613.9
genius	mental caracter.	136
socicties, Amer.		369.1
succession	law	347
	pol. sci.	321
Heredity	evolution	575
	hygiene	613.9
	origin of the soul	129
mental		136
spiritual	doctr. theol.	233
Heresies		273
Heretics, persecutions of		272
Hermeneutics	Bible	220.6
Hermetic art	alchemy	540.1
Hermits	biografy	920
	relig. biografy	922
Hernia	diseases	616
Herodotus	Greek literature	888
Heroism	ethics	179
Herpetology		598.1
Herzegovina	history	943.9
Hessian fly	pests	632
Heven	theology	237
Hexapoda	zoology	595.7
Hibbert lectures	religion	290
Hibernation	zoology	591.5
Hicksites	Friends	289
Hieroglyfics		419
	Egyptian	493
High church	Anglican church	283
license	temperance ethics	178
pressure	heating	697
schools	pub. sch. system	379.1
	sec. educ.	**373**
Higher education	**academies**	**373**
	colleges	**378**
	of women	**376**
Highlands, Scotland	description	914.1
Hight of atmosfere		523
Hights, mesurement of	survey'g	526
Highwaymen	law	343
Highways	law	347
	local government	352
	road engineering	625
	transportation	388
travel on	protec. of life	614.8

Topics in blackface type ar subdivided in the Tables

Hildebrand	Italian history	945
	religious "	270
Himalayan architecture		722
Himalayas	travel	915.4
Himyaritic language		492
Hindi language		491
Hindostan	history	954
Hindrances	farming	632
Hindu architecture		722
	filosofy	181
	languages	491
	law	349
	religion	294
Hinduism	religion	294
Hindustan	history	954
Hindustani language		491
Histogenesis	zoology	591
Histology	animals	591
	botany	581
	human anatomy	611
Historians	biografy	928
Historic atlases		911
	books Bible	222
	charts and tables	902
	geografy	911
	magazines, general	905
	class special with subject	
	painting	756
	societies, general	906
	class special with subject	
	theology	209
History		**900**
	ancient	**930**
	bibliografy of	016.9
	constitutional	342
	ecclesiastic	**270**
	filosofy of	901
	literary, general	809
	modern	**940–999**
	natural zoology	**590**
	naval, see spec. countries	
	of civilization	901
	sacred	220.9
	of special topics, see subject	
Histrionics		792
Hobbes	materialism	146
Hocky	outdoor sports	796
Hog	domestic animals	636.4
Hoisting machinery	mil work	621
	mining engineering	622
Holiday opening	library economy	024
Holidays	customs	394

Holidays	hygiene	613.7
	school, education	371.2
Holiness	doctrinal theology	234
Holland	history	949.2
	reformation in relig. hist.	274.9
	travel	914.92
Holley system	waterworks	628
Holtz machine	electricity	537
Holy alliance	European history	940.28
	communion	265
	Ghost knights	929.7
	theology	231
	grail legends	398.2
	land history, ancient	933
	modern	956
	travel	915.6
	orders church	265
	Roman empire	943
	rood ecclesiology	247
	scriptures	**220**
	see	282
	Spirit theology	231
	water ecclesiology	246
Homage	feudalism	321
Home customs		392
	domestic economy	643
	economics	**640**
	education self education	**374**
	vs public	373
	life ethics	173
	rule Irish history	941.5
	political parties	329
	study, societies for	374.4
	woman in	396
Homeopathy	therapeutics	615
Homer	Greek poetry	883
Homeric hymns		883
Homes	hygiene	613
	institutional architec.	725
	sociol.	362
	private architec.	728
	working girls' institutions	362
	polit. econ.	331.8
Homested bil	U. S. law	347
Homicide	law	343
Homiletics	theology	251
Homilies	sermons	252
Homoeopathy		615
Homologies	biology	574
	botany	581
	zoology	591
Homonyms	English language	424

Topics in blackface type ar subdivided in the Tables

Homonyms   other language 434, 444, etc.
Homoptera   entomology   595.7
Honduras, Central Amer.   history   972.8
                           travel   917.28
Honesty   ethics   174
Honey   agriculture   638
Honeymoon   customs   392
Honor   business ethics 174
              student   371.8
Honorary degrees   colleges 378.2
        titles   heraldry 929.7
Hood, Robin   legends   398.2
Hoods, academic   378.2
Hookworm disease   path.   616
                    pub. helth 614.5
Hoosac tunnel   engineering 625
Hoover, H. C.   presidency   973.91
Hopkinsianism   Calvinism   284
Hops   agriculture   633
              brewing   663
Horn   organic chemistry 547
              wind instrument 788
Horns, drinking   customs   394
Horology   astronomy   529
              watch making   681
Horoscope   occultism   133
Horse cars   railroad engineering 625
    diseases veterinary medicin 619
    domestic animal   636.1
    racing   amusements   798
              ethics   175
    railway   engineering   625
              sociology   388
              useful arts   656
    shoeing   682
    training domestic animals 636.1
    zoology   599
Horsemanship   798
Hortatory theology   243
Horticultural societies   716
                    agricultural 630.62
Horticulture   agriculture   630
              landscape gardening 716
Hosea   Bible   224
Hosiery   clothing   646
              costumes   391
              manufacture   687
Hospice of St Bernard   614.8
Hospital sketches   Amer. civil war 973.7
              Great war   940.47
Hospitalers   knights   929.7
Hospitality   ethics   177

Hospitals   architecture   725
              institutions   362
Host   eucharist   265
Hot springs   physical geology 551
    water   heating   697
Hotels   architecture   728
              home economics 647
              hygiene   613
Hothouses   agriculture   635
              flower culture 716
Hour glasses horology   529
Hours of labor political economy 331.8
    school   371.2
House bilding   690
    domestic economy   643
    flies   dom. pests   648
    furnishing   domestic econ. 645
    of commons   legis. bodies 328
        correction   364
        lords   legis. bodies 328
        refuge   364
        representativs legis. bodies 328
    painting   bilding   698
    sanitation   648
    sewerage   628
Household art decoration   747
Housekeeping   640
              cooperativ   334
Houses   architecture   720
              hygiene   613
    noble   heraldry   929.7
    society   student life   371.8
Housewifery   640
Housing of animals   pub. hygiene 614.9
Huckster licenses   local gov't 352
Hudson bay territory   history 971.2
    river   description   917.47
Huguenots   church   284
              lives   922
              persecutions   272
Hulsean lectures   apologetics 239
Human ability   doctrinal theol. 233
    anatomy   611
    body   art anatomy   743
              and mind   130
    depravity   doctrinal theol. 233
    faculties   psychology   150
    habitations   hygiene   613
    life   protec. from accident 614.8
    nature   dogmatics   233
              mental caracteristics 136
    physiology   612

Topics in blackface type ar subdivided in the Tables

Human race	ethnology	572
	rights polit. science	323
	sacrifice nonchrist. relig.	291
Humane societies		179.2
Humanism	filosofy	144
	literature	880
Humanitarianism unitarianism		288
Humanity	ethics	177
Humbugs	delusions	133
Humility	ethics	179
Humming-birds	zoology	598
Humor	American literature	817
	English "	827
	French "	847
	other " 837, 857, etc.	
Humorists	biografy	928
Hungarian language		494
Hungary	history	943.9
	travel	914.39
Hunger	physiology	612
Huns	**history**	**950**
Hunting	business	639
	sport	799
Huronian strata geology		551
Hurricanes		551.5
Husband and wife law		347
Husbandry	**agriculture**	**630**
Husbands, duties of ethics		173
Hussites	Christian sects	284
Huzwaresh language		491
Hydraulic engineering		627
	sanitary	628
	machinery	621.2
	mining engineering	622
Hydraulics	science	532
Hydrocarbons	chemistry	547
Hydrodynamics	physics	532
	water engins	621.2
Hydrofobia	diseases	616
	protectiv inoculation	614.4
	public helth	614.5
Hydrogen	chemistry	546
Hydrogeology		551
Hydrografy	surveying	526
Hydrokinetics		532
Hydrology		551
Hydromecanics		532
Hydrometry	velocity	532
Hydropathy		615
Hydrostatics		532
Hydrozoa	zoology	593
Hygiene	mental	131

Hygiene	**personal**	**613**
	public	**614**
	school education	371.7
	vocal	784
Hygrometry	meteorology	551.5
Hylozoism	metaphysics	146
Hymn tunes	music	783
Hymns	hymnology	245
	Homeric	883
Hyperboreans	Greek mythology	292
Hypnotics	therapeutics	615
Hypnotism	mesmerism	134
Hypochondria	medicin	616
	mental disease	132
Hypotheses	logic	167
Hypothesis, nebular		523.1
Hypsometry	physical geografy	551.5
Hysteria	diseases	616
Hysterics	mental derangements	132
I W W	labor organizations	331.88
Ice	manufacture	621
	meteorology	551.5
	age geology	551
	dealers trades	689
	impure hygiene	613
	sports	796
Icebergs	physical geografy	551
Iceland	history	949.1
	travel	914.91
Icelandic language		439
	literature	839
Ices	domestic economy	641
Ichnology	paleontology	566
Ichthyology		597
Iconoclasts⌉	heathen art	246
Iconografy		**730**
	Christian	246
Iconology	emblems	246
Idaho, U. S.	history	979.6
	travel	917.96
Idealism	filos. system	141
Idealistic painting		753
Ideas, innate intuition		156
Identity, mistaken law		347
	personal	126
Idiocy		132
Idioms	English language	423
	other lang. 433, 443, etc.	
Idiosyncrasies, mental		137
Idiot asylums		362.3
	schools	371.9

Topics in blackface type ar subdivided in the Tables

Idleness	ethics	179
Idolatry	nonchrist. relig.	291
Igneous rocks	lithology	552
Iguanodon	fossils	568
Ilands	physical geografy	551
isolated	history	997
Iliad	Greek epic poetry	883
Illegitimacy	law	347
Illinois, U. S.	history	977.3
	travel	917.73
Illiteracy	public schools	379.2
	spelling reform	421
	suffrage	324
Illuminated books		096
manuscripts		091
Illuminati	society	366
Illuminating gases	chem. tech.	665
	public helth	614.7
Illumination	decoration	745
	house lighting	644
	sacred ornamentation	247
electric	engineering	621.3
	physics	537
Illusions	occultism	133
Illustrated books	book rarities	096
Illustration of books	publishing	655
	rarities	096
Image worship	idolatry	291
Images in churches	ecclesiology	246
Imaginary books		098
imprints		014
quantities	algebra	512
Imagination	psychology	155
in art		701
science		501
Imbecility	mental derangements	132
Imbecils, asylums for		362.3
education of		371.9
Immaculate conception of Christ		232
	Mary	232
Immersion	baptism	265
	baptist doctrins	230
	sects	286
Immigrants and immigration		**325**
Immoral art and literature	ethics	176
Immortality	doctrinal theology	237
	metaphysics	129
	natural theology	218
	of animals	591.5
Impeachment	administration	351
	constitutional law	342
	criminal law	343
Imperial federation, Gt. Br.		354
robes	ceremonies	394
Implements, agricultural		631
domestic		643
Importation duty free for colleges		337
	libraries	021.8
of books	lib. econ.	025.2
Imports	commerce	382
	duty on	337
Imposture		133
Imprecations	ethics	179
Impressionist school of painting		759
Impressment	military	355.2
	naval	359
Imprints, fictitious	bibliografy	014
	rarities	098
Imprisonment	punishments	343
Impurities of water	hygiene	613
Inability, human	doctrinal theol.	233
Inaugurations	ceremonies	394
Incandescence	heat	536
Incantations	occultism	133
Incarnation	Christology	232
Incas	history	985
Incense	ecclesiology	247
Inclined plane	canal engineering	626
	machines	531
Inclines	railroad engineering	625
Income, public	**finance**	**336**
student		371.2
tax	finance	336.2
Incubation, artificial		636
Incunabula	book rarities	093
Incurables, hospitals for		362.1
Indemnity	international law	341
Independence, American	U. S. hist.	973.3
Independency	church polity	262
Independents	sects	285
Indeterminism	psychology	159
Index error	practical astronomy	522
expurgatorius	book rarities	098
making	literary methods	029
rerums	" "	029
Indexes, Biblical	concordances	220.2
class special with subject		
India	antiquities, ancient	913.34
	modern	913.5
architecture	ancient	722
	Mohammed.	723
botany		581.9
British	history	954
Farther	"	959

Topics in blackface type ar subdivided in the Tables

India	Farther	religious history	275.9
	geology		555.4
	history, ancient		934
		modern	954
	religious history		275.4
	travel		915.4
India rubber manufactures			678
Indian archipelago	history		991
Indian Bureau	U. S. admin.		353
corn	agriculture		633
East, languages			491
literatures			891
filosofers			181
legends			398.2
mutiny	Sepoy rebellion		954
ocean	travels		910.4
religions			299
Territory, U. S.	history		976.6
	travel		917.66
wars	**U. S. hist.**		**973**
Indiana, U. S.	history		977.2
	travel		917.72
Indians, American			**970.1**
	biografy		970.2
	education		371.9
	language		497
	literature		897
Indic languages			491
Indicator for steam engins			621.1
Indicators	library economy		025.6
Indictments	criminal law		343
Indies, East, Dutch	**history**		**991**
	travel		**919.1**
Indigestion	medicin		616
Indigo	chemic technology		667
Individual psychology			137
soul, origin of			129
Individuals and the state	ethics		172
bibliografy of			012
Indo-European languages, minor			**491**
literature			**891**
Germanic languages			**491**
Indoor amusements			**793**
Indorsement	law		347
Induction	electricity		537
	logic		161
	magnetism		538
	reasoning faculty		153
Inductiv logic			161
sciences			**500**
Indulgencies	Roman church		282
	doctrin		230
Industrial arts			**600**
	classes	political econ.	331
	depressions	" "	338
	drawing		744
	economy		**330**
	education	educ. systems	371.4
		useful arts	607
	exhibitions		606
	history		609
	legislation	polit. econ.	338
	museums		606
	sanitation		628
	schools		607
	statistics	political econ.	331
	Workers of the World		331.88
Industries	**chemic technol.**		**660**
	primitiv		571
	useful arts		**600**
Industry	ethics		179
Inebriate asylums			362.1
Inebriates	temperance		178
Inebriety	diseases		616
Infallibility, divine			231
	eccles. polity		262
	Roman church		282
	schism	old catholics	284
Infancy, psychology of			136.7
Infant baptism			265
	education	elementary educ.	372.2
	mortality	public helth	614.1
	salvation		234
Infanticide	customs		392
	ethics		173
	law		343
Infantil paralysis	diseases		616
	pub. helth		614.5
Infantry	army		356
Infants, care of	childbirth		618
	home		649
food for	hygiene		613.2
	nursery		649
Infectious diseases	pathology		616
	pub. helth		614.4-.5
Infernal machines	explosivs		662
Infidelity			211
Infinit	metaphysics		125
Infinitesimal calculus			517
Infirm	charities		362.6
Infirmaries	hospitals		362.1
Inflammation	surgery		617
Inflation	paper money		332
Inflection	English filology		425

Topics in blackface type ar subdivided in the Tables

Influenza	pathology	616
Infusoria	zoology	593
Infusorial earth	petrografy	552
Ingenuity	inventions	608
Inheritance	law	347
of soul	metaphysics	129
Inherited disability	hygiene	613.9
Initials	bibliografy	014
	decoration	745
Injections	collectors' manuals	579
	medicin	615
Injectors	steam engin	621.1
Injured, aid to	protection of life	614.8
Injuries	surgery	617
	torts	347
effects of	diseases	616
Injurious animals	agriculture	632
	zoology	591
insects	agriculture	632
occupations	hygiene	613
plants	botany	581
Ink	manufacture	667
Inland navigation	engin'g	626
	transport	656
quarantine	public helth	614.4
seas	physical geografy	551
Inlay	architectural decoration	729
	art furniture	749
Innate ideas		156
Inns	architecture	728
	hotels	647
of court	English law	340
Inoculation, protectiv	pub. helth	614.4
Inorganic and organic matter, differ.		577
	chemistry	546
Inquisition	persecutions by	272
Insane, criminal	law	340
hospitals	architecture	725
	institutions	362.2
lives of		920
Insanity	law	347
	nervous diseases	616
	psychology	132
Inscriptions, comparativ		417
	English language	421
Insectivora	mammals	599
Insects	fertilization of plants	581
	metamorfosis	591
	paleontology	565
	zoology	595.7
injurious	agriculture	632
	zoology	591
Insects	productiv	638
Insessores	birds	598
Insolvency	law	347
Insomnia	disease	616
	hygiene	613
Inspection of bildings, explosivs, etc.		614.8
food, etc.	pub. helth	614.3
Inspiration	Bible	220.1
Installation of ministers		262
Instinct, animal		591.5
human		158
Institute of France		064
Institutes	Roman law	349
	teachers	370.7
Institutions	**Christian**	**260**
	educational	**370**
	musical	780
	of credit	pol. econ. 332
	political science	321
	sociology	**360**
Instruction	**education**	**370**
class special with subject		
Instrumental errors	practical astr.	522
	music	**780**
	public worship	264
Instrumentation	music	781
Instruments, drawing		**744**
making		681
for special uses, class with subject		
Insular faunas	zoology	591.9
floras	botany	581.9
Greece	ancient history	939
modern	"	949.9
Insurance		368
compulsory	polit. econ.	331.2
societies	cooperativ	334
Insurrections	internal relations	323
Intaglios	sculpture	736
Intarsia	arch. decoration	729
Integrity	business ethics	174
Intellect	psychology	151
Intellectual		
development	**education**	**370**
	history	809
	influence of church	261
	relation of church	377
filosofy		**150**
life	**self education**	**374**
Intelligence, human		151
of animals		591.5
Intemperance	ethics	178
	hygiene	613

Topics in blackface type ar subdivided in the Tables

Intercommunication	**sociology**		**380**
	useful arts		**650**
Interdicts	excommunication		262
Interest	political economy		332
and usury	law		347
calculation of	arithmetic		511
securities	finance		336.3
tables			651
Interference	optics		535
Interior decoration			747
department	U. S. admin.		353
of earth	geology		551
Interlude	English drama		822
Intermarriages of families	hygiene		613.9
races	etnics		173
Intermediate education, private			**373**
public			**379**
state	theology		236
Interment	customs		393
public helth			614.6
Intermolecular forces	physics		539
Internal heat	geology		551
relations	political sci.		323
revenue laws	finance		336.2
International association, the			335
coinage			332
congresses			341
class special with subject			
copyright	private law		341
publishing			655
ethics			172.4
exchange	money		332
exchanges	lib. econ.		021.8
exhibitions			606
law			341
relations	pol. sci.		327
standard	money		332
Interoceanic canals	engineering		626
sociology			386
Interstate commerce commission			385
Intervention	international law		341
Intolerance, relig.	persecutions		272
state ethics			172
Intonation	music		781
Intoxicating drinks, traffic			178
Intoxication	alcoholism		616
ethics			178
Intransigentes	Spanish history		946
Intrenchments	military engineering		623
Intuition	ethics		171
psychology			156
Intuitionalism	filosofic systems		143
Intuitiv filosofy			143
Inundations	meteorology		551.5
protection ag'st	engin'g		627
Invalids	domestic econ.		649
Invention of printing			655
rhetoric			808
Inventions	patents		608
Inventors	biografy		926
Invertebrates	**paleontology**		**562**
productiv	agric.		638
zoology			**592**
Investiture	ecclesiastic polity		262
Investitures, war of, 1074–84			270
Investments	private finance		332
Invincible armada	Spanish history		946
Invocation	ritual		264
Invoices	accounts		657
Involution	algebra		512
arithmetic			511
geometry			513
Ionic filosofy			182
Greek	dialects		487
order of architecture			729
Iowa, U. S.	history		977.7
travel			917.77
Iran	history		955
travel			915.5
Iranian languages			491
Ireland	antiquities		913.4
botany			581.9
geology			554.1
history			**941.5**
religious history			274.1
travel			**914.15**
zoology			591.9
Irish bards	lives		928
buls	Eng. humor		827
church, Anglican			283
Roman catholic			282
home rule	history		941.5
polit. parties			329
land question	political econ.		333
language			491.6
literature			891.6
music	**vocal**		784
politics			329
Iron age	prehist. archeol.		571
bearing waters	econ. geol.		553
bilding material			691
chemistry			546
clads	naval arch.		623.8
manufacture			672

Topics in blackface type ar subdivided in the Tables

Iron	mask, man in biografy	92	
	materia medica	615	
	metallurgy	669	
	mining	622	
	ores economic geology	553	
	roofs bilding	695	
	ships	623.8	
	structures arch. construc.	721	
	work manufactures	672	
	ornamental	739	
Irony	rhetoric	808	
Irrigation	agriculture	631	
	canal engineering	626	
	sewage	628	
Irritability in plants botany		581	
Irvingism	catholic apostolic	289	
Isaiah	Bible	224	
Islam	Mohammedanism	297	
Islands	physical geografy	551	
	isolated history	997	
Isle of Man, England history		942	
Wight, " "		942	
Isles of Shoals history		974.2	
	travel	917.42	
Isoeteae	botany	587	
Isografy		652	
Isomerism	chemistry	541	
Isometric projections geometry		515	
Isomorfism crystallografy		548	
Isothermal lines physical geog.		551.5	
Israelites	history, ancient	933	
	modern	296	
Isthmian games Greek antiq.		913.38	
Italian cyclopedias		035	
	essays, collected	045	
	filosofy	195	
	journalism	075	
	language	**450**	
	literature	**850**	
	newspapers	075	
	painting	759	
	periodicals, general	055	
	republics aristocracies	321	
	history	945	
	school of Greek filosofy	182	
	societies, general	065	
Italic languages, minor		479	
Italy	antiquities	913.4	
	botany	581.9	
	geology	554.5	
	history, ancient	937	
	modern	945	

Italy	reformation in	274.5	
	religious history	274.5	
	travel	914.5	
	zoology	591.9	
Ivory carving		736	
	Coast, Africa hist.	966	
	painting	751	
	supply	679	
Jackson, Andrew presidency		973.5	
Jacobins	French history	944	
	political clubs	363	
Jacobite church		281	
Jacobites	Eng. pol. party	329	
Jacotot's system of education		371.4	
Jacquerie	French history	944	
Jade	mineralogy	549	
Jails	prisons	365	
Jaina architecture		722	
Jainas	Hindu sect	294	
Jamaica	history	972.9	
James, St	epistle	227	
1–2	English history	942.06	
Jansenism	heresy	273	
Japan	botany	581.9	
	geology	555.2	
	history	952	
	religious history	275.2	
	statistics	315	
	travel	915.2	
Japan	chemic technology	667	
Japanese architecture		722	
	color prints	761	
	language	495	
	literature	895	
Japanning varnishing		698	
Jasher, book of		229	
Java	history	992	
	travel	919.2	
Jealousy	ethics	179	
Jeanne d'Arc French history		944	
Jefferson, T: presidency		973.4	
Jehovah	doctrinal theology	231	
Jelly fish	zoology	593	
Jeremiah	Bible	224	
Jeremy, Epistle of Bible		229	
Jersey iland	history	942	
	travel	914.2	
Jerusalem	history, ancient	933	
	travel	915.6	
	St John of, knights	929.7	
Jesters	customs	394	

Topics in blackface type ar subdivided in the Tables

Jests	English literature	827
Jesuit missions		266
Jesuits	religious orders	271
Jesus	Christology	232
society of	religious orders	271
Jet	economic geology	553
Jetties	engineering	627
Jewelry	customs	391
	fine arts	739
	manufacture	671
	toilet	646
Jewish architecture		722
calendar		529
filosofy		181
language		492
literature		892
religion		296
Jews, disabilities of		296
history, ancient		933
modern		296
restoration of		296
Job	Bible	223
Jockies	horse racing	798
Joel	Bible	224
John, king	English history	942.03
St	epistles	227
	gospel	226
	knights of	929.7
	Revelation of	228
Johnson, A.	presidency	973.8
Joinery	carpentry	694
Joint stock companies	law	347
Jokes	English humor	827
Jonah	Bible	224
Joshua	Bible	222
Journalism		**070**
Journalists	biografy	920
Journeys around the world		910.4
Judaism		296
vs Christian church		239
Jude, epistle of	Bible	227
Judea	antiquities	913.33
history, ancient		933
modern		956
Judges, book of	Bible	222
law courts		347
lives		923
Judgment, private	eccles. polity	262
psychology		153
theology		236
Judicial chemistry	law	340
control	administration	351

Judiciary, electiv	law	347
Judith	Bible	229
Juggernaut		299
Jugglery		791
Jugoslavia	history	949.7
	travel	914.97
Julian calendar		529
Junior colleges		**378**
Junius letters	Eng. satire	827
Jupiter	astronomy	523.4
	mythology	292
Jurassic age	geology	551
Jurisdiction	civil trials	347
Jurisprudence		**340**
Jurists, *see* Lawyers		
Jury trial	law	340
Justis	ethics	179
department	U. S. gov't	353
Justises of the peace	law	347
Justification	doctrinal theology	234
Jute	agriculture	633
	manufactures	677
Juvenil books	reading and aids	028.5
class special with subject		
courts		364
criminals	law	343
mortality	public helth	614.1
reformatories		364
Kabala	Jewish filosofy	181
Kafirs	history	968
Kaleidoscope	optics	535
Kalendar		529
Kalifs	Mohammedanism	297
Kalmucks	description	915
	history	950
Kamchatka	history	957
Kamerun, Africa	hist.	967
Kangaroo	zoology	599
Kansas, U. S.	history	978.1
	travel	917.81
struggle in	U. S. hist.	973.6
Kant	German filosofy	193
Keltic antiquities		913.36
Druids	religion	299
history, ancient		936
languages		491.6
Kelts	ancient history	936
Kempis, Thomas à		242
Kentucky, U. S.	history	976.9
	travel	917.69
Kenya colony, Africa	history	967

Topics in blackface type ar subdivided in the Tables

Keramics	art	738
	chemic technology	666
Kerosene	" "	665
	inspection, protec. of life	614.8
Keys and locks	manufactures	683
	mathematical student honor	371.8
Khiva	travel	915.8
Kidnapping	criminal law	343
Kindergarten	education	372.2
Kindness	ethics	177
Kinematics	physics	531
Kinetic theory of gases		533
Kinetics	physics	531
Kinetograf	fotografy	778
Kinetoscope	"	778
King Philip's war	N. E. history	974
	U. S. "	973.2
King's daughters		267
	bench	347
Kings, book of	Bible	222
	lives	923
	political science	321
Kinship	genealogy	929
Kissing	customs	392
Kitchen economy		643
	gardening	635
	middens archeology	571
Kitchens	architecture	728
	dom. econ.	643
Kite flying	sports	796
Kleptomania	mental disease	132
Klondike, Can.	hist.	971.21
Knightage	heraldry	929.7
Knighthood	chivalry	394
Knights hospitalers		929.7
of labor	labor unions	331.88
Malta		929.7
Pythias	secret societies	366
Rhodes		929.7
St John		929.7
Templars		929.7
	masons	366
Knitting	domestic economy	646
Knives	cutlery	672
	stone	571
Know-nothing party	U. S. politics	329
Knowledge	metaphysics	121
Kodaks	fotografy	771
Kongo, Africa	hist.	967
Koordistan	travel	915.6
Koran	Mohammedanism	297
Krishna	Buddhism	294

Kroatian language		491.8
Ku Klux Klan	political ass'ns	363
Kurdish language		491
Kurdistan	travels	915.6
Kurile ilands	travel	915.2
Labels in museums	biology	579
	museum econ.	069
Labor laws		331
	obstetrics	618
	of children	331.3
	party polit. parties	329
	political economy	**331**
Laborsavers, literary		029
Laboratories	architecture	727
	biologic	570
	chemic	542
	school equipment	371.6
	state adulterations	614.3
Laboratory work	educ. methods	371.3
Laborers cottages	architecture	728
	occupation hygiene	613
Laboring classes	**political econ.**	**331.8**
Labrador	history	971.9
Labyrinths	prehistoric archeol.	571
Lace-making	art needlework	746
	textil manufactures	677
Lacker work	artistic furniture	749
	manufactures	667
Laconics	English literature	828
Lacquer work	artistic furniture	749
	manufactures	667
Lacrosse	games	796
Lactometer	public helth	614.3
Ladrone ilands	history	996
Laissez faire	pol. econ.	330
Lake drainage		627
	dwellings prehistoric arch.	571
	states, U. S. history	**977**
	travel	**917.7**
Lakes, artificial	landscape gard.	714
	physical geografy	551
	water supply	628
Lamaism		294
Lambertypes		773
Lamellibranchiata	zoology	594
Lamentations	Bible	224
Lampoons	English satire	827
Lampreys	fishes	597
Lamps	chemic technology	665
	elec. lighting	621.3
Lancaster and York	Eng. hist.	942.04

Topics in blackface type ar subdivided in the Tables

Lancaster system   education   371.4
Land   law   347
            political economy   333
            public domain   336
            surveying   526
    slides   geology   551
    titles   insurance   368
Landed gentry   heraldry   929.7
Landlord and tenant   law   347
                    polit. econ.   333
Landscape   drawing   741
                fotografs   779
                gardening   710
                natural   719
                painting   758
                sketching   741
Landtag   German central gov't   354
                    local   "   352
Language   400
            lessons   elemen. educ.   372
            of flowers   716
            sign   def and dum   371.9
                    hieroglyfics   419
            universal   408
Lantern, astronomic   523.8
        magic   optics   535
        slides   education   371.3
Lapland, Russia   history   947
La Plata   travel   918.2
Larceny   law   343
Lard   adulterations   614.3
            chemic technology   664
Larva   embryology   591
Laryngoscope   616
Laryngotomy   surgery   617
Larynx   acoustics   534
                anatomy   611
Last supper   sacraments   265
Late hours   hygiene   613.7
Lath   plastering   693
Lathe work   mecan. engin'g   621
Latin antiquities   913.37
        biografy   920
        church   282
        classics   870
        epic poetry   873
        erotica   874
        geografy   912
        hymns   hymnology   245
        inscriptions   471
        language   470
        literature   870

Latin lyric poetry   874
        medieval and modern   479
        mythology   292
        union   332
Latitude at sea   navigation   527
            determinations   geodesy   526
            finding   525
Latium   ancient history   937
                modern   "   945
Latter-day saints   Mormonism   289
Laughing gas   anesthetics   615
Laughter   emotions   157
                hysteria   616
Laundry   domestic economy   648
Lava   lithology   552
Lavatories   school furniture   371.6
Law   340
        addresses   347
        and miracles   theology   231
            order leags   temperance   178
        making   pol. sci.   328
        moral   ethics   170
        of nations   341
            nature   science   501
                    sociology   340
        parish   ecclesiastic polity   262
        parliamentary   328
        reports, American   345
                English   346
        Sunday   263
        class special with subject
Lawn games   796
Lawns   712
Laws, bilding   bilding   692
                protection of life   614.8
        conflict of   341
        medical practis   614.2
        of language   Eng. etymology   422
Lawyers   ethics   174
                lives   923
Laying out of
        towns and streets   city planning 711
                        engin'g   625
                        public helth   614.7
Lazarettos   contagious diseases   614.4
                hospitals   362.1
Lead, see Led
Leading cases, American law   345
                English   "   346
        class special with subject
Leading   glazing   698
Leag of nations   341

Topics in blackface type ar subdivided in the Tables

Leags, law and order	temperance	178	
Learned societies		060	
Learning	psychology	154	
Leases	law	347	
Leather manufacture		675	
	stampt bilding	698	
Leaves	botany	581	
Lecompton constitution	Kan. hist.	978.1	
	U. S. "	973.6	
Lectern	sacred furniture	247	
Lectionary	Anglican ritual	264	
Lectures, Amer. oratory		815	
	halls for architecture	725	
	instruction methods	371.3	
	library	021	
	popular education	374.5	
	class special with subject		
Led, black	economic geology	553	
	chemistry	546	
	manufacture	671	
	metallurgy	669	
	mining	622	
	ores economic geology	553	
	poisoning toxicology	615	
	roofs bilding	695	
	water pipes	628	
Leding	glazing	698	
Leeches	culture	639	
	medicin	616	
	zoology	595	
Legacies	law	347	
	taxation	336.2	
Legal anecdotes		340	
	bibliografy	016.3	
	capacity of persons law	347	
	education	340	
	ethics	174	
	hermeneutics	347	
	status of women	396	
	tender paper money	332	
Legends	folklore	398.2	
	monastic	271	
	mythology	291	
	of the Madonna	232	
Legerdemain		791	
Legislation	American statutes	345	
	British "	346	
	comparativ	340	
	industrial	338	
	library, founding of libs.	021.8	
	sumptuary ethics	177	
	class special with subject		
Legislativ bodies and annals		328	
Legitimacy	family law	347	
Legs, artificial	surgery	617	
Leinster, Ireland	history	941.8	
	travel	914.18	
Lemons	agriculture	634	
Lenses	fotografy	771	
	optics	535	
Lent	church fast	264	
Lenten mass	music	783	
Lepidoptera	zoology	595.7	
Lether manufacture		675	
	stampt bilding	698	
Lettering, ornamental		745	
Letters	American literature	816	
	English alfabet	421	
	literature	826	
	other "	836, 846, etc.	
	patent patents	608	
	on special topic, class with subject		
Letterwriting		808	
Lettic languages		491	
Lettish "		491	
Levant	history	956	
	travel	915.6	
Levees	canal engineering	627	
Leveling	geodesy	526	
Lever	mechanics	531	
Levitation	spiritism	133	
Leviticus	Bible	222	
Lex mercatoria	law	347	
Lexicografy, comparativ		413	
	English language	423	
Lexicons, see special language			
	on special topics, see subject		
Liability insurance	business	368	
	pol. econ.	331.2	
	to military servis	355.2	
Libel	law	347	
Liberal Christianity	rationalism	211	
	unitarianism	288	
Liberality	ethics	179	
Liberia	history	966	
Liberty	ecclesiastic polity	262	
	metaphysics	123	
	civil law	347	
	political science	323	
	of conscience eccles. pol.	262	
	press	323	
	wil psychology	159	
	personal doctrin	233	
	law	347	

Topics in blackface type ar subdivided in the Tables

Liberty personal	pol. science	323	
	salvation	234	
religious	church	261	
	state ethics	172	
Librarian, duties, etc.		023	
Librarians	biografy	920	
Libraries	**history**	027	
	lib. economy	020	
for work'g class	pol. econ.	331.8	
	lib. "	027.6	
imaginary	book rarities	098	
parochial	library econ.	027.8	
	parish work	257	
school	education	371.6	
	library economy	027.8	
special	" "	026	
	polygrafy	080	
Sunday opening, lib. econ.		024	
	theology	263	
in sense of series, see subject			
Library	**administration**	025	
	bildings	022	
	architecture	727	
	catalogs	017–019	
	economy	020	
	gov't and servis	023	
	legislation	lib. econ.	021.8
	rules	024	
	schools	020.7	
Librettos	opera	782	
License	local government	352	
Licenses	public helth	614.2	
	taxation	336.2	
	temperance	178	
maritime	commerce	387	
Lichens	botany	589	
Licinian laws	pol. econ.	333	
	Roman hist.	937	
Lien laws		347	
Life	**biology**	**570**	
	ethics	179	
	ontology	111	
conditions of	biology	577	
contingencies	probabilities	519	
elixir of	alchemy	540.1	
future	doctrinal theology	237	
	natural "	218	
insurance		368	
	probabilities	519	
protection of, from accidents		614.8	
saving servis	protect. of life	614.8	
	transport	656	
Life tables	life insurance	368	
Light	optics	535	
	therapeutics	615	
and air	hygiene	613	
effect on	plants	581	
electric	engineering	621.3	
	physics	537	
infantry	military science	356	
of earth		525	
moon, stars and sun		**523**	
zodiacal	astronomy	523	
Lighthouses	engineering	627	
	navigation	656	
	optics	535	
	protec. of life	614.8	
Lighting	engineering	628	
decorativ	fine arts	745	
electric	engineering	621.3	
	physics	537	
library bildings		022	
mediums	chem. tech.	665	
Lightning and lightning rods		537	
shock	surgery	617	
Lights	chemic technology	665	
	ecclesiology	246	
and fuel	domestic economy	644	
shades	drawing	742	
	perspectiv	515	
Lignite	economic geology	553	
Lima, Peru	history	985	
	travel	918.5	
Limbo	escatology	236	
Limbs, artificial	surgery	617	
Limbus	escatology	236	
Limes	bilding material	691	
	chemic technology	666	
	economic geology	553	
Limestone	" "	553	
	lithology	552	
Limited editions		094	
Lims, artificial	surgery	617	
Lincoln, A.	presidency	973.7	
Lincrusta	paperhanging	698	
Line engraving		765	
Linear perspectiv		515	
Linen manufacture		677	
Lines	analytic geometry	516	
	descriptiv "	515	
	geometry	513	
Linguistics		**400**	
Linguists' lives		924	
Linnaean system	botany	580	

Topics in blackface type ar subdivided in the Tables

Linnaean system	zoology	590
Linoleum	manufactures	677
Lions	zoology	599
Lip reading	education	371.9
Liquefaction	heat	536
Liquid air	physics	533
wastes	sanitary engin'g	628
Liquids	physics	532
Liquor laws	temperance	178
Liquors	manufacture	663
	taxation	336.2
	temperance	178
Lisbon	history	946.9
	travel	914.69
Litanies	sacred music	783
Litany	church servis	264
Literary addresses		804
class special with topic		
clubs self education		374.2
criticism, art of		801
class special with subject criticized		
esthetics		801
frauds and forgeries		809
history		809
institutions colleges		**378**
men biografy		928
methods library econ.		029
miscellanies, English		828
occupations hygiene		613
periodicals		805
property law		347
publishing		655
societies student life		371.8
style rhetoric		808
Literature		**800**
bibliografy of		016.8
biografy of		928
classic, Greek & Latin		**880**
immoral ethics		176
lib. econ.		025.2
woman delineated in		396
Lithografy	engraving	763
Lithology	geology	552
Lithozincografy		767
Lithuania	history	947
Lithuanian language		491
Liturgies		264
Live stock	**agriculture**	**636**
	insurance	368
Liverworts	botany	588
Lives	Amer. Indians	970.2
	biografy	**920**
Lives	gipsies	397
	slaves	326
Living, cost of	dom. econ.	647
Living matter, properties of		577
Livonian language		494
Lizards	reptils	598.1
Loadstone	economic geology	553
	magnetism	538
Loan institutes	polit. economy	332
systems	library "	025.6
Loango, Africa	travel	916.7
Loans	private finance	332
	public "	336.3
of books	library economy	024
Lobsters	fisheries	639
	zoology	595
Local government	administration	352
histories, see name of place		
option		178
taxes	public finance	336.2
	schools	379.1
Location of library bildings		022
Locke, J.	English filosofy	192
Locks	canal engineering	626
	manufacture	683
Locomotion	communication	656
	physiology	612
animal	comp. anat.	591
Locomotivs	steam engineering	621.1
Locusts	economic zoology	591
	entomology	595.7
	pests	632
Lodestone	economic geology	553
	magnetism	538
Lodging houses for poor		362.5
Log book	seamanship	656
Logarithms		510
Logging	timber trade	674
Logic		**160**
Logical catalogs		017
machines		164
Logos	Christology	232
Lollards	religious sect	289
Lombard street	banking	332
London, England	history	942.1
	travel	914.21
Longevity	life insurance	368
	physiology	612
	probabilities	519
	statistics	312
Longitude at sea	navigation	527
determinations	geodesy	526

Topics in blackface type ar subdivided in the Tables

Longitude, methods of finding		525
theoretic astronomy		521
Loo-choo ilands travel		915.2
Loom, power manufactures		677
Lord chancellors biografy		923
Lord's day		263
prayer		226
supper sacraments		265
Lost books book rarities		098
library economy		024
Lotteries ethics		174
Lotus Egyptian religion		299
Louisiana, U. S. history		976.3
travel		917.63
purchase U. S. hist.		973.4
Louvre gallery fine arts		708
Love ethics		177
feasts pub. worship		264
of God theology		231
Low Countries history		949.2
Dutch language		439
German literature		839
Latin language		479
literature		879
Lower empire Byzantine		949.5
Guinea, Africa hist.		967
Loyalty state ethics		172
Lubrication mecan. engin'g		621
Lucretius ancient filosofy		187
Latin poetry		871
Luke gospel		226
Lumber bilding material		691
manufacture		674
Lunacy law		347
psychology		132
Lunar caustic therapeutics		615
tables		523
Lunatic asylums		362.2
Lungs anatomy		611
diseases of		616
functions of physiol.		612
Luray caverns description		551
Lusitania (Portugal) history		946.9
Luster ware pottery		738
Lute stringd instruments		787
Lutheran church		284
confession creeds		238
Lutherans biografy		922
Luxury economics		339
hygiene		613
Lycanthropy insanity		132
Lyceum Greek filosofy		185
Lyceums self education		374.2
Lycopodinae botany		587
Lyddite chem. tech.		662
Lying ethics		177
Lying-in hospitals		362.1
Lynch law		343
Lyric poetry, Greek		884
Latin		874
Mabinogion Welsh literature		891.6
Macaronics English literature		827
Maccabees Bible		229
Macedonia Greek hist.		938
Machine engraving		768
guns military engin'g		623
Machinery engineering		**621**
farm		631
in industry pol. econ.		338
Machines hydraulics		532
mecanics		531
Mackerel fishery		639
McKinley, W. presidency		973.8
Madagascar geology		556.9
history		969
religious history		276.9
travel		916.9
Madeira ilands history		946.9
Madhouses		362.2
Madison, J. presidency		973.5
Madness psychology		132
Madonna in art		709
painting		755
legends of		232
mariolatry		232
Madrid travel		914.6
Madrigal music		784
Magazines general periodicals		**050**
literary		805
class special with subject		
Magellan straits travels		918.2
Magic lanterns optics		535
natural occultism		133
Magicians lives		920
Magistrates law		347
Magna charta constitutional history		342
English history		942.03
Magnetism		538
animal psychology		134
Magneto-dynamos electricity		537
Magnets, properties of		538
Magnifiers optics		535
Magyar language		494

Topics in blackface type ar subdivided in the Tables

Magyars	history	943.9
Mahabharata	Sanskrit literature	891
Mahometanism		297
Mails	postoffis	383
Maine, U. S.	history	974.1
	travel	917.41
law	temperance	178
ship	Span. war	973.8
Maize	agriculture	633
Majolica	pottery	738
Majorca	history	946
Malabar	"	954
Malacca	"	959
Malachi	Bible	224
Malacology		594
Malacostraca	zoology	595
Malaria	hygiene	613
Malarious soils	public helth	614.7
Malay archipelago	**history**	**991**
	travel	919.1
	Polynesian languages	499
	literatures	899
Malaysia	**geology**	**559.1**
	history	**991**
	religious history	**279.1**
	travel	**919.1**
Malformations, animal	comp. anat.	591
human	deformities	617
	somatology	573
vegetable	botany	581
Malleability	molecular physics	539
Malpractis	law	343
	public helth	614.2
Malt liquors	brewing	663
Malta	history	945
knights of		929.7
Malthusianism	population	312
Mamelukes	Egyptian history	962
Mammalia	paleontology	569
	zoology	599
Mammoth	paleontology	569
	zoology	599
cave	physical geografy	551
Man	anatomy	611
	doctrinal theology	233
	ethnografy	572
	mammals	599
	mental caracteristics	**136**
	physiology	612
	psychology	**150**
antiquity of	prehist. arch.	571
	nat. hist. of man	573
Man in the iron mask	biografy	92
Isle of	history	942
origin of	evolution	575
	nat. hist. of man	573
	natural theology	213
Management	**library economy**	**025**
	of state properties	336
Manasses, prayer of	Apocryfa	229
Mandolin	stringd instruments	787
Manganese ores	economic geology	553
Mania	psychology	132
Maniacs	lives	920
Manicheism	heresies	273
Manifolding	writing	652
Manipulation	practical chemistry	542
Manitoba, Canada	history	971.27
Manly exercises	**outdoor sports**	**796**
Manners and customs		**390**
	for local, see special countries	
Manometer	pneumatics	533
Manor houses	architecture	728
Manors	political economy	333
Mansions	architecture	728
Manslaughter	law	343
Mantels	fixt furniture	729
Manual training	education	371.4
Manuals, business	commerce	658
collectors'	biology	579
legislativ		328
class special with subject		
Manufactories	architecture	725
Manufactures		**670**
	chem. technology	**660**
	production	338
	public helth	614.7
Manufacturing works	engineering	621
Manures	agriculture	631
	sewage	628
Manuscripts	Bible	220.4
	book rarities	091
	copyright	655
	diplomatics	417
	Latin diplomatics	471
Manx language		491.6
Map cases	library admin.	025.8
drawing in schools		910.7
projection	geodesy	526
Maps		912
astronomic, general		524
moon, planets, star, or sun		**523**
school apparatus		371.6
Marathi language		491

Topics in blackface type ar subdivided in the Tables

Marble	economic geology	553		Mary, virgin	biografy	232
	inscriptions	417			R. cath. doctrin	232
	Greek	481		Maryland, U. S.	history	975.2
	Latin	471			travel	917.52
	lithology	552		Mashonaland, Africa	history	968
	quarrying	622		Masks	dramatic music	782
	sculpture	731		Mason and Dixon's line	slavery	326
	working bilding	693		Masonry	bilding	693
Marian persecutions in England		272		anti	secret societies	366
Marine animals		591.9		Masons " "		366
	architecture naval engin'g	623.8		Masquerades	amusements	793
	corps navy	359			social customs	394
	engins	621.1		Mass	Rom. catholic ritual	264
	insurance	368			law of gravity	531
	law	347			of earth	525
	plants	581.9			recitative music	784
Mariners compass	magnetism	538			sacred "	783
	occupation hygiene	613		Massachusetts, U. S.	history	974.4
Mariolatry	worship of Virgin	232			travel	917.44
Marionets	amusements	791		Massage	therapeutics	615
Maritime affairs	naval science	359		Master and servant	family ethics	173
	discovery	910.4			law	347
	law	347		Mastersingers	German poetry	831
	surveying	526		Mastodon	paleontology	569
Mark	gospel	226		Matamoras	history	972
Market gardening	agriculture	635		Matches	chemic technology	662
Markets	architecture	725		Materia medica		615
	domestic economy	641		Materialism	filosofy	146
Marking system	education	371.2		Materials	bilding	691
Marks	political science	321			library bookbinding	025.7
Marl	lithology	552		for clothing	dom. econ.	646
Maronites	sects	281			hygiene	613
Maroons	history of Jamaica	972.9		strength of	engin'g	620.1
Marprelate controversy		285			physics	539
Marque and reprisal	intern. law	341		Maternity	ethics	173
Marquetry	artistic furniture	749			hospitals	362.1
	cabinet work	684			medicin	618
Marriage	customs	392		Mathematical	drawing	744
	ethics	173			instruments	510
	law	347			probabilities	519
	registers genealogy	929			tables	510
	registration pub. helth	614.1			theory of music	781
	sacrament	265			tides	525
Mars	planets	523.4		Mathematicians' lives		925
	seasons astronomy	525		**Mathematics**		**510**
Marshes	physical geology	551		Matins	church ritual	264
	hygiene of public helth	614.7		Matriculation	schools	371.2
Marsupialia	mammals	599		Matter	metaphysics	117
Martial law		344			physical chemistry	541
Martinique	history	972.9			**physics**	**530**
Martyrs	persecutions	272			properties of living	577
Mary, queen of Eng.	Eng. hist.	942.05		Matthew	gospel	226

Topics in blackface type ar subdivided in the Tables

Mauritius	geology		556.9
	history		969
	religious history		276.9
	travel		916.9
Mausoleums			718
Maxima and minima	algebra		512
	calculus		517
	geometry		513
Maxims	English literature		828
	law		340
class special with subject			
Maya architecture			722
civilization	antiq.		913.7
language			497
Mayor	local gov't		352
Mazurka	piano music		786
Meals	domestic economy		642
Mean time	solar and sidereal day		529
value	probabilities		519
Measles	diseases		616
	public helth		614.5
Measurements, etc. see Mesurements, etc.			
Meat	domestic economy		641
as food	hygiene		613.2
inspection	pub. helth		614.3
preservation	chem. tech.		664
supply	production		338
Mecanic arts and trades			**680**
Mecanical drawing			744
engineering			**621**
equivalent	heat		536
musical instruments			789
remedies	therapeu.		615
training			607
in schools			371.4
Mecanics	physics		531
applied			620.1
institutes	exhibitions		606
liens	law		347
lives			926
Medallions	numismatics		737
Medals	carving		736
numismatics			737
Media	ancient history		935
Medical analysis	chemistry		543
biografy			926
botany	econ. botany		581
	materia med.		615
diagnosis			616
education			610
state control of			614.2
electricity	physics		537
Medical electricity	therapeutics		615
ethics			174
jurisprudence			340
museums			610
police			614.2
practis	pathology		616
	state control of		614.2
schools			610
societies			610
testimony			614.2
zoology			591
Medicin			**610**
preventiv	**pub. helth**		**614**
Medicinal			
use of stimulants	temperance		178
Medicins	therapeutics		615
patent	public helth		614.3
Medico-legal relations			614.2
Medieval architecture			723
art, history of			709
customs and costumes			**390**
designs			745
Europe	history		940.1
filosofy			189
Latin			479
literature			**800**
science			502
sculpture			734
Meditations	theology		242
Mediterranean sea	physical geology		551
travel			910.4
Mediums	spiritism		133
Medo-Persia	ancient history		935
antiquities			913.35
Medusae	zoology		593
Meekness	ethics		179
Meerschaum	econ. geol.		553
Megaric filosofy			183
Megatherium	paleontology		569
Melancholy	psychology		132
Melanesia	history		993
travel			919.3
Melbourne	history		994
travel			919.4
Meliorism	filosofic systems		149
Melodeon	music		786
Melody	theory of music		781
Melons	agriculture		635
Memoirs	**biografy**		**920**
scientific societies			506
Memorial day	school observ.		371.3
	U. S. civil war		973.7

Topics in blackface type ar subdivided in the Tables

Memorial sermons biografy	920	
sermons	252	
Memory mental derangements	132	
psychology	154	
in animals zoology	591.5	
Menageries amusements	791	
zoology	590	
Mendelism botany	581	
Mendicant orders	271	
Mennonite church	289	
Mensuration arithmetic	511	
surveying	526	
Mental		
capacity psychology	151	
of women education	376	
psychology	136	
caracteristics	136	
derangements medicin	616	
psychology	132	
development childstudy	136.7	
education	370	
disability, inherited hygiene	613.9	
faculties	150	
of animals zoology	591.5	
filosofy	150	
fotografs	139	
healing	615	
heredity psychology	136	
physiology and hygiene	131	
Mercantil law	347	
libraries	027.2–.3	
rules arithmetic	511	
theory and practis	658	
Merchant servis sociology	387	
Merchants business ethics	174	
lives	923	
Mercury chemistry	546	
materia medica	615	
metallurgy	669	
planets	523.4	
poisons	615	
ores economic geol.	553	
Meridian line astronomy	522	
Meridional instruments	522	
Mermaids folklore	398.4	
Mesmerism psychology	134	
Messenger servis	385	
Messiah doctrinal theology	232	
Mesurements, electric	537	
practical chemistry	542	
Mesures and weights metrology	389	
Mesuring surveying	526	

Mesuring instruments metrology	389	
physics	530	
of angles crystallografy	548	
heat	536	
light optics	535	
Metafors rhetoric	808	
Metallic ores econ. geol.	553	
poisons therapeutics	615	
tractors cures	615	
Metallurgy	669	
Metals bilding materials	691	
coinage	332	
history	669	
inorganic chemistry	546	
manufactures	**671**	
mining	622	
organic chemistry	547	
transmutation of	540.1	
Metalwork, artistic	739	
Metalworking tools mach.	621	
Metamorfic rocks geology	552	
Metamorfism physical geology	551	
Metamorfosis botany	581	
of insects	595.7	
zoology	591	
Metaphors rhetoric	808	
Metaphysics	**110**	
Metempsychosis metaphysics	129	
Meteoric showers astronomy	523	
Meteorites lithology	552	
Meteorology	551.5	
natural history of man	573	
Meteors astronomy	523	
Meter weights and mesures	389	
Meters Eng. prosody	426	
water	628	
Method of least squares orbits	521	
probabil.	519	
Methodist church	287	
episcopal church	287	
Methodists biografy	922	
Methodology metaphysics	112	
Methods, business	658	
literary lib. econ.	029	
of education	**371**	
statistics	311	
class special with subject		
Metric system internat'l mesures	389	
Metrology	389	
Mexican Indians	970.1	
war U. S. history	973.6	
Mexico antiquities	913.7	

Topics in blackface type ar subdivided in the Tables

Mexico	fauna	591.9	Military history		355
	flora	581.9		Amer. civil war	973.7
	geology	557.2	of special countries, see country
	history	972	hygiene		613
	religious history	277.2	law		355
	travel	917.2	organization in schools		371.4
Mezzotint		766	pensions		351
Mica	economic geology	553	religious orders		929.7
Micah	Bible	224	**science**		**355**
Michigan, U. S.	history	977.4	signals		623
	travel	917.74	Militia		355.2
Microbes	botany	589	Milk analysis	adulterations	614.3
	etiology of disease	616		chemistry	543
Microfone	physics	537	dairy		637
Microfotografy	fotografy	778	products	adulterations	614.3
	microscopy	578	Mill, see Mil
Micrometers	astronomy	522	Millennium	theology	236
Micronesia	history	996	Millerites		286
Micro-organisms	theory of disease	616	Millinery	clothing	646
Microphotografy	fotografy	778		trades	687
	microscopy	578	Milling tools		621
Microscopes		578	Mils and manuf. works	engineering	621
	optics	535	architecture		725
Microscopic analysis of water		613	**manufactures**		**670**
	life **invertebrates**	**592**	Milwaukee, Wis.	history	977.5
Microscopy		578		travel	917.75
	animal histology	591	Mimeograf	offis fittings	652
	lithology	552	Mimetic arts		792
	study of disease	616	Mimicry	social ethics	177
	vegetable histology	581	**Mind**	**psychology**	**150**
Microspermeae	botany	584	**and body**		**130**
Microtome	microscopy	578	cure	therapeutics	615
Middens and privies	scavenging	628	in animals	zoology	591.5
	kitchen prehist. arch.	571	readers	biografy	920
Middle ages	European history	940.1	reading	mesmerism	134
	high German language	437	Mineral cements	chem. technology	666
	poetry	831		economic geology	553
	states, U. S. history	**974**	oils	chemic technology	665
Middleman	pol. econ.	331.2		economic geology	553
Middlesex, England	history	942.1	springs	" "	553
Migrations of animals		591.5	surveys		622
	men ethnology	572	veins	ore deposits	553
Mil dams	hydraulic eng.	627	waters	adulterations	614.3
	water engins	621.2		chem. tech.	663
work	engineering	621		economic geology	553
Mildew	agriculture	632		hygiene	613
	botany	589		therapeutics	615
	domestic econ.	648	Mineralogy		549
Military academies, e. g. West Point		355	Minerals	rock determination	552
	and naval arts	**355**	Mines	military engineering	623
	biografy	923		mining	622
	engineering	623		ownership pol. econ.	333

Topics in blackface type ar subdivided in the Tables

Minature books		099
Miniatures	painting	757
Minima and maxima	algebra	512
	calculus	517
	geometry	513
Mining	engineering	622
products	political economy	338
Minister	eccles. polity	262
Ministerial work	**religion**	**250**
Ministers	foren government	354
	lives	922
	U. S. government	353
Ministration to sick and ded		265
Ministries	architecture	725
Ministry	ecclesiastic polity	262
	religion	**250**
Minnesingers	German poetry	831
Minnesota, U. S.	history	977.6
	travel	917.76
Minorca	history	946
Minors	law	347
Minstrelsy	English poetry	821
negro	vocal music	784
Mints	political economy	332
Minute books	curiosa	099
Miocene period	geology	551
Miracle plays	Eng. literature	822
	general history	809
	religion	244
	theater	792
Miracles	doctrins	231
	New Testament	226
	post-biblical	231
Mirage	optics	535
Mirrors	"	535
Miscegenation	ethics	173
	hygiene	613.9
	law	347
Miscellanies, see subjects		
Miscellany	American literature	818
	English "	828
	other " 838, 848, etc.	
Misers	biografy	920
Mishna	Judaism	296
Missals	illuminated	096
	Rom. catholic ritual	264
Missing link	origin of species	575
Missionaries	biografy	922
Missionary schools		377
Missions		266
parish		269
Mississippi, U. S.	history	976.2
Mississippi, U. S.	travel	917.62
	bubble loan institutes	332
	river description	917.7
	valley "	917.7
Missouri, U. S.	history	977.8
	travel	917.78
river	description	917.78
Miter	sacred ornaments	247
Mites	zoology	595
Mithraic worship		295
Mixt drinks	adulterations	614.3
	chemic tech.	663
Mnemonic derangements		132
Mnemonics		154
Moabite stone		492
Modeling	elem. educ.	372
	sculpture	731
Models	art study	707
Modern architecture		724
	costumes and customs	390
	filosofers	**190**
	lives	921
	Greek language	489
	literature	889
	history	**940–999**
	literature	**800**
	sculpture	735
Modesty	ethics	179
Moguls	Indian history	954
Mohammedan architecture		723
Mohammedanism		297
Moisture	hygiene	613
	physical geografy	551.5
	soil public helth	614.7
	therapeutics	615
Molasses	chemic technology	664
Mold	fungi	589
Moldavia, Rumania	history	949.8
	travel	914.98
Moldings	architecture	729
Molecular physics		539
Molecules	theoretic chemistry	541
Moles	zoology	599
Molinists	heresies	273
	persecutions	272
Mollusca	paleontology	564
	zoology	594
Molluscoidea		594
Mollusks	fishery	639
Moluccas	history	991
Moments	statics	531
Monachism	theology	271

Topics in blackface type ar subdivided in the Tables

Monaco	history	944
Monarch	foren governments	354
Monarchs	biografy	923
Monarchy		321
Monasteries	architecture	726
	theology	271
Monastic orders	"	271
schools	education	377
Monasticism		271
Monetary congresses		332
Money		332
making	commerce	658
	ethics	174
Mongolian languages		495
Mongols	**history**	**950**
Monism	filosofy	147
Monitorial system of education		371.4
Monitors, iron clads	naval engin'g	623.8
school government		371.5
Monkeys	zoology	599
Monks	relig. orders	271
Monocotyledones	botany	584
Monogamy	family ethics	173
	hygiene	613
Monograms	design	745
Monoliths	prehistoric arch.	571
Monomania	insanity	132
Monopolies		338
	state	336
Monotremata	mammals	599
Monroe, J.	presidency	973.5
doctrin	foren relations	327
Monsoons	meteorology	551.5
Monsters, fabulous		398.4
Monstrosities	nat. hist. of man	573
	animal	591
	vegetable	581
Mont Blanc	travel	914.4
Mont Cenis tunnel		625
Montana, U. S. history		978.6
	travel	917.86
Montanism	heresies	273
Montenegro	history	949.7
	travel	914.97
Months, names of		529
Montreal	history	971.4
	travel	917.1
Monts de piété	loan institutes	332
Monuments	**antiquities**	**913**
	cemeteries	718
	prehistoric	571
Moon	astronomy	523.3
Moon	effect on tides	525
Moorish architecture		723
Moot courts		340
Moraines	glaciers	551
Moral agency, free	theology	233
education		377
expectations	probabilities	519
filosofy		**170**
government in schools		371.5
heridity	doctrin	233
	metaphysics	129
sentiment	ethics	171
systems	"	171
Morals and church		261
history of	ethics	170
of laboring classes		331.8
the press		179
war	ethics	172.4
Moravia	history	943.7
Moravian brethren	sects	284
	language	491.8
Morbid anatomy		616
Morea	history	949.5
Moresnet	"	949.3
Morfology	animals	591
	comparativ filol.	415
	English language	425
	plants	581
Morganatic marriage	customs	392
	ethics	173
Mormonism		289
Morocco	geology	556.4
	history	964
	religious history	276.4
	travel	916.4
Morphin habit	ethics	178
Morphology, see Morfology		
Mortality, law of	insurance	368
	statistics	312
	public helth	614.1
Mortar	bilding material	691
Mortars	chemic technology	666
	ordnance	623
	prehistoric archeol.	571
Mortgages	law	347
Mortification	surgery	617
Mortmain	law	347
Mortuary bildings	architecture	726
	customs	393
	designs sacred ornaments	247
	statistics population	312
	registration	614.1

Topics in blackface type ar subdivided in the Tables

Mosaic law   Old Testament   222
      work   fine arts   747
Mosaics   arch. decoration   729
      floors and flooring   721
      religious ornaments   247
Moslems   297
Mosques   architecture   726
Mosquito shore, C. Amer.   hist.   972.8
Mosquitos   public helth   614.4
      zoology   595.7
Mosses   botany   588
      sea   "   589
Motet   sacred music   783
Mother   ethics   173
      maternity   618
      Goose   folk lore   398
      tung   elem. educ.   372
Mothers pensions   362.6
Moths   agric. pests   632
      domestic pests   648
      zoology   595.7
Motion, beginnings of   biology   576
      in medicin   massage   615
      laws of   astronomy   521
      metaphysics   116
      of earth   astronomy   525
      liquids   hydraulics   532
      plants   botany   581
      solar system   523
      perpetual   mechanics   531
      pictures, see Moving
Motor functions   psychology   158
      vehicles   629.2
Mottos   English literature   828
Mould   fungi   589
Mouldings   architecture   729
Mound bilders   prehistoric arch.   571
      U. S. history   973.1
Mounds   prehistoric arch.   571
Mountain railways   625
      resorts   hygiene   613
Mountaineering   hygiene   613.7
      sports   796
Mountains, attraction of   geodesy   526
      in moon   523.3
      physical geografy   551
Mounting specimens   579
Mourning   customs   393
Movables   chattels   347
Movement cure   615
Movements   psychology   158
      of plants   botany   581

Moving pictures   amusements   791
      education   371.3
      see also Fotoplays
Mowers   agriculture   631
Mozambique   history   967
Mucilage manufacture   668
Muck   agriculture   631
Mud construction   693
Mudie's circulating libraries   027.3
Muggletonians   sects   289
Muhammedans   297
Mulberry   agriculture   634
      silk culture   638
Mule   domestic animals   636.1
      zoology   599
Multiple stars   523.8
Multiplex telegrafs   elec. engin'g   621.3
Mummies   393
Municipal bonds   political econ.   332
      government   admin.   352
      law   "   350
      statutes   340
Municipalities   admin.   352
Munitions of war   military engin'g   623
Munster, Ireland   history   941.9
      travel   914.19
Mural decorations   architecture   729
Murder   criminal law   343
Muscle-reading   133
Muscular exercise   hygiene   613.7
      sense   physiology   612
      psychology   152
Museums and libraries   021
      architecture   727
      arrange. of spec.   biol.   579
      mus. ec.   069
      art   fine arts   708
      general   069
      medical   610
      school   371.6
      scientific   natural science   507
      Sunday opening   263
      class special with subject
Mushrooms   botany   589
      food   641
Music   **art**   **780**
      copyright   655
      ecclesiology   246
      public worship   264
      therapeutics   615
      box   mec. instruments   789
      halls   architecture   725

Topics in blackface type ar subdivided in the Tables

Musical form		781
instruments		780
	acoustics	534
sounds	"	534
Musicians	biografy	927
Muskets	manufacture	683
Mustelidae	zoology	599
Muster rolls		355
Mutilations of library books		024
	war customs	399
Mutiny	maritime law	347
Mutual aid societies	pol. economy	334
insurance	" "	334
Mycenae	ancient history	938
Mycology	botany	589
Myopia	eye diseases	617
Mysteries	occultism	133
Mystery plays	Eng. literature	822
	history	809
	religion	244
	theater	792
Mystic filosofers		189
Mysticism	filosofy	149
	heresies	273
Mystics	medieval	189
Mythology, comparativ		**291**
	German	293
	Greek and Roman	292
	Norse	293
Myths		**291**
Myxomycetes	botany	589
Nahum	Bible	224
Names of days and months		529
	persons and places	929
pen	bibliografy	014
Nantes, edict of	religious history	274
Napkins	customs	394
Naples, Italy	history	945
	travel	914.5
Napoleon, code	law	349
Napoleonic period	Europ. hist.	940.27
Narcotics, action of	hygiene	613
and stimulants	ethics	178
therapeutics		615
Narrativs, personal	Gt war, 1914–19	940.48
Nasmith societies		267
Natal, Africa	history	968
	travel	916.8
Natatores	birds	598
National aid to education		379.1
and state univer.		**378**

National and state univer., state educ.		379.1
banks		332
bibliografy		**015**
cemeteries		718
churches vs organic unity		261
conservation	pol. econ.	339
costumes		391
customs, special		**390**
det	public finance	336.3
flowers	heraldry	929.8
libraries		027.5
music		786
parks		719
politics		329
resources	conservation	339
school supervision		379.1
songs	music	784
Nations, law of	internat. law	341
leag of		341
origin of		901
rise of	Eur. hist.	940.1
Nativ Americans	political parties	329
Natural body	doctrinal theology	233
filosofy		**530**
gas	chem. technology	662
	economic geology	553
	heating	697
history,	Biblical	220.8
	biology	574
	collectors' manuals	579
	museums	507
	of countries	**508.3**
	man	573
	zoology	**590**
law		340
magic	occultism	133
religion		**210**
resources		333
science		**500**
	bibliografy of	016.5
	biografy of	925
selection	evolution	575
Naturalists	biografy	925
Naturalization		323.6
Nature	**metaphysics**	**113**
	science	**500**
law of	sociology	340
of being	metaphysics	111
printing		655
study	elem. educ.	372
	general	507
unity of	metaphysics	113

Topics in blackface type ar subdivided in the Tables

Nature, unity of science	501	
Nautic astronomy	527	
Naval architecture engin'g	623.8	
biografy	923	
engineering	623.8	
history	359	
Amer. civil war	973.7	
Great War 1914–19	940.45	
see also special countries		
hygiene	613	
men, lives of	923	
science	359	
Navarre history	946	
Navies	359	
Navigation astronomy	527	
useful arts	656	
laws	347	
signals communication	654	
Navigator ilands history	996	
Navigators biografy	923	
Navy administration	359	
department, U. S.	353	
Near sightedness medicin	617	
schools	371.7	
Nebraska, U. S. history	978.2	
travel	917.82	
Nebular hypothesis astronomy	523.1	
Nebulas "	523.8	
Necessity metaphysics	123	
Necrology **biografy**	**920**	
colleges	**378**	
Necromancers	133	
Needlework	746	
domestic economy	646	
Negro conditions in U. S.	325	
education	371.9	
race ethnology	572	
mentality	136	
nat. hist. of man	573	
political standing	324	
slavery	326	
songs music	784	
Nehemiah Bible	222	
Neighborhood gilds	367	
Nemean games Greek antiq.	913.38	
Néo-Grec architecture	724	
Neolithic age prehist. archeol.	571	
Neology rationalism	211	
Neoplatonism	186	
Neoplatonists apologetics	239	
Nepotism civil servis	351	
Neptune descriptiv astronomy	523.4	

Nervous functions of animals	591	
physiology	612	
prostration	616	
system, comp. anatomy	591	
human "	611	
Nestorian church	281	
Nests birds	598	
Netherlands history	949.2	
travel	914.92	
Nets for collectors biology	579	
Neuralgia diseases	616	
Neuroptera insects	595.7	
pests	632	
Neuroses diseases	616	
Neuters generation of animals	591	
Neutrality international law	341	
Nevada, U. S. history	979.3	
travel	917.93	
New Brunswick, Canada history	971.5	
church, Swedenborgian	289	
England geology	557.4	
history	**974**	
religious history	277.4	
travel	**917.4**	
France, Canada history	971.01	
travel	917.1	
Granada, S. A. *see* Colombia		
Guinea geology	559.5	
history	995	
religious history	279.5	
travel	919.5	
Hampshire, U. S. history	974.2	
travel	917.42	
Hebrides, Australasia history	993	
Holland, Australia "	994	
Jersey, U. S. history	974.9	
travel	917.49	
Jerusalem church	289	
Mexico, U. S. history	978.9	
travel	917.89	
Platonism	186	
Plymouth colony history	974.4	
South Wales "	994	
Sweden (Penn'a) "	974.8	
travel	917.48	
Testament	**225**	
Greek dialects	487	
thought	131	
year customs	394	
York, U. S. history	974.7	
travel	917.47	
Univ. of the State of	379.7	

Topics in blackface type ar subdivided in the Tables

New Zealand history 993
    relig. hist. 279.3
    travel 919.3
Newfoundland history 971.8
News rooms free 027.9
Newspaper cuttings preservation 029
Newspapers ethics 179
    journalism 070
Newt zoology 598.1
Ngami lake travel 916.8
Niagara Falls description 917.47
Nicaragua history 972.8
    travel 917.28
Nicene, Ante-, church 100–325 281
    councils religious history 270
    creed 238
    Post-, church 325–1054 281
Nicobar ilands history 992
Niello-work arch. decoration 729
Niger river description 916.6
Night soil air pollution 614.7
Nihilism filosofy 149
    socialism 335
Nile description 916.2
Nineveh ancient history 935
    cuneiform lang. 492
Nineteenth century Eur. history 940.28
Nirvana oriental filosofy 181
Nitrogen compounds air pollution 614.7
    fertilizers 631
Nitroglycerin chemic tech. 662
Nobel prizes 378.3
Nobility heraldry 929.7
    social classes 323
Nobles' lives 923
Nomads 397
Nomenclature, botany 580
    theoretic chemistry 541
Nominalism filosofy 149
Non-Christian religions 290
    and education 377
Non-Euclidean geometry 513
Nonconformists Eng. relig. hist. 274.2
    sects 283
Nonjurors Eng. relig. hist. 274.2
Normal schools 370.7
Norman architecture 723
    conquests Europ. hist. 940.1
Normandy, France French " 944
    Scand. " 948
Normans, England history 942.02
Norrland, Sweden " 948.8

Norrland, Sweden travel 914.88
Norse language 439
    literature 839
    mythology 293
Norsemen Scandinavian hist. 948
North Africa geology 556.1
    history 961
    religious history 276.1
    travel 916.1
America antiquities 913.7
    geografy 917
    geology 557
    history 970
    languages 497
    religious history 277
    scientific travels 508.7
    statistics 317
    travel 917
American Indian literature 897
Atlantic states, U. S. geology 557.4
    history 974
    relig. hist. 277.4
    travel 917.4
Carolina, U. S. history 975.6
    travel 917.56
Central Africa geology 556.6
    history 966
    relig. hist. 276.6
    travel 916.6
    states, U. S. geology 557.7
    history 977
    relig. hist. 277.7
    travel 917.7
Dakota, U. S. history 978.4
    travel 917.84
Eastern boundary U. S. hist. 973.5
    passage 919.8
    pole travel 919.8
    west boundary U. S. hist. 973.6
    passage travel 919.8
    territory, U. S. hist. 977
    travel 917.7
Northern lights aurora borealis 523
    mythology 293
Northmen **Scandinavian history** 948
    in America U. S. hist. 973.1
Northwest Territories, Can. hist. 971.2
    territory **U. S. hist.** 977
Norway botany 581.9
    geology 554.8
    history 948.1
    religious history 274.8

Topics in blackface type ar subdivided in the Tables

Norway travel	914.81
Norwegian language	439
literature	839
Romanesque arch.	723
Nosology medicin	616
Nostrums state control	614.2
Notaries public law	347
Notation, arithmetic	511
for book sizes	025.3
systems lib. classification	025.4
theoretic chemistry	541
Notebooks literary methods	029
Notes private finance	332
Notion psychology	153
Nouvelle France history	971.01
Nova Scotia "	971.6
Novel reading ethics	175
reading and aids	028
writing	808
Novelists biografy	928
Novels American literature	813
religious	244
Noxious materials air pollution	614.7
Noxiousness of animals	591
Nubia, Egypt history	962
travel	916.2
Nuisances law	347
public helth	614.7
Nullification in South Carolina	973.5
U. S. constitut. law	342
Number metaphysics	119
Numbering machines offis	652
printing	655
Numbers, book of Bible	222
shelf library econ.	025.8
theory of algebra	512
Numismatics	737
Nuns and nunneries	271.9
Nurseries day	362.7
Nursery domestic economy	649
food hygiene	613.2
lore folklore	398
Nurses physiologic zoology	591
training of	610
Nursing domestic economy	649
medicin	610
Nusairian religion	297
Nutriments physiology	612
Nutrition physiologic botany	581
zoology	591
physiology	612

Oases phys. geog.	551.5
Oaths ethics	179
legal	347
of allegiance pol. sci.	323.6
Obadiah Bible	224
Obedience doctrinal theology	234
Obelisks antiquities	913.32
monuments	718
Oberammergau passion play	792
Obituary addresses biografy	**920**
Object teaching education	372
Obligations social ethics	177
Obliquity of ecliptic to equator	525
Oboe musical instrument	788
Observation psychology	152
errors probabilities	519
Observations astronomy	524
auxiliary astron.	522
Observatories, astronomic	522
meteorologic	551.5
school apparatus	371.6
Observing powers education	372
Obsession occultism	133
Obstetrics	618
Occult sciences	133
Occultations and transits astron.	523
Occultism	133
Occupation, choice of	371.4
Occupations, injurious hygiene	613
mortality in pub. helth	614.1
special diseases from	616
Ocean exploration	910.4
fenomena	551
geografy maps	912
life zoology	591.9
mails	383
telegraf	654
tides	525
transport sociology	387
useful arts	656
travel	910.4
Oceania antiquities	913.9
geografy	**919**
geology	**559**
history	**990**
religious history	**279**
scientific travels	508.9
statistics	319
travel	**919**
Oceans physical geografy	551
Octateuch Bible	222

Topics in blackface type ar subdivided in the Tables

Odd Fellows secret societies		366
Odic force		134
Odontology, animal		591
human anat.		611
surgery		617
Œcumenic councils eccles. pol.		262
relig. hist.		270
Offensiv animals econ. zoology		591
materials public helth		614.7
Offertory alms		264
organ music		786
sacred music		783
Official functions civ. serv. offisers		351
register, U. S. civil servis		351
residences architecture		725
Oficleide music		788
Offis bildings architec.		725
equipment and methods		651
tenure of civil servis		351
training law education		340
Offisers, army and navy lives		923
duties of public ethics		172
Ofidia reptils		598.1
Ofthalmia eye diseases		617
Ofthalmoscope		617
Ohio, U. S. history		977.1
travel		917.71
valley **description**		**917.7**
Oil manufacture		665
coal economic geology		553
painting art		751
bilding		698
refining air pollution		614.7
Oilcloth manufactures		677
Oils adulteration		614.3
chemic technology		665
vegetable agriculture		633
Oklahoma, U. S. history		976.6
travel		917.66
Old Bactrian language		491
catholic church		284
Egyptian language		493
English "		427
French "		447
Norse "		439
literature		839
Prussian language		491
red sandstone geology		551
Saxon language		439
literature		839
Testament		**221**
Oleomargarin adulterations		614.3

Oleomargarin chemic technol.		664
Oleron, laws of admiralty		347
Olfaction physiology		612
psychology		152
Oligarchy political science		321
Oliv oil chemic technology		665
Olivs agriculture		634
Olympiads cronology		529
Olympic games Greek antiquities		913.38
Omens occultism		133
Omnigraf **engraving**		**760**
Omnipotence doctr. theology		231
Omnipresence " "		231
Omniscience " "		231
Oneida community socialism		335
Ontario, Can. history		971.3
Ontogeny embryology zool.		591
Ontology filosofy		111
Oolite geology		551
lithology		552
Oology ornithology		598
Oosporeae algae and fungi		589
Ooze lithology		552
Opal economic geology		553
Open air schools		371.7
shelvs lib. econ.		024
Opera amusements		792
dramatic music		782
ethics		175
houses architecture		725
recitative vocal music		784
Operativ surgery		617
Operetta music		782
Ophicleide "		788
Ophidia reptils		598.1
Ophthalmia eye diseases		617
Opium ethics		178
hygiene		613
materia medica		615
war, 1840–42 Chinese hist.		951
Opossums mammals		599
Oppositions solar system		523
Optics physics		535
Optimism filosofy		149
Optional studies curriculum		375
Oracles occultism		133
Oral examinations education		371.2
Orange associations polit. soc.		363
Oranges agriculture		634
Orations Amer. literature		815
Oratorios sacred music		783
Orators biografy		928

Topics in blackface type ar subdivided in the Tables

Oratory		808	
	American literature	815	
	other "	825, 835, etc.	
	sacred homiletics	251	
Orbits	**descriptiv astronomy**	**523**	
	theoretic "	521	
Orcharding and orchards	agriculture	634	
Orchestral music		785	
	sacred music	783	
Orchestrion	music	789	
Orchids	botany	584	
	fertilization of botany	581	
Ordeal, trial by	law	340	
Orders, holy	ministry	262	
	sacraments	265	
	monastic	**271**	
	of architecture arch. design	729	
	knighthood heraldry	929.7	
	social pol. sci.	323	
Ordinal	church ritual	264	
Ordinances	" "	264	
	religious	265	
Ordination	eccles. polity	262	
	sacraments	265	
	sermons	252	
Ordnance	engineering	623	
Ore deposits		553	
	dressing mining eng.	622	
Oregon, U. S.	history	979.5	
	travel	917.95	
	question U. S. hist.	973.5	
Ores	econom. geol.	553	
	metallurgy	669	
	mineralogy	549	
	mining	622	
Orfan asylums		362.7	
Organ	music	786	
	sacred music	783	
Organic and inorganic matter		577	
	chemic industries	**660**	
	chemistry	547	
	remains paleontology	**560**	
Organization			
	central government foren states	354	
	U. S.	353	
	city government	352	
	civil servis	351	
	cooperation	334	
	courts law	347	
	laboring classes	**331.87**	
	schools education	371.2	
Organografy	botany	581	
Organografy	zoology	591	
Oriental architecture		722	
	art	709	
	churches	281	
	customs	**915**	
	filosofy	181	
	history	**950**	
	languages	**490**	
	literature	**890**	
	music theory	781	
	mythology	291	
	question Turkey	949.6	
	religions	**290**	
	societies	490	
Orientalia	**literature**	**890**	
Orientation	ecclesiology	246	
Origen	early Christian filos.	189	
Origin of English language		422	
	evil natural theology	216	
	individual soul metaphys.	129	
	knowledge "	121	
	language	401	
	life	576	
	man nat. hist. of man	573	
	religious belief	201	
	sexes evolution	575	
	species "	575	
	speech filology	401	
Original home of man	ethnology	572	
	sin doct. theology	233	
Orinoco river	travel	918.7	
Orkneys, Scotland	travel	914.1	
Ornament	architecture	729	
Ornamental botany		716	
	design	745	
	gardening	**710**	
Ornaments	costume	391	
	prehistoric	571	
	toilet	646	
Ornithology		598	
Orology	physical geografy	551	
Orphan asylums		362.7	
Orthodox church, Holy or Greek		281	
Orthodoxy	heresies	273	
Orthoepy	comparativ filol.	411	
	English language	421	
Orthografy	" "	421	
	other "	431, 441, etc.	
Orthopedics	surgery	617	
Orthoptera	articulates	595.7	
Oslo, Norway	history	948.2	
	travel	914.82	

Topics in blackface type ar subdivided in the Tables

Ossetic language		491
Osteology, animal		591
	human anatomy	611
Ostracism	Greek antiquities	913.38
Ostracoda	articulates	595
Ostrich	zoology	598
	farms agriculture	636.6
Otology	anatomy of ear	611
Ottoman empire	**history**	**949**.6
Out-bildings	architecture	728
Outcast races		397
Outcrop	geology	551
Outdoor relief	charity	361
	pauperism	339
	sports	**796**
Outlawry	criminal law	343
Outlines, compends, see subject		
Outlining	drawing	741
Outlooks	landscape gardening	717
Over-hours	hygiene	613
Over-mantels	fixt furniture	729
Overshot wheels	mecan. engin'g	621.2
Overstrain, physical hygiene		613.7
Overstudy	school hygiene	371.7
Overture	orchestral music	785
Overwork	hygiene	613
	mental mental hyg.	131
Owners, land pol. econ.		333
	liability of bilding	692
Ownership, land		333
Oxford, England	travel	914.2
	movement	283
	university	378.4
Oxygen	chemistry	546
Oysters	fisheries	639
	food	641
	fossils	564
	preservd pub. helth	614.3
	zoology	594
Ozocerite	economic geology	553
Ozone	chemistry	546
	hygiene	613
Pachyderms	zoology	599
Pacific ilands, Polynesia hist.		996
	travel	919.6
ocean	physical geografy	551
slope, U. S.	geology	557.9
	history	**979**
states, U. S.	**history**	**979**
	religious hist.	277.9
	travel	**917.9**

Pacific war of Chilean hist.		983
Paddock lectures apologetics		239
Pædiatric medicin		618
Pagan architecture		722
Paganism		**290**
Pageants, dramatic customs		394
	scenario writing	808
	theater	792
processional amusements		791
	customs	394
Paging machines printing		655
Paidology		136.7
Pain sense physiology		612
Painless extinction of animal life		614.9
Paint, prehistoric		571
Painted decoration architec.		729
Painters' lives		927
Painting	**fine art**	**750**
	house, sign, etc.	698
	porcelain	738
Paintings, collections of		708
	engravings from	**750**
Paints	chem. technology	667
Palaces	architecture	728
of rulers	arch.	725
Paleobotany		561
Paleografy	English language	421
	inscriptions	417
Paleolithic age prehistoric architec.		571
Paleontology		**560**
Palestine	ancient history	933
	modern "	956
	travel	915.6
Palestrina	sacred music	783
Pali language		491
Palimpsests	rare mss	091
Palingenesis	metaphysics	129
Pallium	sacred ornaments	247
Palmistry	occultism	133
Palms	botany	584
Pamflet cases	library econ.	025.8
Pamflets	**misc. collections**	**040**
	preservation of	025.8
on special topics, see subject		
Panama	history	986
	relig. hist.	278.6
Pancreatic fluid physiology		612
Pandects	Roman law	349
Panics, commercial money		332
	production	338
	trade com.	380
	dom. com.	381

Topics in blackface type ar subdivided in the Tables

Panjabi language		491
Panopticon	prison system	365
Panoramas	amusements	791
	painting	750
Pantheism	filosofy	147
	natural theology	212
Pantheon	architecture	722
Pantomimes	drama	792
	music	782
Papacy	eccles. polity	262
Paper covers	library books	025.7
hanging trade		698
manufacture		676
money		332
roofing	bilding	695
Papers on special topics, see subjects		
Papua	history	995
Papyrus	manuscripts	091
Parables	English literature	828
	New Testament	226
Paradise, garden of Eden, Genesis		222
primitiv home of race		572
theology		236
Paraffin	chem. technology	665
Paraffining	bilding material	691
Paraguay	geology	558.9
	history	989
	religious history	278.9
	travel	918.9
Parallax	descriptiv astron.	523
	practical "	522
Parallelism	Scripture	220.8
Parallels	gospels	226
Parasites, pathology	animals	591
	plants	581
Parasitic diseases	pathology	616
	public helth	614.5
plants		581
Parcel post	post-offis	383
Parchment	paper-making	676
Parent and child	law	347
Parents	ethics	173
Parian cronicle	Arundel marbles	481
	Greek history	938
Paris, congress of, 1856	intern. law	341
expositions		606
Parish	ecclesiastic polity	262
	law	352
libraries		027.8
missions	theology	269
work		**250**
Parks, public	landscape gardening	712
Parks, public	local government	352
Parliament	constitutional law	342
	England	328
houses of	architec.	725
Parliamentary control	admin.	351
	law	328
Parlor magic	pastimes	793
Parochial libraries		027.8
schools and libraries		257
education		377
Parodies	English literature	827
Parquetry	floors and flooring	721
Parricide	criminal law	343
Parrots	domestic birds	636.6
	zoology	598
Parsee dualism	Christian heresies	273
Parseeism	Parsees	295
Parsifal	legends	398.2
	opera	782
Parsing	English grammar	425
Parsis	biografy	922
	religion	295
Part songs	vocal music	784
Parthenon	architecture	722
Parties, political		329
social	amusements	793
	domestic econ.	642
Partizan warfare	**military science**	**355**
Partnership	law	347
Party conventions	polit. science	329
feeling in religion, use of		280
Parzival	legends	398.2
Passion music		783
plays	English literature	822
	general history	809
	Oberammergau	792
	religion	244
Passions	psychology	157
Pastel drawing		741
Pasteurism	protectiv inoculation	614.4
Pastoral work	**theology**	**250**
Pastors	ecclesiastic polity	262
Patagonia	geology	558.2
	history	982
	religious history	278.2
	travel	918.2
Patent indexes	literary methods	029
law	law	347
	patents	608
medicins	adulterations	614.3
	state control	614.2
	therapeutics	615

Topics in blackface type ar subdivided in the Tables

Patents	useful arts	608
Pathologic anatomy	diagnosis	616
Pathology	botany	581
	medicin	616
	mental	132
	of labor	618
	zoology	591
Patience	ethics	179
Patriarchal institutions	pol. science	321
Patriarchs of Bible	lives	220.9
Patricide	law	343
Patriotism	ethics	172
Patriots	biografy	923
Patristic filosofers' lives		921
filosofy		189
theology		230
Patronage	ethics	177
Pauper asylums		362.5
labor		331.6
Pauperism		339
and illiteracy	pub. educ.	379.2
Pavements	road engineering	625
	sanitation	628
Pawnbroking		332
Peabody fund	education	373.7
Peace and war	ethics	172.4
jubilee	Boston	780
society	international ethics	172.4
Pearl fishery		639
Pearls	gems	553
Peasantry	political economy	331.7
Peasants war	Ger. hist.	943
Peat	economic geology	553
fuel	chem. tech.	662
	domestic econ.	644
Pedagogics		**371**
Pedestrianism		796
	ethics	175
Pediatrics	medicin	618
Pedigrees	genealogy	929
Pedobaptism		265
Peerage	heraldry	929.7
Pehlevi language		491
Pelagianism	heresies	273
Pelasgian architecture		722
Pelew ilands	history	996
Peloponnesus	ancient hist.	938
	modern	949.5
Pen names	bibliografy	014
Penal law		343
Penance	theology	265
Pencils	writing materials	651
Pendulum	geodesy	526
	physics	531
Peninsular war	Spanish history	946
Penitentiaries		365
	architecture	725
Penmanship		652
Pennsylvania, U. S.	history	974.8
	travel	917.48
Penology	criminal law	343
Pens	writing	651
Pensions, government		351
	teachers	371.1
Pentateuch	Bible	222
People's palace	self-education	374.9
party, U. S.	politics	329
Perception	psychology	152
Percussion caps	explosivs	662
	instruments music	789
Perfection	ethics	171
Perfectionists	sects	289
Perfumery	chemic technology	668
	toilet	646
Periodical clubs	self education	374.2
Periodicals, general		**050**
	class special with subject	
Peripatetic filosofers		185
Perjury	law	343
Perkinism	cures	615
Perpetual motion		531
Persecutions	theology	272
Perseverance of the saints		234
Persia	ancient history	935
	geology	555.5
	modern history	955
	religious "	275.5
	travel	915.5
Persian architecture		723
	ancient	722
filosofers		181
languages		491
Person of Christ	doct. theol.	232
Personal appearance	costumes	391
	ethics	177
equation	astron.	522
hygiene	**medicin**	**613**
liberty	Eng. law	347
names	etymology	929
narrativs	**autobiografy**	**920**
Great war 1914–19		940.48
property	English law	347
religion		248
rights		347

Topics in blackface type ar subdivided in the Tables

Personal taxation	political economy	336.2
Personality	dogmatics	233
	metaphysics	126
	psychology	137
Personnel	domestic servis	647
	library "	023
Perspectiv	descrip. geometry	515
	drawing	742
	effect arch. design	729
Perspiration	therapeutics	615
Persuasion	logic	168
Perturbations	earth	525
	hevenly bodies	521
Peru	antiquities	913.8
	fauna	591.9
	flora	581.9
	geology	558.5
	history	985
	religious history	278.5
	travel	918.5
Peruvian ancient architecture		722
Pesants war German hist.		943
Peshito language		492
Pessimism filosofy		149
Pestalozzian system of education		371.4
Pestifuges	dom. econ.	648
	museums	579
Pestilences	public helth	614.4
Pests, agricultural		632
household		648
Petards	military engineering	623
Peter, St	epistles	227
Petition, right of Eng. const. hist.		342
Petitions	administration	351
	legislativ procedure	328
Petrifaction	**paleontology**	**560**
Petrografy		552
Petroleum	chemic technology	665
	economic geology	553
Petrology	geology	552
Peutingerian tables anc. geog.		913
Pew rents	cleric support	254
Pewter		739
Phallism		291
Phanerogamia	**botany**	**582**
Phantoms	occultism	133
Pharmacal drugs adulteration		614.3
Pharmaceutic chemistry		615
Pharmacists registration		614.2
Pharmacopoeias materia medica		615
Pharmacy	econ. botany	581
	materia med.	615

Phases of moon		523.3
Phenicia	ancient history	939
Phenician architecture		722
	filosofers	181
	language	492
Phenomena, nutritiv	physiology	612
	vital biology	577
Phi Beta Kappa		371.8
Philadelphia, Penn.	history	974.8
	travel	917.48
Philanthropists biografy		923
Philanthropy	ethics	177
Philately	postage stamps	383
Philemon	epistles	227
Philharmonics	societies	780
Philippians	epistles	227
Philippines	history	991.4
	relig. hist.	279.1
	travel	919.14
Philip's, King, war New Eng. hist.		974
Philo-, Philos-, see Filo-, Filos-		
Phoenicia	ancient history	939
Phoenician, see Phenician		
Phon-, Phos-, Phot-, see Fon-, Fos-, Fot-		
Phrase books English language		428
Phrenologists biografy		920
Phrenology		139
Phthisis	lung diseases	616
	public helth	614.5
Phyllopoda	zoology	595
Phylloxera	agriculture	632
Physical anthropology		573
astronomy		**523**
capacity of women educ.		376
chemistry		541
conditions mental carac.		136
education hygiene		613.7
school "		371.7
geografy		**551**
geology		**551**
sciences		**500**
units physics		530
Physicians, ethics		174
lives of		926
registration		614.2
Physicochemistry		541
Physics		**530**
Physiognomy		138
Physiografy		**551**
Physiologic acoustics		534
biology		574
botany		581

Topics in blackface type ar subdivided in the Tables

Physiologic chemistry	animals	591
	biology	574
	man	612
	plants	581
optics	physics	535
psychology		131
zoology		591
Physiology		612
	animal	591
	biology	574
	mental	131
	vegetable	581
Phytografy	**descriptiv botany**	**580**
Piano and organ		786
Pianola		789
Picaresque novel		863
Piccolo	musical instrument	788
Pictorial art	**fine arts**	**700**
Picts	ancient history	936
	Scottish "	941
Picture frames	decoration	749
galleries		708
Picturesque beauty	esthetics	701
	views and tours	**910**
Pierce, F.	presidency	973.6
Piers	arch. construction	721
	design	729
	bridges	624
	river and harbor eng.	627
Pietists	heresies	273
Piety, practical		**240**
Pig	domestic animals	636.4
Pigeon holes	offis equipment	651
Pigeons	poultry	636.5
	zoology	598
Pigments	chemic tech.	667
	fine arts	751
	inspection pub. helth	614.3
Pigmies	folklore	398.4
human		573
Pigs	domestic animals	636.4
Pile driving		624
Pilgrimages	religious	248
Pilot	laws	347
Pilots	protection of life	614.8
	seamanship	656
Pineapple	agriculture	634
	botany	584
Pines	"	585
Pinnipeds	mammals	599
Pioneers	biografy	923
Pipes, elefant	American antiquities	913.7
Pipes, hydraulics		532
	prehistoric archeology	571
	sewer	628
	steam heating	697
	transmission	621.1
	waterworks	628
Piracy	history	910.4
	law	343
Pirates' lives	collectiv	923
	individual	92
Pisces	zoology	597
Pisciculture	business	639
Pistols	manufacture	683
Pit dwellings	prehist. archeol.	571
Pitcairn Iland	history	997
	travel	919.7
Placers	economic geology	553
Places, names of	etymology	929
Plagiarism	literary methods	029
Plague	diseases	616
Plagues, history of	public helth	614.4
Plains	physical geografy	551
Plan	architectural design	729
Plane geometry		513
	perspectiv	515
	trigonometry	514
Planetary system	descriptiv astron.	523
Planets	descript. astron.	523.4
	theoretic "	521
Planisfere	astronomy	522
Plans, architectural		720
for bilding		692
	libraries library bildings	022
of cities	maps	912
Plantagenets	English history	942.03
Plantation songs		784
Planting	agriculture	631
Plants	**botany**	**580**
	geologic agents	551
	paleontology	561
and animals	differences	577
nature-printing from		655
ornamental		716
Plaster	bilding materials	691
casts	**sculpture**	**730**
of Paris	agriculture	631
	art	731
Plastering	masonry	693
Plate	carving	736
	domestic economy	642
	manufacture	671
glass	insurance	368

Topics in blackface type ar subdivided in the Tables

Plate glass	manufacture	681	Poisons, vegetable	econ. botany	581
Plated ware	"	671	Poker	amusements	795
Plating books	library econ.	025.2		ethics	175
Plato	ancient filosofy	184	Polabian language		491.8
	Greek literature	888	Poland	history	943.8
Platonic filosofy		184		language	491.8
Platonists, new		186		literature	891.8
Platt Deutsch language		439		travel	914.38
	literature	839		partition of hist.	947
Play, nursery		649		Russian "	947
Players	dramatic biografy	927	Polar regions, antarctic	geology	559.9
Playgrounds, public		796		travel	919.9
Playing cards		795		arctic geology	559.8
Playright		655		relig. hist.	279.8
Plays	English drama	822		travel	919.8
	parlor amusements	793	Polariscope	optics	535
	mystery history	809	Polarization of light	astronomy	522
	religion	244		chemistry	544
	theater	792		optics	535
Pleading		347	Polemic sermons		252
Pleasure	psychology	157		theology	239
Pleuropneumonia	cattle disease	619	Police	local gov't	352
	diseases	616		mesures administration	351
Plow	agriculture	631		medical state control	614.2
Plumbing		696		sanitary administration	351
	house drainage	628	Polish language		491.8
Plurality of worlds	astronomy	523.1		literature	891.8
Plutarch	literature	888	Polish	chemic technology	667
Plutology	**polit. econ.**	**330**	Polishing	painting	698
Plutonic rocks	lithology	552	Politeness	ethics	177
Plymouth brethren	sects	286		etiquet	395
Pneumatic tubes	communication	654	Political associations		363
Pneumatics		533		conventions	329
Pneumatology	**metaphysics**	**128**		economists biografy	923
Poetic books of Bible		223		**economy**	**330**
	selections Eng. lit.	821		ethics	172
Poetry, Amer. civil war		973.7		**history**	**900**
	literature	811		organizations assoc.	363
	English "	821		parties	329
	other "	831, 841, etc.		**science**	**320**
	filosofy of	808		status of woman	396
	humorous Eng. lit.	827	Politicians	biografy	923
	sacred hymnology	245	Politics		329
	satiric Eng. lit.	827		morals of	172
Poets' lives		928	Polity, ecclesiastic		262
Pointed architecture		723	Polk, J. K.	presidency	973.6
Poisonous secretion	animals	591	Polka	piano music	786
Poisons	chemic analysis	543	Poll-tax	political economy	336.2
	medical jurisprudence	340	Pollen	fertilization	581
	therapeutics	615	Pollution, air	public helth	614.7
	effects of diseases	616		water, by cemeteries	614.6
	sale of state control	614.2		supply of towns	628

Topics in blackface type ar subdivided in the Tables

Polo	amusements	796
Polonaise	piano music	786
Polyandry	customs	392
	ethics	173
Polycromatic ornament		747
Polyfonic school	music	783
Polygamy	criminal law	343
	customs	392
	ethics	173
	hygiene	613
	Mormonism	289
Polyglot Bibles		220.5
	dictionaries	413
Polygrafy	**special libraries**	**080**
see subject for topical collections		
Polymorfism	crystallografy	548
Polynesia	geology	559.6
	history	996
	languages	499
	religious history	279.6
	travel	919.6
Polypetalae	botany	583
Polyps	zoology	593
Polytheism		291
Polyzoa	zoology	594
Pomology	agriculture	634
Pompeii	description	913.37
Pompey's pillar	Egyptian antiquities	913.32
	monuments	718
Ponds	landscape gardening	714
Ponies	dom. animals	636.1
	student honor	371.8
Pontificate, Roman	eccles. polity	262
Poolselling	ethics	175
Poor laws	local government	352
	pauperism	339
rates		336.2
Poorhouses	asylums	362.5
Popery	ecclesiastic polity	262
Popes	church history	282
	lives	922
Popham colony	Maine history	974.1
Popish plot, 1679	English hist.	942.06
Popular ballads		784
	delusions occultism	133
	education, public	**379**
	elections suffrage	324
	lectures self educ.	374.5
	science	**500**
Population	statistics	312
Porcelain	chemic technology	666
	fine arts	738

Pork packing	public helth	614.7
	trichinae	614.5
Porosity	properties of solids	539
Port Royal heresy		273
	persecutions	272
Portents	occultism	133
Portland cement	econ. geol.	553
	manufacture	666
vase	pottery	738
Porto Rico	history	972.9
Portrait painting		757
Portraits	engraving	769
	painting	757
Portugal	geology	554.6
	history	946.9
	religious history	274.6
	travel	914.69
Portuguese language		469
	literature	869
Positivism	filosofy	146
Post-mortem examinations	pathol.	616
Post-Nicene apostolic church		281
Postage stamps		383
Postal savings banks		332
servis		383
telegraf		384
Posters	advertising	659.1
	cartoons	741
Postoffises	sociology	383
Potash	chemic technology	661
Potato	field crops	633
	garden crops	635
disease	agriculture	632
	botany	581
Pottery	art	738
	manufacture	666
	prehistoric	571
Poultry, diseases of		619
	domestic animals	636.5
Poverty	pauperism	339
Powder, baking	adulterations	614.3
	chemic. technol.	664
explosiv	manufactures	662
toilet		646
Power, balance of	polit. science	320
transmission	elect. engin'g	621.3
	mec. "	621
Practical astronomy		522
	chemistry	542
	mining	622
	religion	**240**
Practis of medicin		616

Topics in blackface type ar subdivided in the Tables

Pragmatism		144
Prairies	physical geografy	551.5
Praise meetings	public worship	264
Prakrit language		491
Prayer	natural theology	217
	ritual	264
books	"	264
family		249
gage	natural theology	217
Lord's	gospels	226
meetings		264
of Manasses	Apocryfa	229
private	personal relig'n	248
Preachers	biografy	922
Preaching		251
Preadamites	nat. hist.	573
Precedence	heraldry	929.7
Precession	practical astronomy	522
	theoretic "	521
Precious metals	metallurgy	669
	mineralogy	549
stones	econ. geol.	553
	mineralogy	549
Predestination	doctrinal theology	234
Predicting machines	tides	525
Predictions	occultism	133
Preemption	state land	336
Preexistence of the soul		129
Prefixes	English etymology	422
Prehistoric archeology		571
man	nat. hist. of man	573
Prejudis	logic	165
	social ethics	177
Prelacy	ecclesiastic polity	262
Preordination	doct. theol.	234
Preparatory schools, private		**373**
Preparedness, military		355.2
Preraphaelitism		759
Presages	occultism	133
Presbyter	ministry	262
Presbyterians		285
	biografy	922
Presbytery	ecclesiastic polity	262
Prescience	divine attribute	231
Prescription writing	farmacy	615
Presents, Christmas	customs	394
Preservation of food		664
Preservativs	bilding	691
	zoologic collections	579
Preserving	cookery	641
President, U. S.	administration	353
	inauguration	394
Presidential elections		324
Presidents	biografy	923
Press clippings		029
hydraulic	engineering	621.2
	science	532
journalism		**070**
liberty of		323
morals of		179
printing		655
public order		351
writing for	lit. methods	029
Pressure gages	pneumatics	533
of air	meteorology	551.5
blood	physiology	612
clothing	hygiene	613
liquids	hydraulics	532
sense	physiology	612
Prestidigitation		791
Pretenders	English history	942.07
Prevention of contagious diseases		614.4
fire	protection of life	614.8
Priapus	mythology	292
Prices	political economy	338
of books	library admin.	025.2
Pride	ethics	179
Priesthood	Christian ministry	262
Priests, celibacy of		253
	canon law	348
	ethics	176
lives		922
Primacy	ecclesiastic polity	262
Primaries	suffrage	324
Primary schools	methods	372.2
	state system	379.1
Prime meridian	cosmic time	529
Primers	elementary education	372
Primeval man	natural hist. of man	573
	prehist. archeol.	571
Primitiv Christianity		270
church		281
culture		571
Promogeniture law		347
Primrose leag	political ass'ns	363
Prince Edward Is. Can.	history	971.7
Printers	biografy	926
marks		655
occupation	hygiene	613
Printing	library administration	025.1
calico	chemic tech.	667
telegrafs	communication	654
trade		655
Prints, books of		769

Topics in blackface type ar subdivided in the Tables

Prints, cloth   chemic technology   667
Prison associations   365
   contracts   polit. economy   331.5
   disciplin   365
   life   Amer. civil war   973.7
      World war 1914-19   940.47
Prisoners of war   internat. law   341
Prisons   architecture   725
   hygiene   613
   sociology   365
Private banks   332
   grounds   landscape   712
   international law   341
   judgment   eccles. pol.   262
   libraries   027.1
   ownership of land   333
   reading   self education   374.1
   schools   girls   376
      secondary   373
   theatricals   793
      ethics   175
   vs public schools   379
   worship   248
Privateers   341
Privately printed books   rarities   094
Privileges to library readers   024
Prize fighting   ethics   175
Prizes   international law   341
   maritime   "   347
   in school   education   371.5
Probabilities   mathematics   519
Probate   law   347
Probation of malefactors   364
Processes   preservativ   bilding   691
Processions   customs   394
Produce   agriculture   633
Production   political economy   338
Products   field   633
   garden   635
Profanity   ethics   177
Profecy   Bible inspiration   220.1
Professional ethics   174
Professors' salaries   educ.   371.1
Professorships of books and reading   028
Profetic books of Bible   224
Profit sharing   political econ.   331.2
Profits   capital and labor   331.1
Prognostications   occultism   133
Progress   civilization   901
   sociology   301
   of population   statistics   312
Progressiv development of man   575

Prohibited books   rarities   098
Prohibition   temperance   178
   party   political science   329
Projectils   military engineering   623
   physics   531
Projections   analytic geometry   516
   descriptiv   "   515
   map   geodesy   526
Promis   ethics   174
Promissory notes   law   347
   political econ.   332
Promotions of scholars   371.2
   teachers   371.1
Pronunciation   Eng. language   421
Proof and copy   literary methods   029
   legal   law   347
   reading   printing   655
Propaganda, library   021
Propagation of contagious diseases   614.4
Propelling machinery   shipbilding   623.8
Proper names   persons and places   929
Property
   capital   331
   church   254
      monastic foundations   271
      political science   322
      taxation   336.2
   city   local taxation   352
   law of title to   347
   literary   publishing   655
   state   pub. finance   336
   suffrage   324
   tax   336.2
   theory of   polit. econ.   335
Prophecy   Bible inspiration   220.1
Prophetic books of Bible   224
Proportion in art   esthetics   701
   plan   arch. design   729
Proprietary libraries   027.2
Proscription   criminal law   343
Prose composition   Greek   488
      Latin   478
Proslavery   326
Prosody   comparativ filol.   416
   English language   426
   other   "   436, 446, etc.
Prospecting   mining engin'g   622
Prostitution   administration   351
   ethics   176
   hygiene   613
Protection   political economy   337
   of animals   591.5

Topics in blackface type ar subdivided in the Tables

Protection of human life		614.8
Protectiv inoculation	pub. helth	614.4
Protectorate	English history	942.06
Protestant episcopal church		283
	episcopalians biog.	922
	sects, continental	284
Protestantism		284
	and Romanism	282
Protofyta	botany	589
Protoplasm	animal physiology	591
	biology	576
	physiology	612
Protozoa	paleontology	563
	zoology	593
Provençal language		449
	literature	849
	Romanesque architecture	723
Provence, France hist.		944
Proverbs, book of	Bible	223
	folklore	398
Providence, Divine natural theology		214
	theology	231
Provincialisms English lang.		427
Pruning	agriculture	631
Prussia	history	943.1
	travel	914.3
Prussian language, old		491
Prussic acid	toxicology	615
Psalmody	music	783
Psalms	Bible	223
	hymnology	245
Psalter	church ritual	264
Pseudepigrafa		229
Pseudo gospels		229
Pseudomorfs	crystallografy	548
Pseudoneuroptera insects		595.7
Pseudonyms bibliografy		014
Psychiatry		132
Psychic fenomena		133
	medicin mental path.	132
	research psychology	133
Psychoanalysis		131
Psychology		**150**
Psychomancy divination		133
Pteridofyta	botany	587
Pteropoda zoology		594
Public administration		**350**
	analysts adulterations	614.3
	annuities pub. finance	336.3
	baths	613
	bildings architecture	725
	local gov't	352

Public charities		361
	customs	394
	documents	328
	print'g and distrib.	655
	finance	**336**
	gardens	712
	helth	**614**
	local gov't	352
	lands	336
	law	**340**
	libraries	027.4
	sanitation	**614**
	schools education	**379**
	securities polit. economy	336.3
	servis commissions	380
	shows customs	394
	ethics	175
	speaking oratory	808
	spirit patriotism	172
	utilities commerce	**380**
	works administration	352
	worship	264
Publishers catalogs and circulars		015
	lives	920
Publishing		655
Pueblos	dwellings	571
Puerperal diseases obstetrics		618
Puerto Rico	history	972.9
	travel	917.29
Pugilism	amusements	796
	ethics	175
Pulpit	clergy	262
eloquence homiletics		**250**
Pulpits	architec. accessories	729
	sacred furniture	247
Pump	pneumatics	533
	practical chemistry	542
Pumping engins mecan. engin'g		621.6
	waterworks	628
Pumps	engineering	621.6
Punctuation English language		421
Punishment, future theology		237
	law	343
	school	371.5
Puppet plays		791
Pure food	pub. helth	614.3
sciences		**500**
	bibliografy	016.5
Purgatory	theology	236
Puritanism	"	285
Puritans	English history	942.06
	religious hist.	274.2

Topics in blackface type ar subdivided in the Tables

Puritans	Mass. history	974.4		Quebec, Can.	history	971.4
	persecutions by	272		Queen Anne architecture		724
Purpose	ethics	171		Queens	biografy	923
Puseyism	theology	283		Questions	*Class with subject*	
Pushtu language		491		Quicksilver, *see* Mercury		
Puzzles		793		Quietism	heresies	273
Pygmies	folklore	398.4		Quietists, persecution of		272
	human	573		Quincy system	education	371.4
Pyramids	Egyptian	913.32		Quoits	amusements	796
Pyrenees mountains	travel	914.6		Quotations	English literature	828
Pyrites	mineralogy	549			general collections	808.8
Pyrografy		736				
Pyrometry	temperature	536		Rabbinic learning	Judaism	296
Pyrotechnics	chemical tech.	662		Rabbits	domestic animals	636.9
Pyrrhonism	Greek filosofy	186		Race	influence on mind	136
Pythagorean filosofy		182			suffrage	324
Pythias, knights of	secret societies	366			betterment	613.9
					horse amusements	798
Quackery	delusions	133			mortality public helth	614.1
	medical state control	614.2		Races of man		572
Quadrant	astron. instrument	522		Racing	amusements	798
Quadrature	integral calculus	517			ethics	175
	of circle geom.	513		Radiant energy of sun		523.7
Quadrumana	zoology	599			matter	539
Quadrupeds	"	599			points meteors	523
Quadruplex telegrafs	engin'g	621.3		Radiates	paleontology	563
Quakers	lives	922			zoology	593
	persecutions	272		Radiation	heat	536
	sects	289			physics	535
Qualifications of readers	lib. econ.	024		Radio	business	654
	teachers educ.	371.1			engineering	621.3
	voters suffrage	324		Radio-chemistry		541
Qualitativ analysis	chemistry	544		Ragged schools		377
Quality	metaphysics	111		Rags	public helth	614.4
Quantics	algebra	512		Railroad accidents		656
Quantitativ analysis	chemistry	545			corporations	385
Quantity	English prosody	426			electric	621.3
	metaphysics	119			engineering	625
Quarantine	administration	352			law	385
	contagious diseases	614.4			officials' lives	923
	laws local admin.	352			passenger stations arch.	725
Quarries, prehistoric		571			rate regulation	385
Quarrying	mining engineering	622			transport business	656
Quarrymen's occupation	hygiene	613			sociology	385
Quartermasters	military admin.	355			travel protect. of life	614.8
Quartet	sacred music	783		Railroading		656
Quartets	vocal "	784		Railway guides		656
Quartz	lithology	552		Rainfall	meteorology	551.5
	mineralogy	549		Raising funds for libraries		021.9
Quarternary age	geology	551		Ram, hydraulic	engineering	621.2
Quaternions	mathematics	516			water hydraulics	532
Quays	harbor engineering	627		Ranch, cattle		636.2

Topics in blackface type ar subdivided in the Tables

Rank	heraldry	929.7
	polit. science	323
Rape	law	343
Rare binding	book rarities	095
illustrations	book rarities	096
printing	" "	094
Rarissima		**090**
Rat	disease carrier	614.4
	domestic pests	648
	noxious animals	591
	zoology	599
Rationalism	natural theology	211
Rationalistic age	religious history	270
Rationalists, apologetics against		239
Raw materials, duties on		337
Readers, aids to		**028**
	English language	428
	rules library econ.	024
Reading and aids		**028**
	art of	808
	books, higher, Eng.	820.8
	clubs self education	374.2
	desks offis equipment	651
	elementary education	372
	private self education	374.1
	proofs printing	655
	rooms, free lib. econ.	027.9
	bildings	022
Ready-reckoners		651
Reagents	chem. anal.	544
Real estate	law	347
	taxation polit. econ.	336.2
presence	theology	265
Realism	filosofy	149
Reapers	agriculture	631
Reason in animals zoology		591.5
innate	intuition	156
natural theology		**210**
Reasoning	psychology	153
Rebellion	political science	323
Southern	U. S. hist.	973.7
Rebuses	amusements	793
Receits	cookery	641.5
	medicin	615
	useful arts	602
workshop	chem. tech.	660
class special with subject		
Receptiv functions	psychology	152
Recipe books	cookery	641.5
Reciprocity	free trade	337.9
Recognition hereafter doct. theol.		237
Reconstruction	U. S. history	973.8
Recreation	hygiene	613.7
	bildings architecture	725
Recreations	school hygiene	371.7
Recreativ arts		**790**
Recruiting	military science	355.2
Red Cross societies		361
River settlement, Canada hist.		971.27
	travel	917.1
Redemption	theology	234
Redy reckoners		651
Reference books	library admin.	025.5
	use of aids	028
department	lib. econ.	025.5
exact	literary methods	029
use of libraries		024
Referendum	legislation	328
	polit. sci.	321
Reflecting instruments	astron.	522
	optics	535
Reflection	heat	536
	light	535
	psychology	153
Reflections	perspectiv	515
Reflex action	zoology	591
Reform bil, 1832 English suffrage		324
	civil servis	351.6
	parliamentary	328
	prison sociology	365
	schools	364
education		371.9
sociology		301
spelling	English lang.	421
Reformation, age of European hist.		940.2
	religious history	270
Reformatories	architecture	725
	delinquents	364
	inebriates	362.1
Reformatory associations		364
Reformd church, Dutch		284
	in Amer.	285
episcopal church		283
Reformers	biografy	923
Refracting telescopes		522
Refraction	heat	536
	optics	535
	practical astronomy	522
Refrigerators	domestic economy	643
Refuge, houses of		362.5
Regattas	amusements	797
	college and school	371.7
Regeneration	theology	234
Regicides	biografy	923

Topics in blackface type ar subdivided in the Tables

Regimen	**hygiene**		**613**
Regiments, history of			353
	U. S. civil war		973.7
Registers, family			929
	of deeds	law	347
	U. S. army and navy		353
Registration	public helth		614.1
	statistics		311
Regulation of medical practis			614.2
Regulations, army			**355**
	navy		359
	readers	library econ.	024
Regulators	see special subject		
Reincarnation			129
Relations, domestic, political science			323
	foren	" "	327
	of capital and labor		331.1
	church and state	ethics	172
		pol. sci.	322
Relationship			929
Relativ location	library economy		025.8
Relativity, Einstein theory	astron.		521
	gravity		531
	physics		530
Relics	miracles		231
Relief decoration	architecture		729
	maps	phys. geog.	551
	work	charity	361
		parish	258
Religion			**200**
	and education		377
	science	apologetics	239
		nat. theol.	215
	bibliografy of		016.2
	biografy of		922
	Christian		**200**
Religions, non-Christian			**290**
Religious anecdotes			244
	architecture		726
	art		**246**
	associations, Bible, etc.		206
		general	**267**
		parish	256
		special sects	**280**
		Y. M. C. A.	267.3
		Y. W. C. A.	267.5
	biografy		922
	ceremonies	ritual	264
		sacraments	265
	controversy	**history**	**270**
		theology	239
	on special subjects, see subject		

Religious education	education		377
	religion		268
	of clergy		207
	fiction		244
	history		**270**
	institutions		**260**
	liberty		261
	orders, monastic		**271**
	painting	art	755
		ecclesiology	247
	poetry		245
	sects		**280**
	societies, see Religious assoc.		
	on special subjects, see subject		
	symbolism		246
Remains, paleontology			**560**
Remedies	pathology		616
	therapeutics		615
	legal		347
Remonstrants	sects		284
Remuneration	library econ.		023
	political "		331.2
Renaissance	architecture		724
	European history		940.2
	fine arts		709
	religious history		270
	sculpture		735
Rent	political economy		333
	of state property	finance	336
Rents, pew	cleric support		254
Repentance	doctrin		234
Reporting	journalism		070
	shorthand		653
Reports, law,	American		345
	British		346
	library administration		025.1
	class special with subject		
Repoussé work	fine arts		739
Representation			324
Representativ gov't	polit. sci.		321
Reprisal	international law		341
Reproduction	botany		581
	physiology		612
	zoology		591
Reproductiv power	psychology		154
Reptils	paleontology		568
	zoology		598.1
Republic	political science		321
Republican party, U. S.			329
Repudiation	public finance		336.3
Reredos	sacred furniture		247
Rescue	protection of life		614.8

Topics in blackface type ar subdivided in the Tables

Research, endowment	educ.	378.3
	psychic	psychology	133
Reservoirs		628
Residences	architecture	728
	official	"	725
Resin-producing invertebrates		638
Resins	chemic technol.	668
	fossil	economic geol.	553
Resistance of materials	engineering	620.1
		molec. phys.	539
	water	hydraulics	532
Resonators	acoustics	534
Resorts, helth	hygiene	613
Resources, conservation of	national	339
		natural	333
Respiration	animals	591
	physiology	612
Respiratory system	anatomy	611
Responsibility, human	doct. theol.	233
		ethics	171
Rest and sleep	hygiene	613.7
Restaurants		642
	architecture	725
Restoration of the Jews		296
Restriction of contagious diseases		614.4
Resumption	U. S. finance	336
Resurrection	Christology	232
	doctrinal theol.	236
Resuscitation of the drownd		614.8
Retreats, religious		269
Retribution	doctrinal theol.	237
Reuchlin	medieval filos.	189
Revelation, Book of	Bible	228
	divine	theology	231
Revenue	**state finance**	**336**
Reviews	*Class with subject reviewd*	
Revised statutes	American law	345
	version	Eng. Bible	220.5
		New Test.	225
		Old "	221
Revival of letters	literary history	809
Revivals	architecture	724
	music	783
	of religion	269
Revolts	political science	323
Revolution, American	history	973.3
	English, 1688	"	942.06
	French, 1789	"	944
	of the earth	astronomy	525
Revolutionary societies, patriotic Am.		369.1
Revolutions	political science	323
Rewards and punishments	school	371.5

Rewards and punishments	theology	233
Rhaeto-Romansch language		459
Rhetoric		808
	sacred	homiletics	251
Rheumatism	diseases	616
Rhine	travel	914.3
Rhinoceros	zoology	599
Rhizopoda	"	593
Rhode Island, U. S.	history	974.5
		travel	917.45
Rhodes	ancient history	939
	knights of	929.7
	modern history	949.9
Rhodesia, Africa	history	968
Rhymes	English prosody	426
Rhyming dictionaries	Eng. lang.	426
Rhynchota	insects	595.7
Richard 1–2	English history	942.03
3	" "	942.04
Riddles	amusements	793
	popular life	398
Riding	recreations	798
Rifle manufacture		683
	military equipment	355
	shooting	amusements	799
Rifled ordnance	military engin'g	623
Right of search		341
	standard of	ethics	171
Righteousness	personal religion	248
Rights	political science	323
	and liberties	const. law	342
	land	political economy	333
Rimes	Eng. prosody	426
Rinderpest	veterinary medicin	619
Rings, finger	costume	391
	sacred ornaments	247
Rio Janeiro	history	981
	travel	918.1
Riots	law	343
	political science	323
	in any locality, class with its hist.	
Riparian rights	pol. econ.	333
Ripple-marks	geology	551
Rites and ceremonies	customs	394
Ritual and ritualism	pub. worship	264
River engineering		627
	transport	sociology	386
Rivers	physical geografy	551
	water supply	628
Rivets	machine tools	621
Roads	engineering	625
	military	military eng.	623

Topics in blackface type ar subdivided in the Tables

Robbery	criminal law	343
Robin Hood	English ballads	821
	legends	398.2
Rock analysis	chemistry	543
salt	economic geology	553
Rocks	lithology	552
Rocky mountains, U. S.	travel	917.8
Rococo style	architecture	724
Rodentia	zoology	599
Roland	legends	398.2
song of	Fr. poetry	841
Rolling mils	metal manuf.	671
Rolls of honor, military		355
	school	371.5
Romaic language		489
literature		889
Roman antiquities		913.37
architecture		722
art		709
catholic church		282
catholics	biografy	922
empire, Holy		943
history, ancient		937
modern		945
inquisition	persecutions	272
law		349
literature		**870**
mythology		292
orders, monastic		271
sculpture		733
Romance, English		823
languages		479
literatures		879
religious		244
Romanesque architecture		723
revival	architecture	724
Romanism		282
Romans, epistle to	Bible	227
Romansh language		459
Romany	gipsies	397
Rome, ancient	history	937
church of		282
modern	history	945
	travel	914.5
Romish church		282
Rommany	gipsies	397
Rood screen	architecture	729
	sacred furniture	247
Roof construction	architecture	721
coverings	bilding	695
Roofs	architectural design	729
	engineering	624

Roosevelt, F. D.	presidency	973.91
T.	"	973.91
Rope making		677
walking	entertainment	791
Rose	botany	583
culture	land. gard.	716
Roses, wars of	English hist.	942.04
Rosetta stone	Egyptian inscript.	493
	Greek "	481
Rosicrucians	secret societies	366
Rotary blowers and pumps	engin'g	621.6
Rotation	physics	531
of earth		525
hevenly bodies		521
sun		523.7
Rote teaching	education	371.3
Rotifera	zoology	595
Roumania	history	949.8
	travel	914.98
Roumanian language		459
Round dances	amusements	793
	ethics	175
table	Arthurian romances	398.2
Roundheds	English history	942.06
Rowing	sport	797
Royal houses	heraldry	929.7
lives	collected biografy	923
Rubber manufactures		678
Rubies	economic geology	553
Rubrics	Anglican ritual	264
Rugs	manufactures	677
	oriental	745
Ruins	antiquities	913
	modern	**914–919**
Rulers	collected biografy	923
palaces	architecture	725
Rules for readers	library econ.	024
staf	" "	023
of order, parliamentary		328
school		371.5
Rumania	history	949.8
	travel	914.98
Rumansh language		459
literature		859
Ruminants	zoology	599
greater	agric.	636.2
smaller	"	636.3
Runes		439
Anglo-Saxon		429
German		437
Running	hygiene	613.7
sports		796

Topics in blackface type ar subdivided in the Tables

Rural architecture		728	Sacrifice	birth customs	392
economy	agriculture	631		Christology	232
free delivery	post. serv.	383	Sacrifices	Bible	220.9
life	agriculture	630.1		sacraments	265
	sociology	323	Sacrilege		265
schools		379.1	Saddlery	trade	685
sports		796	Safes	manufactures	672
water supply		628	Safety lamps	mining engineering	622
Russia	fauna	591.9	Sagas, Norse		839
	flora	581.9	Sage foundation		306
	geology	554.7	Sahara desert	physical geografy	551.5
	history	947		travel	916.6
	religious history	274.7	Sailing directions		656
	statistics	314		navigation	527
	travel	914.7	Sailmaking	trade	689
in Asia	history	957	Sailors	biografy	926
Russian America, Alaska	history	979.8	Saint Albans raid	U. S. history	973.7
architecture		723		Vermont hist.	974.3
baths	hygiene	613	Bartholomew massacre		272
church sects		281	Bernard, hospice of		614.8
cyclopedias		037	Helena	history	997
essays, collected		047	John of Jerusalem, knights of		929.7
journalism		077	Lawrence river	hist.	971.4
language		491.7	Louis, Mo.	history	977.8
literature		891.7		travel	917.78
newspapers		077	Simonism	socialism	335
periodicals, general		057	Saints	doctrin	235
societies, general		067		lives of	922
Russo-Japanese war	Jap. hist.	952	in art	ecclesiology	246
	Rus. "	947		painting	755
Turkish wars	" "	947	Latter day		289
Rust, anti, processes	bilding	691	Salamanders	batrachia	597
Ruth	Bible	222	Salary	polit. econ.	331.2
Ruthenian language		491.7	**Sale catalogs**	**of books**	**017–019**
Ryswick, peace of	treaties	341	Salic laws	German law	349
			Salin waters	economic geology	553
Sabbatarians	Christian sect	289	Saloons	temperance	178
Sabbath		263	Salt	lithology	552
schools		268		manufactures	664
Sabeism	filosofy	181	rock	economic geology	553
Sabellian heresies		273	Salts	chemic technology	661
Sacraments		265		theoretic chemistry	541
ritual		264	Salvage	maritime law	347
Sacred art		**246**	Salvation	doctrinal theology	234
biografy		922	army	associations	267
drama	miracle plays	792		Great war, 1914–19	940.47
	religion	244	Samaritan language		492
furniture		247	Samaritans	sects	296
history		**270**	Samoa, Polynesia	history	996
music		783	Samuel	Old Testament	222
poetry		245	San Francisco, Calif.	history	979.4
rhetoric		251		travel	917.94

Topics in blackface type ar subdivided in the Tables

San José scale	pests	632
Salvador	history	972.8
Sanctification	doctrinal theology	234
Sanctuary	legal antiquities	340
Sanctus	sacred music	783
Sand storms		551.5
Sandals	costumes	391
Sands	economic geology	553
Sandstone	" "	553
	lithology	552
old red		551
Sandwich Islands	history	996
Sangreal	legends	398.2
Sanguification	physiology	612
Sanhedrim	Judaism	296
Sanitariums	helth resorts	613
	institutions	362.1
Sanitary affairs	**pubic helth**	**614**
commissions	local gov't	352
	U. S.	361
engineering		628
police	administration	351
science	engineering	628
Sanitation, engineering		628
public		**614**
veterinary	pub. helth	614.9
Sanskrit language		491
literature		891
Santo Domingo	history	972.9
Saracenic architecture		723
empire	history	953
Sarcofagi	burial customs	393
Sardinia	ancient history	937
	modern "	945
Saskatchewan, Can.	hist.	971.24
Sassanian architecture		722
Sassanians	ancient history	935
Satan and Satanism	doctrin. theol.	235
	witchcraft	133
Satellites	theoretic astronomy	521
Satire	American literature	817
	other " 827, 837, etc.	
Satires, religious		244
Satiric music, dramatic		782
Satirists	biografy	928
Saturn	astronomy	523.4
Saurians		598.1
Sauroptergia	reptils	598.1
Savings banks	political econ.	332
Savoy, declaration	doct. theology	238
France	history	944
house of	Ital. hist.	945

Saw mils		674
Saws	machine tools	621
Saxon, Anglo-,	language	429
	literature	829
old	language	439
	literature	839
Saxony	history	943
Saybrook platform	creeds	238
Scalds	surgery	617
Scales	instrument making	681
	mesuring instrument	530
	music	781
	practical chemistry	542
	weights and mesures	389
wage	pol. econ.	331.2
Scalping	war customs	399
Scandal	ethics	177
Scandinavia	history	948
Scandinavian	cyclopedias	038
	essays, collected	048
	filosofy	198
	journalism	078
	language	439
	literature	839
	newspapers	078
	periodicals, gen.	058
	protestants	284
	societies, gen.	068
Scarecrows	agriculture	632
Scavenging of towns		628
Scene painting	painting	750
	theater	792
Scenery	natural	719
Scepticism, Sceptics, see Skepticism, etc.		
Schism	eccles. history	270
	polity	262
Schists	lithology	552
Schizomycetes	botany	589
Schleswig-Holstein	Ger. hist.	943
Scholar's life	**self culture**	**374**
Scholarships	research	378.3
	school tuition	371.2
Scholastic filosofers' lives		921
filosofy		189
School architecture		727
funds	state education	379.1
furniture		371.6
hygiene	education	371.7
libraries	"	371.6
	library economy	027.8
texts	English language	428
Schools	architecture	727

Topics in blackface type ar subdivided in the Tables

Schools   education   370
    and libraries   library econ.   021.3
    library   library econ.   020.7
    music   mus. education   780
    of painting   759
    parochial   education   377
                   parish work   257
    public   **379**
    reform   364
                   architecture   725
    Sunday   268
    class special with subject
Science and religion   apologetics   239
                   natural theol.   215
    applied   **600**
    bibliografy of   016.5
    biografy of   925
    elementary education   372
    in Bible   220.8
    mental   **150**
    military   **355**
    moral   **170**
    natural   **500**
    naval   359
    of religion   201
    political   **320**
    sanitary   628
    social   sociology   **300**
    study and teaching   507
Sciences, classification of   501
    natural   **500**
    occult   133
Scientific bildings   architecture   727
    management   business   658
    men   lives of   925
    surveys and travel   **508.3**
Scientists, apologetics against   239
Scope and usefulness of libraries **021**
Scorpions   zoology   595
Scotch churches, presbyterian   285
    covenant   creeds   238
    English dialects   427
    episcopal church   283
    filosofy   192
    language   491.6
    poetry   821
    presbyterians' lives   922
Scotland   antiquities   913.4
              flora   581.9
              geology   554.1
              history   941
              religious history   274.1

Scotland   travel   914.1
              zoology   591.9
Scottish, *see* Scotch
Scrap book methods   029
    books   general collections   082
    class special with subject
Screening   mining engineering   622
Screens   arch. construction   721
             fixt furniture   729
Screw   physics   531
    cutting   621
    propellers   engineering   621.1
Script   writing   652
Scriptural biografy   Bible   220.9
                       N. T.   225
                       O. T.   221
Scripture commentaries   220.7
          concordances   220.2
          cronologies   220.9
          dictionaries   220.3
          harmonies of gospels   226
          histories   220.9
          readings   public worship 264
Scriptures, holy Bible   **220**
Scroll-sawing   749
Sculptors   biografy   927
Sculpture   **730**
              prehistoric   571
              sacred ornamentation   247
Scutage   feudalism   321
Scythian language   494
Sea anemones   zoology   593
    cucumbers   "   593
    fishery   trade   639
    laws   347
    mosses   algae   589
    power   359
    serpent   delusions   133
    shore resorts   hygiene   613
    urchins   zoology   593
Seal engraving   736
    fishing   639
Seals   heraldry   929.8
           zoology   599
Seamanship   656
Seamen's lives   926
Search, right of   international law 341
Seasickness   616
Seaside cottages   architecture   728
        resorts   hygiene   613
Seasons   astronomy   525
Seating capacity   architecture   729

Topics in blackface type ar subdivided in the Tables

Seats, country	architecture	728
Seaweeds	botany	589
	fertilizers	631
Secession	church of Scotland	285
	law	342
	U. S. history	973.7
Second advent of Christ		232
	adventists sects	286
	sight occultism	133
Secondary schools		**373**
	public	379.1
Secret ballot	suffrage	324
	servis Amer. civil war	973.7
	Great war 1914–19	940.48
	societies	366
	college	371.8
	writing cryptografy	652
Secretion	animals	591
	physiology	612
Sects, Christian		**280**
Secular education		377
Sedentary life	hygiene	613
Sedimentary rocks lithology		552
Sedition	law	343
See	eccles. polity	262
Seismology		551
Selection	evolution	575
Self defense, art of athletics		796
	education	**374**
	government polit. science	321
	school discip.	371.5
Sematology	filology	419
Seminaries	architecture	727
	education	**373**
	theologic religion	207
	for special topics, see subject	
Seminary method of instruction		371.3
Seminole wars, U. S. history		973.5
Semitic languages		492
	literatures	892
Senegambia history		966
Sennar, Egypt "		962
Sensation, beginnings of biology		576
	in animals zoology	591
	plants botany	581
	psychology	152
Sensationalism filosofy		145
Sense	psychology	152
Sensibility	"	157
Sensitiv plant botany		583
	physiol. botany	581
Sepia	painting	751

Sepoy war, India history			954
Septuagint	Bible		221
Sepulcher	cemeteries		718
Sepulture	customs		393
	public helth		614.6
Serbia	history		949.7
	travel		914.97
Serbian language			491.8
Serfs	Russian history		947
	slavery		326
	social classes		323
Serials	*Class with subject*		
Sericulture			638
Sermons			252
		public worship	264
Serpent charming			591
	worship		291
Serpentine	economic geology		553
	lithology		552
Serpents	zoology		598.1
Servants	domestic economy		647
	ethics		173
	law		347
Servia	history		949.7
Servian language			491.8
Servis	military science		355
	books church ritual		264
	library		023
	table dom. econ.		642
Servitude	slavery		326
	military		355.2
Session laws, American			345
	English		346
Seven champions			398.2
	sages		398.2
	sleepers		398.2
	wonders of the world anc.		722
	med.		723
Seventh day adventists sects			286
	baptists "		286
	Sabbath		263
Sewage	disposal of		628
Sewerage	city administration		352
	engineering		628
Sewers	public helth		614.4
Sewing	domestic economy		646
	machine		687
Sex customs			392
	in education		**376**
	nature		577
	influence of therapeutics		615
	mortality public helth		614.1

Topics in blackface type ar subdivided in the Tables

Sex, origin of	evolution	575
production of	embryology	591
Sexes	mental characteristics	136
Sexual ethics		176
science		612
selection	evolution	575
variation	animals	591
Sferic astronomy		522
projections	descr. geom.	515
Sfinx	Egyptian mythology	299
Sfygmograf	diagnosis	616
Shades and shadows	descrip. geom.	515
Shaft sinking	mining	622
Shafting	mil work	621
Shakers	sects	289
Shakespere	Eng. drama	822.3
Shale	lithology	552
Sharks		597
Shay's rebellion	Mass. history	974.4
Sheep, diseases of	vet. medicin	619
domestic animals		636.3
Shel banks	prehist. archeology	571
fish	business	639
	zoology	594
Shelf dep't	library economy	025.8
Shels	fossil	564
	prehist. archeology	571
	projectils	623
	zoology	594
Shelter	domestic econ.	643
of laboring classes	pol. econ.	331.8
Shelving	library bilding	022.4
Shemitic languages		492
Sheol	escatology	236
Sherifs	law	347
	local government	352
Shetland ilands	travel	914.1
Shields	heraldry	929.8
	wepons	399
Shintoism		299
Ship canals	engineering	626
	sociology	386
life	hygiene	613
propulsion	engineering	623.8
railways	"	625
Shipbilding	"	623.8
Shipping business	useful arts	656
history of	sociology	387
laws		347
Shipwrecks	adventures	910.4
	lifesaving methods	614.8
Shipwreckt, rescue of	prot. of life	614.8

Shoals, Isle of	history	974.2
	travel	917.42
Shock	result of injury	617
Shoemaking	manufacturing	685
Shoes	costume	391
	domestic econ.	646
Shooting	gunnery	623
	sport	799
Shop girls	labor of women	331.4
Shorthand		653
Shortsightedness	eye diseases	617
Shows	entertainments	791
	public customs	394
Shrimps	zoology	595
Shrubbery	landscape gardening	715
Shrubs	botany	582
Siam	history	959
	travel	915.9
Lower	history	959
Siamese architecture		722
language		495
twins	deformities	617
	nat. hist. of man	573
Siberia	geology	555.7
	history	957
	religious history	275.7
	travel	915.7
Sibyllin books	magic	133
Sicilian Norman architecture		723
Sicily	ancient history	937
	modern "	945
Sick, food for	hygiene	613.2
hospitals for		362.1
	architecture	725
ministry of	sacraments	265
parish care of		258
room	domestic economy	649
Sidereal month	astronomy	523.3
time	cronology	529
Siege operations	mil. engin'g	623
warfare	" science	355
Sight	anatomy	611
	asylums for the blind	362.4
	diseases of	617
	optics	535
	physiology	612
	psychology	152
Sign boards	advertising	659.1
language	educ. of def	371.9
	hieroglyfics	419
painting		698
Signal servis	meteorology	551.5

Topics in blackface type ar subdivided in the Tables

Signals in navigation acoustics	534	
military military engin.	623	
telegrafic	654	
Silesia, Austria history	943.7	
Prussia "	943.1	
Silhouets	741	
Silk culture	638	
dyeing chemic technology	667	
manufacture	677	
worm agriculture	638	
zoology	595.7	
Silo agriculture	631	
Silurian age geology	551	
Silver inorganic chemistry	546	
metallurgy	669	
mining	622	
money	332	
ores economic geol.	553	
plating manufacture	671	
Silverfish agric. pests	632	
dom. "	648	
Silversmiths work fine arts	739	
Silverware domestic economy	642	
fine arts	739	
manufactures	671	
Simony canon law	348	
eccles. polity	262	
Sin doctrin	233	
Sinai ancient history	939	
modern "	953	
Sinaitic inscriptions	492	
Singers biografy	927	
Singing public worship	264	
vocal music	784	
Single standard coinage	332	
Sinking fund public finance	336.3	
Sintuism	299	
Sirocco meteorology	551.5	
Sisterhoods parochial work	255	
religious orders	271.9	
Size notation for books	025.3	
Sizes of books lib. econ.	025.8	
standard literary methods	029	
Skating	796	
Skeeing sports	796	
Skeleton, human	611	
of animals anat.	591	
Skeletons, preparations of	579	
Skepticism ancient filos.	186	
filosofic systems	149	
heresies	273	
natural theology	211	
Skeptics biografy	922	
Sketching drawing	741	
Skiing sports	796	
Skil, games of, amusements	794	
ethics	175	
Skild labor political economy	331.7	
Skul anatomy	611	
craniology	573	
Slander ethics	177	
Slang English language	427	
other "	437, 447, etc.	
Slater fund education	373.7	
Slates bilding stones	553	
lithology	552	
Slating bilding	695	
Slaughter houses air pollution	614.7	
industrial sanit'n	628	
Slavery	326	
abolition of U. S. history	973.7	
Slaves biografy	326	
Slavic filosofy	197	
languages	491.8	
literatures	891.8	
see also Russian		
Slavonic church language	491.8	
Sleep	135	
and rest hygiene	613.7	
of plants botany	581	
Sleepwalking	135	
Sliding friction mechanics	531	
Slight of hand	793	
Slöjd education	371.4	
Sloth ethics	179	
Slovakian language	491.8	
Slovenian "	491.8	
Sloyd education	371.4	
Sluices engineering	621.2	
Small arms manufacture	683	
Smallpox diseases	616	
inoculation, pub. helth	614.4	
public helth	614.5	
Smel, nervs of anatomy	611	
physiology	612	
senses psychology	152	
Smelting metallurgy	669	
Smithsonian exchanges lib. econ.	021.8	
institution	506	
Smoke air pollution	614.7	
flues heating	697	
nuisance sanitation	628	
Smoking ethics	178	
hygiene	613	

Topics in blackface type ar subdivided in the Tables

Smuggling	criminal law	343	Solar spectrum	astronomy	523.7
Smut	agriculture	632		system	descriptiv astron.	523
	fungi	589		time	cronology	529
Snakes		598.1	Soldiers' cemeteries, national		718
Snow	meteorology	551.5		homes	institutions	362
Snowshoeing	sports	796		lives	biografy	923
Soapmaking	air pollution	614.7		**military science**		**355**
	chemic technology	668		orfan schools		362.7
Sobriquets	bibliografy	014	Sol-fa method	music	784
Sociability	animals	591.5	Solids	geometry	513
Social clubs		367		properties of	physics	539
	customs and manners	394	Solitary confinement	punishments	343
	democracy	socialism	335	Solitude		177
	distinction	ethics	177	Solomon ilands	history	993
		rank	929.7		song of	Bible	223
	drinking	temperance	178	Solubility	theoretic chemistry	541
	ethics		177	Solutions	quantitativ analysis	545
	evil		176	Somatology	anthropology	573
	science		**300**	Somnambulism		135
		bibliografy	016.3	Somnambulists	biografy	920
	surveys		**914-919**	Song festivals	music	784
		sociology	309.1		of Solomon	Bible	223
	worship		264		the three children	Bible	229
Socialism		335	Songbooks	folklore	398
Societies, debating		374.2	Songs and ballads, English lit.		821
	dress reform	646		music		784
	for home study	374.4	Sonnets	English literature	821
	parish work	256	Sophist filosofy		183
	learned		**060**	Sorcery	occultism	133
	religious, *see* Religious assoc.		Sores	surgery	617
	welfare		**360**	Sorghum	agriculture	633
	special, class with subject			manufactures	664
Society	ethics	177	Soteriology	doctrinal theology	234
	for ethical culture	170		**hygiene**		**613**
	houses	student life	371.8	Soudan, Africa, history		966
	ilands	history	996		Egypt, "		962
	of Christian endevor	267	Soul	doctrinal theol.	237
	Jesus	monastic orders	271		**metaphysics**		**128**
	the Cincinnati	369.1		natural theol.	218
Socinians	heresies	273		destiny of	129
	unitarian church	288		in animals	591.5
Sociology		**300**		origin of	metaphysics	129
	bibliografy of	016.3	Sound	physics	534
	biografy of	923	South Africa	geology	556.8
Socratic filosofy		183		history	968
Soda	chemic technology	661		religious history	276.8
Sodalities	parish work	256		travel	916.8
Sofist filosofy		183		America antiquities	913.8
Soil	public helth	614.7		**description**		**918**
Soils	agriculture	631		**geology**		**558**
	chemic analysis	543		**history**		**980**
Solar engins	engineering	621.4		**religious history**		**278**

Topics in blackface type ar subdivided in the Tables

South America scientific travels	508.8	
statistics	318	
travel	918	
American Indian languages	498	
Atlantic states, U. S. geology	557.5	
history	975	
religious hist.	277.5	
travel	917.5	
Carolina, U. S. history	975.7	
travel	917.57	
Central Africa geology	556.7	
history	967	
religious hist.	276.7	
travel	916.7	
states, U. S. geology	557.6	
history	976	
relig.hist.	277.6	
travel	917.6	
Dakota, U. S. history	978.3	
travel	917.83	
Sea ilands history	996	
travel	919.6	
scheme stocks	332	
West, U. S. history	979	
travel	917.9	
Southern states U. S. history	975	
Soverens biografy	923	
Soverenty pol. science	320	
Space astronomy	523.1	
metaphysics	114	
sense physiology	612	
Spain antiquities	913.4	
botany	581.9	
geology	554.6	
history	946	
religious history	274.6	
travel	914.6	
Spanish America history	980	
travel	918	
art	709	
cyclopedias	036	
essays, collected	046	
filosofy	196	
inquisition persecutions	272	
journalism	076	
language	460	
literature	860	
newspapers	076	
periodicals, general	056	
societies, general	066	
war U. S. hist.	973.8	
Spar economic geology	553	

Spark, induction electricity	537	
Sparring amusements	796	
Sparta ancient history	938	
Spas hygiene	613	
Speakers oratory	808	
Speaking tubes communication	654	
Specie payment banking	332	
Species, origin of	575	
Specific customs taxation	336.2	
gravity chemistry	542	
physics	531	
of liquids physics	532	
Specifications for bilding	692	
Specifics therapeutics	615	
Specimens, arrangem't in museums	579	
Spectacles disorders of vision	617	
optics	535	
Specters occultism	133	
Spectroscope optics	535	
Spectroscopy astronomy	522	
Spectrum analysis astronomy	523	
chemistry	544	
optics	535	
Speculation ethics	174	
finance	332	
Speech filology	400	
fonology	414	
physiology	612	
freedom of polit. science	323	
impediments of	612	
organs of acoustics	534	
human anatomy	611	
visible comparativ filol.	414	
Speeches Amer. oratory	815	
Spelling books English language	428	
fonetic " "	421	
reform " "	421	
Sph-, see also Sf-		
Sphagna botany	588	
Spices adulterations	614.3	
chemic technology	664	
Spiders zoology	595	
Spies international law	341	
Spindles stone age	571	
Spine, curvature of diseases	616	
Spinning manufactures	677	
Spires architec. construction	721	
design	729	
Spirit doctrinal theology	233	
leveling geodesy	526	
Spiritism occultism	133	
Spiritual body doctrinal theology	233	

Topics in blackface type ar subdivided in the Tables

Spiritual heredity	doctrinal theology	233
	mental caracteris.	136
	metaphysics	129
Spiritualism	"	111
	occultism	133
	sects	289
Spirituous liquors	chem. tech.	663
	temperance	178
Spitzbergen	history	998
	travel	919.8
Spoils system	civil servis	351.6
Sponges	zoology	593
Spontaneity	metaphysics	127
Spontaneous combustion	chemistry	541
	generation	576
Sports, outdoor		**796**
parlor		**793**
Springs	physical geology	551
	mineral economic geol.	553
	waterworks	628
Sprinkling of streets	sanit. engin'g	628
Squares, least	geodesy	526
	probabilities	519
magic	arithmetic	511
tables of		510
Squaring the circle	geometry	513
Squids	zoology	594
Squinting	eye diseases	617
Stables	agriculture	636
	air pollution	614.7
	architecture	728
Stacks	library economy	022.4
Staf	" "	023
	military science	355
	music	781
Stage	ethics	175
	theater	792
coach	transport	656
Staind glass		748
Staining	chemic tech.	667
Stairbilding	bilding	694
Stalactites and stalagmites		551
Stammering		616
Stamp act	U. S. history	973.3
collecting		383
laws	public finance	336.2
Stamping designs	fancywork	746
Stamps, postage	post-offis	383
Standard sizes	literary methods	029
time		529
Standing army		355
Star chamber	Eng. history	942.05

Star fish		593
see also Stars		
Starch	adulterations	614.3
	manufacture	664
Stars	descriptiv astron.	523.8
Starvation	dietetic diseases	616
	hygiene	613.2
State and church	church	261
	political science	322
	state ethics	172
banks		332
bildings	architecture	725
control of cities	adminis.	352
department	U. S. gov't	353
dets	public finance	336.3
education		**379**
ethics		**172**
governments		353
laboratories	adulterations	614.3
law reports, U. S.		345
libraries		027.5
medicin		**614**
monopolies		336
ownership of land		333
political science		**320**
properties	public finance	336
rights	U. S. const. law	342
socialism		335
supervision of schools	educ.	379.1
trials	criminal law	343
universities	**colleges**	**378**
	state education	379.1
Statecraft		320
States-general	French legislature	328
Statesmanship	political science	320
Statesmen	biografy	923
Static electricity		537
Statics		531
Stationary engins		621.1
Stationery	paper manufacture	676
Statistical methods		311
Statistics		**310**
	labor	331
	library administration	025.1
class special with subjects		
Statuary		**730**
Statute law	American	345
	British	346
Steam boilers		621.1
	inspection	614.8
engin	mech. engin'g	621.1
	physics	536

Topics in blackface type ar subdivided in the Tables

Steam fitting		696
heating	bilding	697
	engineering	621.1
navigation	sociology	387
	useful arts	656
physics		536
pipes	bilding	696
pumps		621.6
ships	naval engin'g	623.8
transport	useful arts	656
Stearin	organic chemistry	547
Steel	bilding material	691
	manufactures	672
	metallurgy	669
engraving	fine arts	762
structures	arch.	721
works	"	725
Steeples	"	729
Steering	seamanship	656
Stellar astronomy		523.8
Stencil decoration		747
Stencils		652
Stenografy		653
Stephen	English history	942.02
Stereometer	specific gravity	531
Stereometry	gaging	511
Stereopticon	optics	535
Stereoscopes	"	535
Stereotomy	descr. geometry	515
Stereotyping	printing	655
Stethometry	physiology	612
Stethoscope	diagnosis	616
Sties, hog	air pollution	614.7
Stigmata	devotional	248
Stıl-life	painting	758
Stils	chemic technology	668
	prac. chem.	542
Stimulants	ethics of using	178
	hygiene	613
	manufacture	663
	therapeutics	615
Stipple engraving		765
Stock exchanges		332
jobbing		332
live	**agriculture**	**636**
Stockholm	history	948.7
	travel	914.87
Stockings	clothing	646
	costume	391
Stocks	political economy	332
Stoic filosofy		188
Stone age		571
Stone and iron structures	architec.	721
artificial	chemic technology	666
bilding materials		691
carving	sculpture	736
construction	masonry	693
cutting	masonry	693
	sculpture	731
	stereotomy	515
remains		571
ware	manufactures	666
Stonehenge	English antiquities	913.4
Stones	econ. geology	553
Storage of electricity	engin'g	621.3
	science	537
rooms	library economy	022.4
Stores, cooperativ	political econ.	334
department		658
Stories	English fiction	823
	kindergarten	372.2
of animals		591.5
Storms, electric		538
	meteorology	551.5
Story-telling	library econ.	027.62
Stoves	heating systems	697
	kitchen equipment	643
	manufactures	672
Strategy		355
Stratification	geology	551
Stratified ore deposits	econ. geol.	553
Stratigrafic geology		551
Strawberries	agriculture	634
Street cleaning		628
railways	engineering	625
	management	656
	sociology	388
Streets	engineering	625
	local administration	352
laying out	pub. helth	614.7
trees in	sanitary engin'g	628
Strength of materials	engineering	620.1
	molec. phys.	539
Stresses	bridge engineering	624
Strikes	political economy	331.89
Stringd instruments		787
Strofe	English prosody	426
Structural biology		574
botany		581
geology		551
Structure, molecular	physics	539
of the universe	astron.	523.1
Strychnin	materia medica	615
Stuarts	English history	942.06

Topics in blackface type ar subdivided in the Tables

Stucco	masonry	693
Student life and customs		371.8
Students	biografy	923
Study, Bible		**220**
	clubs, relation to library	021
	furniture	651
	methods	371.3
	rooms library economy	022
	self-culture	**374**
of special topic, see subject		
Stuttering		616
Style	dom. econ.	646
	fashion	**390**
	literary rhetoric	808
Subject bibliografies		**016**
	catalogs bibliografy	017
	library admin.	025.3
Subjectivity	knowledge	121
Sublime and beautiful esthetics		701
Submarine armor		627
	cables telegrafy	654
	mines military eng.	623
	telegraf communication	654
	sociology	384
	tunnels mining eng.	622
	vessels shipbilding	623.8
	warfare naval eng.	623
Subscription libraries		027.3
	to creeds eccles. pol.	262
	39 articles Ang. ch.	283
Subsidies	protection	337
	ship	387
Substance	metaphysics	111
Subways	hygiene of ground	614.7
	road engineering	625
	sanitation	628
Success in life ethics		174
Succession, apostolic eccles. pol.		262
	monarchic pol. science	321
	to Eng. crown const. law	342
	property law	347
Suction pump	physics	533
Sudan, Africa	history	966
	Egypt "	962
Suez canal	engineering	626
	sociology	386
Suffixes	English etymology	422
Suffocation	protection of life	614.8
Suffrage	political science	324
Sugar	adulterations	614.3
	manufacture	664
	organic chemistry	547

Sugar cane	agriculture	633
	refining air pollution	614.7
	chem. tech.	664
Suggestion	hypnotism	134
	therapeutics	615
Suicide	customs	394
	ethics	179
Suits in equity law		347
Sulfates	chemic technology	661
Sulfur	chemistry	546
	compounds air pollution	614.7
	waters econ. geol.	553
Sulfuric acid	chemic technology	661
Sumatra	history	992
Summer houses arbors		717
	resorts amusements	791
	architecture	728
	schools self education	374.8
Sumptuary laws ethics		177
Sun	descriptiv astronomy	523.7
	motors engineering	621.4
	pictures **fotografs**	**770**
	worship	291
Sunda	geology	559.2
	history	992
	religious history	279.2
	travel	919.2
Sunday		263
	closing library economy	024
	school libraries	027.8
	schools	268
Superintendence, bilding		692
	school	379.1
Superior, Lake travel		917.7
Supernatural	metaphysics	125
	theology	231
Supernaturalism occultism		133
Superstitions		133
Supervision	bilding	692
	school governmental	379.1
	professional	371.2
Supply and demand pol. econ.		338
Support, library		021.9
	public school	379.1
Supremacy, papal eccles. polity		262
Supreme court reports, U. S.		345
Surface features of the earth		551
Surgeons	biografy	926
Surgery		617
Surinam, S. Amer. hist.		988
Surnames	genealogy	929
Surveying	geodesy	526

Topics in blackface type ar subdivided in the Tables

Surveys, general scientific		508.3
	sanitary public helth	614.7
	social description	**914–919**
Survival of the fittest evolution		575
Susceptibility psychology		157
Suttee	treatment of the ded	393
Svealand, Sweden	history	948.7
	travel	914.87
Swastika	ecclesiology	246
	heraldry	929.6
Swearing	ethics	179
Sweating system laboring classes		331.2
Sweden	antiquities	913.4
	botany	581.9
	geology	554.8
	history	**948.5**
	religious history	274.8
	travel	**914.85**
	zoology	591.9
Swedenborgian church		289
Swedish church sects		284
	language	439
	literature	839
Swimming		797
	animal locomotion	591
Swindling	ethics	174
	law	343
Swine, diseases of vet. medicin		619
	domestic animals	636.4
Switzerland	antiquities	913.4
	botany	581.9
	geology	554.9
	history	949.4
	religious history	274.9
	travel	914.94
	zoology	591.9
Sword exercise		796
Syenite	lithology	552
Syfon	physics	532
Syllogism	logic	166
Symbolic logic		164
Symbolism	Bible	220.6
	religious art	**246**
Sympathy	emotions	157
Symphony	orchest. music	785
Symptoms	diagnosis	616
Synagogs	architecture	726
Syncronology	history	902
Synod	ecclesiastic polity	262
Synonyms	English language	424
	French "	444
	other " 434, 454, etc.	

Syntax	comparativ filology	415
	English language	425
Synthesis	chemistry	545
	logic	**160**
Syphilis	diseases	616
	public helth	614.5
Syphon	physics	532
Syria	ancient history	939
	modern "	956
Syriac language		492
Syrian church sects		281
	desert travel	915.3
Syrup	adulterations	614.3
Systematic catalogs bibliog.		017
Systems manuals *Class with subject*		
	filosofic	**140**
Tabernacle	Biblical antiquities	220.9
	sacred furniture	247
Table	domestic economy	642
	and parlor games	793
	talk English literature	828
	tipping spiritism	133
Tableaux	amusements	793
Tables	astronomy	524
	furniture	645
	library	022.9
	interest	651
	life insurance	368
	mathematical	510
	mercantil	658
	tide	525
	time transport	656
Tablets, memorial monuments		718
Tachygraphy shorthand		653
Tactics, military		**355**
Taft, W. H. presidency		973.91
Tailoring		687
Taiwan history		952
Takigrafy		653
Talbotypes		772
Talent	psychology	151
Tales	English literature	823
Talipes	surgery	617
Talismans	occultism	133
Talmud	Judaism	296
Tambourine	instruments	789
Tamil language		494
Tammany political associations		363
Tanganyika Ter. history		967
Tanning		675
	air pollution	614.7

Topics in blackface type ar subdivided in the Tables

Taouism		299
Tapestry		746
Tar	chemic technology	668
roofing	bilding	695
Target-shooting		799
Targums	Chaldee versions	221
Tarifs		**337**
Tartary	**history**	**950**
	travel	**915**
Tasks	school disciplin	371.5
Tasmania	history	994
Taste	esthetics	701
	psychology	152
Taverns	home economics	647
Tax titles	law	347
Taxation	local government	352
	political econ.	336.2
Taxes, exemption from		336.2
tarif		**337**
Taxidermy		579
Taylor, Z.	presidency	973.6
Tea	adulterations	614.3
	cultivation	633
	domestic economy	641
Teachers and teaching		**371**
	institutes education	370.7
	lives	923
	training	370.7
Teaching, freedom of education		378.1
	pol. sci.	323
	of special topics, see subject	
Teas, commercial mixing of		663
Technical dictionaries		603
	class special with subject	
	education	607
	on special topics, see subject	
	troops mil. sci.	358
Technologic schools		607
	on special topics, see subject	
Technology	•	**600**
Teeth	animals	591
	dentistry	617
Teetotalism	temperance	178
Tehuantepec, Mexico history		972
	ship canal	626
Telefone	business	654
	electric engin'g	621.3
	physics	537
	sociology	384
Telegraf	business	654
	engineering	621.3
	military signals	623

Telegraf	physics	537
	sociology	384
codes	writing	652
Telegrafy	engineering	621.3
	useful arts	654
Teleology	metaphysics	124
Telepathy	psychology	133
Telephot	fotografy	778
Telescope	astronomy	522
	optics	535
Telescopes	famous	522
Telferage	mec. engin'g	621
Temper	ethics	179
Temperament	piano	786
Temperaments	psychology	137
Temperance		178
	hygiene	613
Temperature	conditions of life	577
	hygiene	613
	in disease diagnosis	616
	mesurement	536
	of air meteorology	551.5
	body physiology	612
	earth geology	551
	sense physiology	612
	therapeutics	615
Tempering	manufactures	671
	molecular physics	539
Templars	knights	929.7
	masons	366
Temples	architecture	726
	student society halls	371.8
Temporal power papacy		262
Temptation	doctrinal theology	233
Tenants	law	347
Tender, legal paper money		332
Tenement houses architecture		728
Tenements	hygiene	613
Teneriffe	description	914.6
Tennessee, U. S.	history	976.8
	travel	917.68
Tennis, lawn		796
parlor		794
Tension	strength of materials	620.1
Tent life	hygiene	613
Tenting	outdoor sports	796
Tents as dwellings prehistoric arch.		571
Tenure of land law		347
	political economy	333
offis	civil servis	351
	library economy	023
	teachers	371.1

Topics in blackface type ar subdivided in the Tables

Teratology   animals   591
                  natural hist. of man   573
                  plants   581
                  surgery   617
Terminology   metaphysics   112
Terms   schools   371.2
Terra cotta   art   738
                  manufactures   666
                  construction   masonry   693
Terra del Fuego   travel   918.2
Terraces   physical geology   551
Terrapin   zoology   598.1
Terrestrial magnetism   538
Tertiary age   geology   551
Test laws   Eng. religious history   274.2
Testacea   594
Testament, New   225
          Old   221
Testamentary law   347
Testimony   probabilities   519
                  legal   evidence   347
Tests   chemic analysis   543
                  psychology   151
Testudinata   zoology   598.1
Tetanus   diseases   616
                  surgery   617
Teutonic knights   929.7
                  minor languages   439
                  literatures   839
                  mythology   293
Texas, U. S.   history   976.4
                  travel   917.64
                  annexation   U. S. history 973.6
Textbooks   instruction   371.3
        for writ'g verse Eng. prosody   426
        free   pub. schools   379.1
Textil fabrics   dom. econ.   646
                  inspection   614.3
                  manufactures   677
                  prehistoric archeol.   571
        fibers   agriculture   633
        hangings bilding   698
                  dom. econ.   645
        roofing   bilding   695
Texts   comparativ filology   418
        for learning Eng. lang.   428
                  other "   438, 448, etc.
        original Bible   220.4
Thallofyta   botany   589
Thanksgiving day customs   394
                  schools   371.3
                  sermons   252

Thatch   roofing   695
Theaters   amusements   792
                  ethics   175
Theatricals, private   793
Theft   law   343
Theism   natural theology   211
Theodicy   God   231
                  providence   214
Theofanies   231
Theologians   biografy   922
Theologic doctrins   230
                  education   religion   207
Theology   200
                  biografy of   922
                  natural   210
Theophanies   231
Theoretic astronomy   521
                  chemistry   541
                  ethics   171
Theories of construction   bilding   690
                  special subject, with subj.
Theosofy   212
Therapeutics   615
Thermal springs   seismology   551
Thermochemistry   541
Thermodynamics   536
Thermometers heat   536
                  mecanic trades   681
Thermometry   meteorology   551.5
Thermoscope   536
Thessalonians   Bible   227
Thinking   psychology   153
Thirst   physiology   612
Thirty-nine articles   creeds   238
Thirty years' war   European history   940.2
                  German   "   943
                  Scandinavian hist.   948
Thomas à Kempis   242
Thomsonianism   cures   615
Thoracostraca   595
Thorobass   music   781
Thought   psychology   153
                  transference   133
Thrift, laboring classes   polit. econ.   331.8
Throndhjem, Norway   history   948.4
                  travel   914.84
Thugs   religious sect   299
Thunder   physics   537
                  storms   meteorology   551.5
Tibet, China   history   951
Tide tables   525
                  waters   law   347

Topics in blackface type ar subdivided in the Tables

Tides	astronomy	525
	physical geografy	551
Tierra del Fuego	travel	918.2
Tigers	zoology	599
Til	physical geology	551
Tiles	architectural construction	721
	bilding material	691
	manufactures	666
Tiling	masonry	693
	roofing	695
Timber	architecture	724
	bilding material	691
	forestry	634.9
	manufacture	674
	trade	338
Timbuctoo	travel	916.6
Time	cronology	529
	metaphysics	115
keepers	watchmaking	681
standard		529
tables, railroad		656
Timothy	Bible	227
Tin	chemistry	546
	manufactures	671
	metallurgy	669
	mining	622
	prehistoric	571
ores	econ. geol.	553
roofing	bilding	695
Tissues	animal histology	591
	vegetable "	581
Tithes		254
	taxation	336.2
Title catalog	library admin.	025.3
to property, law of		347
Titles and duties	library economy	023
changed book	bibliografy	014
of honor		929.7
Titus	Bible	227
Toads	zoology	597
Toadstools	botany	589
Tobacco	adulterations	614.3
	cerebro-cardiac pois.	615
	cultivation	633
	ethics	178
	hygiene	613
	internal revenue	336.2
	manufactures	679
	state monopoly	336
pipes	manufac.	679
Tobit	Apocryfa	229
Toes, extra	deformities	617
Toilet articles	customs	391
	domestic economy	646
Token money	numismatics	737
Tokio	history	952
	travel	915.2
Toleration, religious	state ethics	172
Tolls, road and bridge		352
Tomb-burial	public helth	614.6
Tombs	cemeteries	718
	disposal of ded	393
Tongue	diagnosis	616
Tonic sol-fa	vocal music	784
Tonics	aids to digestion	615
Tonkin	history	959
Tonnage	gaging	389
	shipping	656
Tools	agriculture	631
	bilding	690
	mecanic trades	680
	prehist. archeol.	571
	printing	655
machine	mecanical engin'g	621
Toothake	dentistry	617
Topical method	instruction	371.3
Topografy	hygiene of ground	614.7
	maps	912
	military engin'g	623
	surveying	526
Tories	political parties	329
Tornadoes	meteorology	551.5
Torpedoes	explosivs	662
	naval engineering	623
Torrens system		333
Tortoises	zoology	598.1
Torts	law	347
Torture	customs of war	399
	law	340
	persecutions	272
Total abstinence		178
depravity	doctrinal theol.	233
Totemism		392
Touch	physiology	612
	psychology	152
Tournaments	customs	394
Town halls	architecture	725
offisers	local gov't	352
planning		711
Towns	government	352
	sanitation	628
Toxicology	therapeutics	615
Toys	amusements	796
	domestic econ.	649

Topics in blackface type ar subdivided in the Tables

Tract societies		206
Tractarianism Anglican church		283
Tracts, religious, practical		240
class special with topic		
Trade, balance of commerce		382
boards of "		381
depressions "		380
domes. com.		381
money		332
production		338
domestic		381
foren		382
free		337
list of books, publishers'		**015**
marks copyright		655
law		347
patents		608
schools		607
slave		326
winds meteorology		551.5
Trades, mecanic		**680**
unions polit. econ.		331.88
Trading companies		338
stamps		658
Traditions folklore		398
Traffic commerce		656
Tragedies English literature		822
Training, physical hygiene		613.7
outdoor sports		796
school hygiene		371.7
teachers		371.1
class special with subject		
Trains railroad business		656
engineering		625
Traitors biografy		923
Tramps pauperism		339
Tramways city transit		388
engineering		625
mining engineering		622
Trance hypnotism		134
Transactions gen. soc.		**060**
special, see subject		
Transcendentalism		141
Transit instruments astronomy		522
local sociology		388
Transits astronomy		523
Translating, art of		808
Translations *Class with originals*		
principle of comp. filol.		418
Transliteration comparativ filol.		411
in cataloging		025.3
Transmigration of souls		129
Transmission, heredity evolution		575
hygiene		613.9
machinery of engin'g		621
of disease pub. helth		614.4
elec. power engin'g		621.3
power mec. "		621
Transmutation of energy physics		531
metals chemistry		540.1
species, evolution		575
Transplanting agriculture		631
Transport criminal law		343
military science		355
sociology		**380**
useful arts		656
bildings architec.		725
Transubstantiation		265
Transvaal, Africa history		968
Transylvania history		943.9
Trap lithology		552
Trapping business		639
Traps agriculture		632
domestic econ.		648
Traumatic fever surgery		617
Travelers, manuals for		910
protection pub. helth		614.8
Travelers' conversation books, Eng.		428
lives		923
Traveling, art of		910
Travels bibliografy		016.9
general		**910**
scientific		**508.3**
special, see subject		
Treason law		343
Treasury notes paper money		332
U. S. administration		353
Treaties international law		341
Treating temperance ethics		178
Treatises priv. law		347
class special with subject		
Treatment of captivs war customs		399
disease		616
the ded customs		393
pub. helth		614.6
Treaty of Washington		341
Tredmils mecanical engin'g		621.4
punishments		343
Trees botany		582
forestry		634.9
fruit culture		634
in streets sanitation		628
ornamental		715
Trefining surgery		617

Topics in blackface type ar subdivided in the Tables

Trent creed of Pius 4	238
Trials, civil law	347
criminal "	343
ecclesiastic	262
military law	344
Triangle musical instruments	789
Triassic age geology	551
Tribes form of state	321
Trichinae economic zoology	591
parasitic diseases	616
Trichiniasis public helth	614.5
Tricks, card amusements	793
slight of hand	791
Tricycling	796
Trieste history	943.6
travel	914.36
Trigonometry	514
Trilobites paleontology	565
zoology	595
Trinity doctrinal theology	231
Tripoli, Africa history	961
Triumfs student customs	371.8
Trombone wind instruments	788
Tromso, Norway history	948.4
travel	914.84
Tropical plants geog. distrib.	581.9
Trotting racing	798
Troubadours Provençal literature	849
Trout culture	639
Trouvères French literature	841
Troy ancient history	939
Truces international law	341
Truck farming	635
system labor and wages	331.2
Trumpet wind instruments	788
Trunkmaking	685
Trusses engineering	624
surgery	617
Trust companies banks	332
Trustees, library	023
Trusts and trustees law	347
Truth ethics	177
Tubes communication	654
Tudor architecture	724
Tudors English history	942.05
Tungusic language	494
Tunicata	594
Tunis history	961
travel	916.1
Tunneling mining engineering	622
railroad engineering	625
Tunnels aqueducts	628

Turanian languages	494
literatures	894
Turkestan geology	555.8
history	958
religious history	275.8
travel	915.8
East history	951
Turkey in Asia geology	555.6
history	956
religious history	275.6
travel	915.6
Europe botany	581.9
history	949.6
travel	914.96
Turkish architecture	723
baths hygiene	613
harems customs	392
language	494
literature	894
Turning manufactures	674
lathes	621
Turnpikes road engineering	625
Turtles zoology	598.1
Tuscany, Italy history	945
Twilight	525
Tyler, John presidency	973.5
Type printing	655
Types psychology of	137
Typewriters communication	652
Typografers biografy	926
Typografy	655
Typology Bible	220.6
Tyre ancient history	939
Tyrian architecture	722
Tyrol history	943.6
travel	914.36
Tyrone, Ireland history	941.6
Tyrotoxicon animal poisons	615
U boats Great war 1914–19	940.45
naval engin'g	623.8
Uganda, Africa history	967
Ukraine, Russia "	947
Ulcers surgery	617
Ulster, Ireland history	941.6
travel	914.16
Ultramontanism catholic church	282
eccles. polity	262
Unconsciousness metaphysics	127
Unction, extreme theology	265
Underground roads engineering	625
mining engin'g	622

Topics in blackface type ar subdivided in the Tables

Understanding psychology	**153**	
Undulation	dynamics	531
	heat	536
	light	535
	sound	534
Uniformity, act of	Eng. relig. hist.	274.2
Uniforms, domestic		647
	military	355
Union of Soc. Soviet Rep.	hist.	947
	trav.	914.7
Unionidae	zoology	594
Unions, trade	polit. econ.	331.88
Unique books	rarities	094
Unitarian church		288
Unitarians	biografy	922
United Americans	political soc.	363
brethren	sects	284
Kingdom	**history**	**942**
Netherlands	"	949.2
presbyterian church	sects	285
Provinces	history	949.2
servis, military and naval		355
States administration		353
	antiquities	913.7
	bank	332
	botany	581.9
	boundaries	**973**
	Christian com. ass'ns	267
	hist.	973.7
	coast survey	526
	constitutional law	342
	finance	336
	geology	**557.3**
	history	**973**
	laws	345
	literature	**810**
	religious history	**277.3**
	sanitary com. charity	361
	hist.	973.7
	statistics	317
	travel	**917.3**
	zoology	591.9
United States of Colombia	geology	558.6
	history	986
	relig. hist.	278.6
	travel	918.6
Unity	metaphysics	111
of God	doctrin	231
human race		572
knowledge		121
language		401
nature		501
Univalvs	mollusks	594
Universal gravitation	physics	531
	history	909
	language	408
	military servis	355.2
Universalism		289
Universalists	biografy	922
Universals	**metaphysics**	**113**
Universe	astronomy	523.1
Universities		**378**
	architecture	727
University education		378
	extension	378.1
	of the State of New York	379.7
	people's, library as the	021
Universology	**cosmology**	**113**
Unregenerate	doctrinal theology	233
Upholstering	trades	684
Upholstery	dom. econ.	645
Upper Guinea	history	966
Ural-Altaic languages		494
Uranografy	**astronomy**	**523**
Uranus	planets	523.4
Urchins, sea	radiates	593
Uruguay	geology	558.9
	history	989
	religious history	278.9
	travel	918.9
Usages, social	customs	395
Use of words	Eng. filology	428
Useful arts		**600**
	bibliografy of	016.6
	biografy of	926
Usefulness of animals, econ. zool.		591
	libraries	**021**
	plants econ. bot.	581
Usury	banking	332
	law	347
Utah, U. S.	history	979.2
	travel	917.92
Utilitarianism	ethics	171
Utilities, public		**380**
Utility of filosofy		101
	special subjects, see subject	
Utopias	political science	321
Vacation schools	adult	374.8
Vaccination	pub. helth	614.4
Vagabondage	pauperism	339
Vagrancy	"	339
Valleys	physical geografy	551
Value, standards of	pol. econ.	332

Topics in blackface type ar subdivided in the Tables

Values, average	probabilities	519
educational	curriculum	375
food	dom. econ.	641
Valvs	hydraulics	532
	mecanical engin'g	621
Vampire	folklore	398.4
	zoology	599
Van Buren, M.	presidency	973.5
Vancouver iland	history	971.1
Vapor engins	mec. engin'g	621.4
Vaporization	heat	536
Vapors	meteorology	551.5
	properties of	533
Varangian kingdom	hist.	947
Variation	evolution	575
in animals	phys. zool.	591
of compass		522
Variolation	public helth	614.4
Varnishes	chemic technology	667
Varnishing	painting	698
Varnishmaking	air pollution	614.7
Vases	pottery	738
Vassalage		321
Vassar college	educ. of women	376.8
Vatican council, 1870	infallibility	262
Vaticination	occultism	133
Vaudois	Christian sects	284
	persecution	272
Vaults	air pollution	614.7
	arch. construction	721
	design	729
Vedas	Sanskrit literature	891
Vegetable anatomy		581
chemistry		547
diet	hygiene	613.2
drugs	mat. med.	615
dye plants	agric.	633
fats	chem. tech.	665
food	dom. econ.	641
gardening		635
oils	chem. tech.	665
parasites	diseases	616
physiology		581
substances, analysis of		543
trades	air pollution	614.7
world	**botany**	**580**
Vegetables	field crops	633
	garden crops	635
	inspection pub. helth	614.3
	preservation chem. tech.	664
Vegetarianism	hygiene	613.2
Vegetation	**botany**	**580**
Vehicles	carbilding	699
	carriage making	684
motor	engin'g	629.2
Vehmgericht	criminal law	343
Veins, mineral	economic geology	553
Vellum, books printed on	rarities	096
Velocipede	amusements	796
	engineering	629.2
Venders	law	347
Veneer	architectural decor.	729
Veneering	cabinetmaking	684
Venesection	therapeutics	615
Venezuela	geology	558.7
	history	987
	religious history	278.7
	travel	918.7
Venice	history	945
Ventilating	science	536
Ventilation	bilding	697
	domestic econ.	644
	library economy	022
	mining engin'g	622
	sanitary "	628
Ventriloquism		791
Venus	planets	523.4
transits of	astron.	523
Vermes	articulates	595
Vermont, U. S.	history	974.3
	travel	917.43
Verse, science of		416
	text-books for writing Eng.	426
Versification	English prosody	426
Vertebrates	**paleontology**	**566**
	zoology	**596**
Vespers	music	783
	ritual	264
Vestments	ecclesiology	247
Veterans	societies	369.1
Veterinary medicin		619
	sanitation pub. helth	614.9
Viaducts	bridges	624
Viaticum	sacraments	265
Vice	criminal law	343
	education	379.2
Vices	**ethics**	**170**
Victoria, Queen	English history	942.08
Australia	"	994
Victorian Gothic architecture		724
Victrola	mec. instruments	789
Vienna, congress of	Europ. hist.	940.27
	internat. law	341
history		943.6

Topics in blackface type ar subdivided in the Tables

Vignettes	**engravings**	**760**
Vikings	history	948
Village communities		321
Villas	architecture	728
Villeins	feudalism	321
Vine culture	agriculture	634
Vinegar		664
Vines	botany	581
Vinyards		634
Violins	stringd instruments	787
Virgin ilands	history	972.9
Virgin Mary	catholic doctrin	232
Virginia, U. S.	history	975.5
	travel	917.55
West, U. S.	history	975.4
	travel	917.54
Virginity	religious asceticism	248
Virtues		**170**
Visible speech	fonology	414
Visigoths	German history	943
Vision	optics	535
	psychology	152
disorders	blind asylums	362.4
	diseases of eye	617
Visions and dreams		135
Visitation and search	internat. law	341
pastoral		253
Visitations	English heraldry	929.7
Vital fenomena, biology		577
functions	animal physiol.	591
	human "	612
statistics	population	312
	public helth	614.1
Vitalism	biology	577
Vitality	zoology	591
Vivisection	animal anatomy	591
	ethics	179.4
laws	public helth	614.2
Vocal culture	elocution	808
	music	784
music		784
organs	acoustics	534
	human anatomy	611
	physiology	612
Vocalists	biografy	927
Vocation, choice of		371.4
Vocational education		371.4
Voice	elocution	808
	physiology	612
	singing	784
Volapük	universal language	408
Volcanic rocks	lithology	552
Volcanoes	physical geology	551
Volition		159
Volkslied	vocal music	784
Voltaic electricity	physics	537
Volumetric analysis	chemistry	545
	geometry	513
Voluntary	music	786
Volunteers	army	355.2
Vomiting	pathology	616
Voodooism		133
Vortex rings	molecular physics	539
Voting	suffrage	324
machines	suffrage	324
Vowels	English language	421
Vows	asceticism	248
Voyages, Antarctic		919.9
Arctic		919.8
round the world		910.4
scientific		**508.3**
travels		910.4
Vulgarisms	English language	428
Vulgate	Bible	220.4
Wager of battle	legal antiquities	340
Wagers	ethics	175
Wages	domestic economy	647
	farm economics	631
	polit. economy	331.2
Wagnerian music		782
Wagons	manufacture	684
Wake	funeral customs	393
Wakefulness	hygiene	613
	psychology	135
Waldenses	persecutions	272
	sects	284
Wales	geology	554.2
	history	942.9
	language	491.6
	religious history	274.2
	travel	914.29
Walking	animal locomotion	591
	pedestrianism	613.7
matches	amusements	796
Walks	landscape gardening	713
Wall papers	decoration	745
	manufacture	676
	paper hanging	698
street	banking	332
Wallachia	history	949.8
	travel	914.98
Wallachian language		459
literature		859

Topics in blackface type ar subdivided in the Tables

Walls	arch. construction	721
	design	729
Waltz	music	786
Waltzing	amusements	793
	ethics	175
Wandering Jew	legends	398.2
War, civil	U. S. history	973.7
customs of		399
department, U. S.		353
ethics		172.4
French and Indian, U. S. history		973.2
Great	**1914–19**	**940.3**
law of		341
Mexican	U. S. history	973.6
military science		**355**
of 1812,	U. S. history	973.5
Roses	English "	942.04
revolutionary	U. S. history	973.3
woman in	customs	396
Warehouses	architecture	725
Warming	bilding	697
	sanitary engineering	628
Warnings	omens	133
Warrants	law	343
Warships	shipbilding	623.8
Warts	skin diseases	616
Washing	laundry	648
Washington, George	presidency	973.4
Washington, D. C.	history	975.3
	travel	917.53
state	U. S. history	979.7
	travel	917.97
treaty of		341
Wasps	insects	595.7
Wastes, disposal of	sanitation	628
Watches	horology	529
Watchmaking		681
Water, artificial ponds, etc.		714
as a beverage	hygiene	613
chemic analysis		543
closets	house drainage	628
colors		751
cure	therapeutics	615
engins	mecanical engin'g	621.2
filters	hygiene	613
gas	heating	697
glass	chem. tech.	666
hydraulics	physics	532
	useful arts	621.2
mineral, artificial		663
physical geografy		551
pollution		628
Water power	hydraulic engin'g	627
	mecanical "	621.2
products		338
rights	pol. econ.	333
supply, agric.		631
	canal engineering	626
	sanitary "	628
towers	fire extinction	614.8
travel	protection of life	614.8
wheels	hydraulics	532
	mec. engineering	621.2
works		628
	city administration	352
Watering places	hygiene	613
Waterloo, battle of	French hist.	944
Waterproofing	bilding	691
Waters, mineral	adulterations	614.3
	artificial	663
	geology	553
	hygiene	613
	therapeutics	615
Wave theory	optics	535
	sound	534
Waves, theory of	hydraulics	532
Wax flowers		746
Wealth, *see* Welth		
Weapons, *see* Wepons		
Weather	meteorology	551.5
Weaving		677
Wedding customs		392
Wedgewood ware	pottery	738
Weeds	economic botany	581
	pests	632
Week, names of days of		529
Weems	prehistoric archeol.	571
Weighing and mesuring	chem.	542
Weights and mesures		389
Wel water	hygiene	613
Welding	metal manuf.	671
Wels	physical geografy	551
	water supply	628
Welsh history		942.9
language		491.6
literature		891.6
travel		914.29
Welth	**political economy**	**330**
and rank	soc. ethics	177
consumption	final	339
	productiv	331
Wepons	customs	399
	mil. engin'g	623
	science	355

Topics in blackface type ar subdivided in the Tables

Wepons	prehist. archeol.	571
Werewolvs	folklore	398.4
West Indies	geology	557.2
	history	972.9
	travel	917.29
West Point	academy	355
U. S.	**history**	**978**
	travel	**917.8**
Virginia, U. S.	history	975.4
	travel	917.54
Western		
church	Rom. catholic	282
hemisfere	**geog.**	**917**
states, U. S.		
Mountain	geology	557.8
	history	**978**
	relig. hist.	277.8
	travel	**917.8**
Pacific	geology	557.9
	history	**979**
	relig. hist.	277.9
	travel	**917.9**
Westminster confession	creeds	238
Wether	meteorology	551.5
Whale	fisheries	639
	zoology	599
Wheat	adulterations	614.3
	agriculture	633
trade	agric. products	338
Wheel and axle	physics	531
cycling	amusements	796
Wheels, cog	mecanical engin'g	621
water	hydraulics	532
	mecanical engin'g	621.2
wooden	manufactures	674
Whigs	political parties	329
Whirlpools	ocean currents	551
Whirlwinds	meteorology	551.5
Whisky	chemic technology	663
insurrection, Penn.	hist.	974.8
tax	pub. finance	336.2
Whist	games	795
White hair	dermatology	616
led	chemic technology	667
Whooping cough	pathology	616
	public helth	614.5
Wife's duties	ethics	173
Wigs	customs	391
Wil	psychology	159
	theology	234
of God	ethics	171
William 1, Conqueror, Eng. history		942.02
William 2 Rufus	Eng. history	942.02
3 and Mary	" "	942.06
4	" "	942.07
Wilmot proviso	U. S. history	973.6
Wils	genealogy	929
	law	347
Wilson, W.	presidency	973.91
Wind and current charts		551
instruments	music	788
mils	air engins	621.4
Window gardens		716
Windows	arch. construction	721
	design	729
	staind glass	arch. decor.	729
Winds	meteorology	551.5
Windsor, house of	Eng. hist.	942.08
Wine	adulterations	614.3
	manufacture	663
	temperance	178
Wings	animal locomotion	591
Winter sports		796
Wire	manufacture	671
Wireless communication	business	654
	engin'g	621.3
Wisconsin, U. S.	history	977.5
	travel	917.75
Wisdom	Apocryfa	229
divine	doct. theology	231
Wit	American humor	817
	English "	827
	other " 837, 847, etc.	
Witchcraft	occultism	133
Witches	persecutions	272
Witnesses	evidence	347
Wives' duties	family ethics	173
Woman	customs	396
	education	**376**
	suffrage	324
	political parties	329
Woman's position and treatment		396
rights	customs	396
Women, diseases of		618
duties of	family ethics	173
	social "	177
labor of	political econ.	331.4
lives of	collections	920.7
Women's religious societies		267
rights	customs	396
work in church		259
Wood	bilding material	691
alcohol	chem. tech.	661
carving	fine arts	736

Topics in blackface type ar subdivided in the Tables

Wood construction	carpentry	694
	engraving	761
	implements manufactures	674
Woodburytypes	fotografy	773
Woods	economic botany	581
	forestry	634.9
Woodworking	carpentry	694
	manufactures	674
Wool	agriculture	636.3
	manufactures	677
	dyeing chemic technology	667
Word method	elemen. education	372
Words	English etymology	422
	slang	427
	use and abuse, Eng.	428
Work, parish, societies for		256
	Sunday	263
Workhouses, asylums		362.5
Working classes	**political econ.**	**331.8**
Workmen's insurance	law	368
	pol. econ.	331.2
Workshop receits	chem. tech.	660
World, atlases of		912
	voyages round	910.4
	war	**940.3–.4**
World's fairs		606
Worlds, plurality of		523.1
Worms	diseases	616
	paleontology	565
	zoology	595
Worship, family		249
	of animals idolatry	291
	public	264
Worsteds	manufactures	677
Wounded, hospitals for		362.1
Wounds	surgery	617
Wrecking and life-saving		614.8
Wrestling		796
Writing	useful arts	652
	elementary educ.	372
	for the press lit. methods	029
	machines	652
	of history	907
Writs	law	347
Written examinations	education	371.2
Wrongs	law of torts	347
Wyoming, U. S.	history	978.7
	travel	917.87
	massacre Penn. history	974.8
X-rays	pathology	616
	radioactivity	539
Yacht-bilding		623.8
Yachting	amusements	797
Yarns	manufactures	677
Yearbooks	**statistics**	**310**
	class special with subject	
Yeast	adulterations	614.3
	botany	589
	chemic technology	664
Yellowstone park	description	917.87
Yiddish dialects		492
	literature	892
York, house of	English history	942.04
Yosemite, Cal.	description	917.94
Young, counsels to	ethics	173
	education of education	372
	men, advice to, bus. ethics	174
	men's Christian ass'n	267.3
	unions	267
	people's religious societies	267
	reading of	028.5
	women, advice to, soc. ethics	177
	women's Christian ass'n	267.5
Yucatan, Mexico	architecture	722
	history	972
	travel	917.2
Yukon	history	971.21
Zambezi	travel	916.7
Zanzibar, Africa	history	967
Zechariah	Bible	224
Zend Avesta	Persian lit.	891
	religion	295
	language	491
Zephaniah	Bible	224
Zinc	metallurgy	669
	ores economic geology	553
	roofs bilding	695
Zincografy		767
Zither	music	787
Zodiac and zodiacal light	astron.	523
Zoofytes		593
Zoologic gardens		590
Zoology		**590**
Zoosporeae	botany	589
Zootechny		636
Zoroaster	Parseeism	295
Zouaves	military science	356
Zululand	history	968
Zuñis	Indians	970.3
Zwinglians	Protestant sects	284
Zygosporeae	botany	589

Topics in blackface type ar subdivided in the Tables